OLWIBULO LWA LWANDE WESONGA

OLWIBULO LWA LWANDE WESONGA

Owahwania
Elizabeth Masiga Kakembo

Owakonyeresa Embosi
Abner Ekudu MA

Lwande Books

Bedford, UK

First published in the UK by Lwande Books, 2018
Copyright © 2018 by Elizabeth Masiga Kakembo
This book is copyright under the Berne convention.
No reproduction without permission.
All rights reserved.

The right of Elizabeth Masiga Kakembo to be identified as
the author of this work has been asserted by her
in accordance with sections 77 and 78 of the
Copyright, Designs and Pantents Act, 1988.

Lwande Books
Bedford (UK)

The author and publisher have made all reasonable
efforts to contact copyright holders for permission,
and apologize for any omissions or errors in the form of
credits given. Corrections may be made to future printings.

A CIP catalogue record for this book is available from
The British Library
The AU Library

ISBN 978-0-9955998-0-2 (Hb)
ISBN 978-0-9955998-1-9 (Pb)

Book design by Myrene McFee
Printed by Ingram Spark (UK) Group,
Milton Keynes.

Lwande Books UK are committed to sourcing paper made from wood grown
in sustainable forests and from recycled paper.

DEDICATION

First, I dedicate this book to Abner Ekudu MA, of Buyore Village. Without him I would not have managed to accomplish what is in this book.

Secondly, to my father Yeremiah Masiga Wa Mbakulo and my mother Miriamu Nakoli Ojanjo Masiga. They instilled in me the beauty of learning, preserving artefacts, taught me a lot about Abatabona, and made me to be highly appreciative of my clan.

Also, to the late Nimulodi Lwagula Masiga and Mrs Deborah Nimulodi Masiga, late Philemon Bubolu Opeda, late Lameka Akongo, Wilson Okwenje, Faisi Nora Makoha, and the late Justice Alikipo Ouma. They always encouraged me in all my endeavors for education. Without them, I would probably have not been able to write this book.

Finally, to my immediate family, Suleiman Ssenyonga Kakembo, Tendo, Sanyu, Bona and Jago. Without their encouragement and participation in the other work of daily living I would have found it impossible to devote attention to the important work Ekudu left for us to preserve and carry forward.

Elizabeth (Beti) Natabona Masiga Kakembo
January 2018

OLUKONGO LWA SAMIA YIYATULA KVR, EGYPT

EBIRI MU STABO

FOREWORD (NEW EDITION)

I absolutely admire and respect Abner Ekudu. His work on ABATABONA is masterful and enlightening. By researching and documenting the lineage and legacy of Omutabona Lwande Wesonga and his descendants, as a branch of Abatabona, Ekudu accomplished a unique task. It is unparalleled in the annals of the Samia Bugwe community. Even in a broader contex I am not aware of a similar undertaking among the Luhya ethnic group, of whom Abasamia are a part. It is an achievement the importance of which cannot be overstated. Let me say, in passing, that Ekudu's story about the relationship between Samia and Kintu and their journey together from Misiri (Egypt) has become a Samia folk lore. Perhaps not so among the Baganda. However, one day someone should research and expand on the nature of their relationship, as well as their territorial / human conquests on their way south. In all honesty I have no new information to add to what Ekudu did and what the Editor, Natabona Betty Masiga Kakembo has reviewed.

Wilson Okwenje
Canada
16 May 2016

OHUSIMA

- Omwami Barnabas Abwoka (Kubengi) omusiani wa Semeyi Ngundira, e Lunyo, Samia, Uganda. Omuyaku wuno yaali omulwayee naye yafubaho muno ohugoba biyaali amanyire. Syekesa ohubasa hwaye koti huli ohweyaale muno. Yaamanya ati abana beffe bahadahe ebindu bitudiraho emyaka cyo mumoni eyo, mani yakesaho ohwetamo amani ohuhola emirimu cino. Otyo muno lukali mwana weffe Abwoka Kuka.

- Omwami Disani Mbakulo wuno muwandikireho ebingi biyahonya hulu-papula lundi.

- Omwami Edwardi Oguti natafwamu mwaka 2015. Muwandikireho hulu-papula lundi koti yahonya. Handi natafwa, yaali amalire ohunyandikira biyenya muboleho, handi biri mu papula cilondaho asi awo.

- Dr. George Bwire Oundo omusiani wa Gideon (Gasundi) Oundo, e Busia nende e Butenge, Samia, Uganda, yangoberaho ameta ka beho beffe. Otyo muno Kuka.

- Dr. Peter W. Obanda omusiani wa Chango Machio, e Lumino, Samia, Uganda, yangobera ameta kabeho beffe. Hwebasa muno handi muno.

- Dr. James M. C. Wafula (Wuno Mujabi. Omusiani wa Yafesi Musungu handi mwanangina wa Lord Ben Odoki owali Chief Justice of Uganda) Yahonya muno ohuteresa olusamia. Handi ndali muberese esiha esidudu ohutingala mu papula, handi nga ali nende emirimu chindi emingi, ecyebikanda bindi. Naye James, siyahaya, yafukirira yasomeramo mu papula. Yeca yateresa ebindu ebyolulimi lu Samia muno. Otyosa muno handi muno lukali.

- Omuhaye Edisa Nabwire (Natabona) omuhana wa Chango Machio, oholera handi yamenya mu London, Great Britain, yongesaho ameta kabeho beffe. Edisa otyo muno.

- Omwami Enosi Ogambo omusiani wa Daudi Ngundira, e Bulondani, yesi yahonya muno handi muno koti lumuwandikireho hulupapula lulondaho. Omuyaku wuno womwoyo omulayi handi abona eyaale. Mwebasa lukali muno.

- Omwami Paulo Namatte, omusiani wa Nyikola Egesa wo Ololo owe Butenge, Lunyo, Samia. Omuyaku wuno yaali omwangu muno ohuhola hu beho beffe ba Bukeko. Yesi yamberesa esibaso mbwe aboona eyaale muno. Otyosa lukaali muno.

- Omuhaye Faisi Norah Makoha Natabona omuhana wa Yeremia Masiga, owe Butenge, Musamia, odeha Mungasti e Buhayo, yangobera ameta ka beho beffe bandali njibirire. Otyo muno handi muno.

- Omuhaye Florence Ogoola, omuhana wa Wandera, handi Omuhaye wa Justice Munange Ogoola, e Virginia, USA. Omuhaye wuno yambolera ameta kosi akadira hu becuhulu beffe abomudala lyaye. Otyo muno handi muno.

- Omwami Gefrrey Ogambo omusiani wa Enosi Ogambo, Leeds, UK. Omusiani wuno wo mwoyo omulayi. Natali niye esitabo sino sisyahaberewo. Niye owekesa simwana koti lungonya ebindu Ekudu biyatulehera. Enosi huyemewo amuberese ohundetera e Bulaya.

- Owa Natabona, Justice James Munange Ogoola. Otyo muno handi muno. Yahonya mumakesi handi niye owicha ohucusa esitabo sino mu Lusungu Nasaye nahonya.

- Omuhaye Rose Masiga omuhana wa Mirika Machio Natabona wa Yeremia Masiga, e Butenge. Rose ali Nairobi, Kenya. Rose yangobera ameta kabana bo mwana weffe Mirika Machio. Otyo muno handi muno.

- Omutabona, Stephen Oundo omusiani wa Alex Oundo, e Nairobi, Kenya. Stephen yakesaho muno ohubola abeho beffe be Kenya ohumuba ameta naye byahaya. Yemawo yangoberaho ameta ka bana babwe bongene. Otyo muno handi muno.

- Omwami Thomson Mangeni Odoki (Wuno Mujabi, omusiani wa Yafesi Musungu) naye yahonyera muno ohuteresa olulimi lu Samia. Mwebasa lukali muno handi muno.

- Owa Natabona, Wilson Okwenje, omusiani wa Simeoni Wafubwa, bulano amenyere e Canada. Eppapula cyo Omutabona Abner Ekudu ciyatulehera, cyali cikofule muno handi muno. Okwenje yaciyira mu bandu bamakesi e Canada baciholaho muno cihaye hukofula mangu. Ohuhola omulimo okwo kuyira ebindu ebingi, naye Okwenje yaali amalirire mu mwoyo ohucya abiholeho. Handi, yasoma mu papula nitaciyira mu hutusamo esitabo. Otyo muno lukali. Mwesi mbebasa lukali muno handi muno, ohuhonyera mu mirimu chino ecyo Olwibulo lweffe Lwa Lwande Wesonga.

- Omuhaye Ruth Osinya Natabona handi Omukoko; omuhana wa Charles Oundo ewe Butenge, yahonya muno ohungobera ameta kabeho beffe. Otyo muno Natabona.

- Omwami Stephen Oundo, omusiani wa Charles Oundo owe Butenge, yahonya muno ohunyandikira ameta ka beho beffe. Kuka otyo muno lukali.

- Omwami Benyamin (Bennya) Odwori, owe Butenge lero yatulawo, yaali ali nomwoyo kwohuhonya naye yeca yalwala. Mani hulwomwoyo mulayi kuyaali nakwo mwebasa lukali muno.

- Naye nitamalirisa, ndaha ohwebasa lukali Omwami Ssenyonga Kakembo, nabana bange, Tendo, Sanyu, alala na becuhulu bange Bona nende Jago. Abandu bano bahonyera lukali muno handi muno. Ssenyonga yangonyeranga ebitabo ebidira hu "Bantu People, Ugandans and the early Egyptians", some humbone embosi Ekudu ciyalomalomaho niciri ecyadieri ati hwatula Emisiri. Huhandi, yahonyanga nende emirimu cyosi hunyemewo fune esiha syohuhola omulimo kuno. Naye abana bange babolanga bati noli nesindu siosi siodaha humanye tuwandikirenge hwahasomenge buli luhuduhana esiha. Abecuhulu bosi bamboleranga baati nonyala ohuwandika ebihudiraho syehabi muno. Mani abandu bange bo muddala bosi basembanga muno handi bamberesa amani ohubiholaho. Mutyo sa muno lukali handi lukali muno.

- *SPECIAL ACKOWLEDGEMENT*: This book would not have been made without the help of Mrs Myrene McFee. American born, she has no single word of Lusamia language in her vocabulary — only long experience in bookmaking and publishing, a keen eye to detail, and a determination to do good work for Lwande Wesonga generation and for me as her friend. On behalf of all Lwande Wesonga generation, I thank Myrene for her contribution to this work.

OHUTUMBULA HWOHUBIRI

Ese nise Beti Natabona omuhana wa Yeremiya Masiga wa Mbakulo. Olukongo lwe Butenge, esiha esyo e Gombolola yaali e Lumino. Esaza lyaali Samia Bugwe. Mama niye Miriamu Nakoli (Masiga). Ndadehera aba Ganda abe Njovu, Omwenengo yibalanga bati Ssenyonga Kakembo. Nguhwa yebula baba bali bamulanga Debora Nachaki, omuhana wa Owori Dadi, Omucaki we Ebucaki. Naye Ngina mama yaali Nasicongi omuhana wa Nasiye. Kuka yebula mama yali Onyito wo Oguta, Omwakoli. Ndasomera mumasomero mu Uganda handi nindacya e Bulaya ndeyongera ohusoma. Ndamalirisa ebyohusoma nende Ohusoma ebidira hu hutusa ebitabo. Ndeca ndahola nende Omuhaye yi Plesidenti we Ghana otangira yibalanga baati Kwame Nkrumah, yiyalehera ebindu byaye ebye bitabo ohutusanga. Omuhaye wuno bamulanga bati June Milne. Ndahola naye emyaka ecihiraho emyaka kabiri. Niyawuluha, ninjiriirira nomulimo kuyaali ahola ohwola fesi luhuwuluhire. Nitawuluha ndeca ndatingala hu luya lweffe ndabona endi syangu muno ebindu abandu ohwibirira. Esyomukisa mulayi Omuyaku Abner Ekudu yaali a konyerese embosi mu bahulundu baliwo esiha esyo. Syesi holere biholereho.

Siridaha abeho beffe bandi bahongereho humulimo kuno. Abandu bandi ndakesaho ohubasaba ametta kabeho beffe naye sibanyala ohukamberesa. Mani emirimu ciohuhola esitabo sino cisisiri emingi. Syesi saba abo abanyala ohuhola omulimu okuhiraho ano, bacye mumoni bawandike esitabbo sindi. Babolanga bati enyumba sibayombahanga hu ludalo lulala. Hambase endi hwengwe abasoma esitabo sino, mwica ohubaho abanyala ohuhola omulimo kuhiraho ano. Sino syohutandikiraho musambo ye bitabo. Ekuddu yaleha epapula ciyawandikaho ebindu ebihira obungi musitabo sino, cibalanganga (Manuscript), ecialimo ohukonyeresa embosi cyosi ciyawandika (research) sakira yaabola ati "kuno nomuka nikwo wesi caakiraho nga lwoba nobona". Ese holere esitabo sitangira nende ISBN (International Standard Book Number). Bulanu syekesa mbwe esitabo sio simanyibwe mubyalo koti esitabo ohwekesa ebyafayo nga siri mu Register yebitabo. Sino mumirimu cyohutusa ebitabo, basilanga esitangira (First Edition). Saba lukali muno abeho beffe abanyala ohuhola omulimo mulayi okuhiraho ano, batandike, bongereho handi bakololose ebindi bitakolosa bilayi. Koti esyohu-boneraho, banyala bahola amasaga kekesa olwibulo luno (Family Tree). Nayee, olwibulo lwa Lwande Wesonga luhulahulane muno. Mani syekesa mbwe syenya esiha esihongo muno ohuhola omulimo kuno. Humalirisa ndaha ohwiculisa Abatabona bomumoni endi omusiro kweffe ffessi nikwo "EMBONGO NA HADYEDYE".

Elizabeth (Beti) Natabona Masiga Kakembo
January 2018

ESITUNDU SITANGIRA

OHUTUMBULA

OLWIBULO LWA NGWENO MULEMA

Ndi omusangafu muno ohuwandika esitabo sino. Silayi muno ohusisoma nohumanya olwibulo lwa Ngweno Mulema omwana wa TEBINO. Ngweno mulema niye omwana wohune hu bana ba Tebino ngina niye Nanyinya, naye baba abamahwana nende ODON-GO; naye Ngweno niye OPIYO. Ngweno yali yalema, yatula munda niyalema ngabak-ingasa. Bamwanangina: Giryenda (Omanyi), Aburi (Omuburi), Odongo (Omudongo) nende Onyango (Omukuhu).

Ngweno yebula omwana waye Musiani mulala ati, olangwa LWANDE MULUNGO, Lwande Mulungo oyo, yakeka abahasi babiri, Nabaholo nende Nabongo. Nabaholo nimwo omutula abatabona balwande. Naye Nabongo niye owebula Lwande Wesonga, ni mu Lwande Wesonga niye owibula abaana bano: Nabooli, Ngweno Lununi, Namudu; Ngweno Hadu/Mahola, Kagenda, Nehema, ni bulano humandika esitabo ndabukulaho esaga lya Lwande Wesonga lyongene, mani esitabo sino sihoya siakulihwa OLWIBULO LWA LWANDE WESONGA, mbwene nisitebwaho Ngweno Mulema, siba esia BATABONA boosi nga aba Lwande baliho nga batula hu Lwande Mulungo.

Bakuka befwe nende balata befwe bebusanga hu siosyo nabaana babwe abasimbuha, bacha ohubakaniayira ebidira hu luya, amayee, engano, emibayo, ebyohudehisania nende ebidira humasika.

Ndabona nga bulano sasisiriwo ebyosi, bulanu esiri nisio amekero Schools, ndahire omwaana asoma esitabo musifo syohukaniayirwa nabahulundu boosi mbano sibasiboneha dawe bafwire babwere, bulanu abandu ba 1900 badudu muno sibasiboneha muno haba abahanyalire bakaniay ira abaraga bababonaho.

Nameta ako akali musitabo esio: sindaduhira ameta kabana ababaandi mani mbawo sindakandika dawe nende ameta ka bahasi sakira husaba omulamu olibawo yahateresa esitabo sino alinyala ohwicusa ameta ako humwene yikadiraho. Manya oti; ochaaka sanyala ohumalayo byoosi ohwola ebindi bimudoondobanaho; ebindi yaba nga sabitekehe bilayi, naye owenyuma niye oteresanga ebyahyama/ ebyadoondobana. Mbasa nimubona ebihyamu mulowe hunjolobya, hunjakire. Ebikobolwangamo ohuteresa amahabi amangi; sakira kuno nomuka nikwo wesi chaakiraho nga lwoba obona.

Abner Ekudu M.A.
Bunyore Village, 1995

1

EBICHAKIRWAHO

Nyandikire esitabo sino, nga nyenya buli lwibulo lwa Tebino lusome bino ebituhoyera ohumanya.

Ohutula hubakuka befwe behalanga hu siosyo engolobe nibahamala ohulya, mani wabechangawo omuhulundu achaaka ohubakaniayira ebyabechangawo, handi babuciranga musidwoli, nibangua amalwa akesubudi aangolobe, mani awo abandu bahulundu na baraga batekeresanga oyo okaniaya.

1. Bibakaniayanga nibyo bino:

   (a) Amayee nga lukalasananga, eryebulebe nomulasani walyo mululu.

   (b) Emibayo nga luchiabechanga; e.g. amalengo nabalwani, endolo, endika, namalwachani kakhwo, amataratara.

   (c) Obuhana nabobbi mgolobe nibabucha nabakhana bahina.

   (d) Enjia ngalubebulana nohulya enyama, ohukabana ahmakumba, e. g. enyumba lebe (enyumba nichio enono chiabahasi abadeha mu daala eryo). Buli mwaana musiani owibulwa mu muhasi wenono eyo alwangwa enono yangina e. g. Abatabona bali nenyumba chino:

01. Nanyanga	Lwande
02. Nahone	Ogoola
03. Namudde (Esibewo)	Hamiripo, Olweni
04. Namangale	Waida
05. Namakangala	Lwande
06. Nehere	Sombi
07. Nasonga	
08. Namiripo	Awori Naholi
09. Neroba	Lwande Magongolo
10. Nahayo	Hakwe, Wamira mboko
11. Nasonga II	Basoga.

2. Namudu = Ngweno Mahola
                Lwande Muliamboka

3. Nehema = Kagenda – (Ababakwa)
                Lwande

Abandu bano baali omundu mulala, naye enyumba (enono chiabahasi) nichio echikabulanga amasaga.

Enyumba chino chiatula hale nende Bible chiosi chirimo, e.g. abaana ba Isirael mulimo enjia ehumi nachibiri.

Olwande lwo lupapula 2

(Soma obufwimbuli 7.5-8)

Bulanu endalo chino abaana sibasibucha ali abahulundu, olwohuba saliwo esidwooli, esiosyo siosi sibulawo, mani bulanu abahulundu abahira obungi abemiaka 1800 sibaliwo dawe, bulanu abaliwo 1910 nibo abahira obungi, naye mwabo simulimo omanyire.

Abaana bulanu engolobe basoma ebitabo, sakira siesi ndahire abaana basomenge ebindu bino nga esitabo nisyo esibakaniayira nga koti luhwibulwana nohukabana enyama.

Enyama chiri chiti: Eyoluyimo, Eyomwino, Eyesibiho, Eyemisambwa, nende Eyomuhana, mbasa echio nichio enyama ehulundu.

Hubira abami bano abahonyanga: ndeberesa (Researches) embosi chino echolwibulo lwa Ngweno Mulema:

01. Eriya Ochieno Ngweno, oyo naye yamanya echiabuli nyumba yitula mu Ngweno Mulema.

02. Samuel Egondi Omulo, yambolera ebidira hu Mboyo – Bulondani.

03. Yekoyada Ngundira Ochieno yambolera ebidira hu Mbakulo.

04. Yowasi Nyabola Lwande, yambolera ebidira hu Lwande II Muliaha.

05. Ekaka Embalwa yambolera ebidira hu Hakwe, Wamira nende Mboko.

06. Morris Ogaani Odooli nende Erisa Odianga Orodi banjekesa ebidira hu Wanga Ofumbuha.

07. Patrick Bbala Balongo yanjekesa ebidira hu Namiripo, Paulo Ngweno.

08. Zablon Wambete Oguna yanjekesa ebidira hu Olwenyi Nyembi.

09. George Ouma Sombi yanjekesa ebidira hu Sombi.

10. Yolamu Masaba yanjekesa ebidira hu Awori.

11. Alfred Omala Olijo yanjekesa ebidira hu Omala.

12. Erasito Obwora Makoha yambolera ebidira hu Ngweno Sisera.

Olwande lwo lupapula 3

OLUKENDO LWA KINTU NENDE SAMIA

Kintu nende Samia batula mu Misiri (KVR) (Egypt). Batula boola mu Sudan, North wa Uganda niboola hulugulu Masaba (Elgon), babukula ohwo esikoko nibeha a Buganda nga Kintu ali nomuhasi waye Naambi.

Lubola mu Buganda ali omwalo nibabuluhira aawo, nibataaka esikoko esio. Omwalo okwo kulangwa MUSAMIA no hwola leero. Nanjala omuhasi wa Samia yakwibula.

Samia luyatula aawo nadira eyomunyanja Sitta Makooli (Lake Victoria) niyengira obwato, nabodoohana nachia ebuleka Esimolo (Kisumu) Bujaluo nakooba musikobo sia Sakwe, Nakenda nachia namenya musyalo sya Banyore ba anganyi mu Kenya niyehala esiribo lere basilanga SIRIBA.

MBAKULIHA (OHUTUBULA) YIBAKULIHA E BUTABONA

(a) Olunyi (Omutuba) niyo engubo yi Samia yefwalanga

(b) Obwato, nibwo bu Samia yambuhiramo nachia ohukonya yamenya

(c) Engeso, niyo eyasibanga endiri chio bwato echingisa amachi

(d) Esyuma.

OHWELAYA HWA BATABONA:

(a) Orubo Sioka Syalali

(b) Makada momu kafuniranga olukendo

(c) Orubo nyumba mbi

(d) Efumo lya mahaa.

ABANA BA SAMIA: Lwande, yebula Tebino

Tebino yebula abaana bano:

1. JINYENDA (Omanyi), esikera nibamulanga OMANYI, waliwo omwami olanga Owinyi yali Esikoma, yachia yangwesa engombe amalwa mani niyimera, nalanga enjia chiosi, mani enjia chiosi nichiebusuba ewa OWINYI mani Jinyenda luyali achia nomuhasi mukofu amulanga namuteba ati, "Omanyire simwami alangire?". Jinyenda yamufunyamo ati haba naye omuhasi oyo yamuboola ati syali ahendo eterangaho. Jinyenda yafukirira, nomuhasi omuboolera ati Nabateba oleha abandu bandi bafunyamo naye ewe ofunyamo olunyuma oti "INGWERE AMALWA" mani Owinyi yateba enjia nga ateba buli luya, naye Jinyenda yafunyamo ati "INGWERE AMALWA" mani abandu boosi bafunyiramo alal bati niwe Omanyi omanyire engombe niyingwere amalwa nohutula awo, nabulano yehola enono "BAMANYI" nibali ABABORO.

2. ABURI NIYE OMWANA WA TEBINO OWO HUBIRI

   Aburi niye omwana wa Tebino owo hubiri, olwola nisiboneha nga Ngweno Mulema niye owabukula obwami, mani Aburi yaali omunyolefu, obwami ohubukulibwa nomwana muyere nga niye omulonda mulwanyi olwo, mani Aburi yakiyanga Ngweno Mulema amwitte abukule obwami.

Aburi babechanga mudembi oba Esirimba, mani Aburi luyawulira ati, Ngweno Mulema mbala bamukingire Hakati, Aburi yekisa abundu, naye omundu owabona Aburi natekehe ohwitta Ngweno Mulema, yachia yekesa Ngweno Mulema. Naye Ngweno Mulema yaboola ati; ese sindi nende embosi nomwana wefe Aburi, Aburi natekeha esio Esanga yinamuloba, ese hanjie Ssa. Ngweno Mulema yabukula obusale nobuyingo naboola abamukinga ati, huchie. Lubaali bahoola abwene awo yi Aburi yali yekisire nalindire ohulasa Ngweno Mulema, ne Aburi yeyinga ohubbeya Ngweno Mulema nefumo, ohumufumita, nihane ahayingo khayiswo, naye Ngweno Mulema luyalehula esikera namalaho, ni Ngweno Mulema yelaaya ati, "HULIHO CHATI AMOLO" ni Aburi luyola mudaala naboolera abana baye ati, "Simusiriraniranga nende olwibulo lwa Ngweno Mulema obusirandamu dawe, nise otangire" Nohutula awo olwibulo lwa Aburi nende olwa Ngweno Mulema sibasiriraniranga obusirandamu. AMOLO olwibulo lwa Ngweno Mulema nibaba nibayima mani bafumita esolo nibelayaa bati, "huliho chati amolo" nga bechulisa ohwelaya hwa Ngweno Mulema nafumitte Aburi.

3. NGWENO MULEMA WA TEBINO

Ngina Ngweno Mulema niye Nanyinya. Ngweno Mulema bebulwa amahwana. Amahwana kano bakalanga bati Opio. Opiyo nirio erita lindi erya Ngweno Mulema. Ehwana lindi balilanga bati Odongo. Ngweno Mulema nimwo omutula ABATABONA.

Olwola nabawo omwana namira esyuma siasimwana muyere, naye omwene syuma nadaha esyuma syaye. Naye omwene mwana naboola ati, "Leha omwana nachia erwanyi hunayibona hubunyaka". Naye omwene nyuma siyafukirisania nende mwanangina dawe, yemeda ohusaba enyuma yaye, mani mwanangina oyo muhulundu, yetta omwana oyo yamubaka yatusamo enyuma eyo, yayiba mwanangina. Luyatusamo enyuma mumwana, omwana yemawo yafa; nalira nabolera mwanangina ati "Otabona enyuma yawo njiyo eyikerere omwana wange yafa". Ohutula olwo nibakabuhana, omuyere achia Boro mu

Olwande lwo lupapula 4

Bujaluwo, naye omuhulundu adonga awo, Nihwo ohutula Abatabona olwembosi "OTABONA".

4. ODONGO WA TEBINO

Odongo, nimwo omutula Abadongo. Ngina niye NANYINYA nibo abebulwa amahwana. Bahindawo muno ohukekana nabatabona. Owachaka ohukeka Natabona niye Reuben Onyero Agula, naye ohutula hu basefwe nende bakuka befwe sisyaliwo dawe. Oluya nilwingiya lukekananga.

5.   ONYANGO WA TEBINO

Omukuhu, niye owali walaaka wa Tebino, Esiakera yalangibwa Omukuhu, yali nende engombe yaye buli yachia achia naboya (Ohuhungira), yaholanga atio, nibulanu abandu bamulanga bati, "OMUKUHU" naye boosi bali "ABABORO" NGWENO MULEMA. Ngweno Mulema nomwana wa Tebino, ngina niye Nanyinya. Ngweno Mulema yali nende omwana mulala ati yengene nga bamulanga bati Lwande Mulungo. Lwande Mulungo yebula Lwande Wesonga. Ngina Lwande Wesonga bali bamulanga bati NABONGO.

ABAHASI BA LWANDE WESONGA NIBO BANO

1.   Namudde Hatoke

2.   Naholi

3.   Namiripo

4.   Namuddu

Boosi haba sibali nibebula dawe. Lwande atule achie alakule. Omulakusi yamubolera ati, wicha ohwakana omuhasi okenda niye owahahuholere olwanyi olwo. Mani hu Lwande yecha yehale embaka. Olwola abakaali baye bachia ohwaya nibabukanana omuhasi. Omuhasi yibabukanana yababolera ati, "Simundoolaho?" Abakaali bachia eyiri Lwande Wesonga bamubolera bati "Aliwo omuhasi undi odaha hu mudoole". Lwande niyeculisa koti omulakusi yamubolera, huyemewo atume abaayi abo bachie baboole omuhasi yeche mudaala. Omuhasi oyo luyecha mudaala yaduhira Lwande Wesonga nangwa amalwa. Omuhasi oyo yolera husyaki, nibamudayira amalwa mu Sikwada bamuyirira, luyamala ohungwa amalwa ako nibamuba nobusuma yalya, yehala aawo ohwola luwerani Lwande atuma abakaali baye muchie mweyee musidwoli omukeni anakonamo, nibwahya muchuli Lwande Wesonga yalanga abahasi baye, Namudde Hatoke, Naholi, Namiripo

Olwande lwo lupapula 5
nende Namuddu omuhasi muyere Lwande yamuboolera ati, ewe chia odehere omukeni oludaabo, hu Namuddu afunyemo ati, "Okunyu kululu kundichanga kuno nikwo kundadehere omuhasi womwami! Lwande Wesonga yamufunyamo ati, "Analichanga hu mbaki change". Okwo nikwo ohwatula olwibulo lwa Namuddu ohubalanga 'ABAHALULU' naye nabatabona abo lwibulo lwa NAMUDDU. Naye Lwande Wesonga ohubola ati, "Analichanga embaki", ohwo nihwo ohwatula olwibulo lwa NEHAMA ohulangwa ABABAKWA.

Omuhasi yibadoola enono yali NEHAMA, yemawo yayera enda, mani abahasi ba Lwande Wesonga, baboolanga bati, siniye owalukenda mani luyaali niyebula omwana omusiani oyo alangwa KAGENDA.

Abahasi ba Lwande Wesonga boosi abaali bakumba bachaka ohuyera enda nibamalire ohwibula Kagenda. Naholi niyebula Ngweno Lumuni, Namuddu niyebula Ngweno Mahola nende Lwande Omulyamboka, Namudde Hatoke haba siyebula omwana nende Lwande Wesonga dawe.

Lwande Wesonga luyafwa babasa ohubekawo Kagenda mulwanyi olwohuba niye omuhulundu owachaaka ohwibulwa munyumba ya Nehama. Namudde Hateke haba siyasima dawe omwana womuhasi wanasikoko ohubekwa oba ohwingira olwanyi, nga ye adaha omwana owamaliriha olangwa Ngweno Lumuni. Namudde Hateke yemawo yabukula ebindu ebyobwami yakisa. Kagenda luyateba ati ebindu byobwami biri ena? Namudde Hateke yakania Kagenda ati, amake kabirya ebindu byosi.

Ngweno Lumuni yali ebuhochangene Ebanda, Namudde Hateke yamulaka yeche nende bahochangene, oludalo olulakane lulwola nende essa Namudde Hateke yabukula esayi yobwami natta musimwero natula erwanyi wedaala yachia ohulinda. Ngweno Lununi luyoola Namudde yabukula esiayi yobwami, nasiyaa Ngweno Lununi. Ngweno Lununi yengira mu daala nolukalakaasa, ohwo nihwo ohwihasa Ngweno Lununi, husisala si Kagenda yadaha yehaleho. Kagenda yafirwa obwami obwo.

Ngweno Lununi niye owakerama Namudde Hateke, yayira olwanyi. Mani abandu ba Namudde Hateke lubecha mudala nga sibaliho nomwiwa nga sibanyala ohuba nende ekono. Bemawo baberesa Ngweno Lununi omuhana nga nisio esibewo sya Namudde Hateke. Esibewo sya Namudde Hateke siebula abaana babiri abasiani, nibo bano:

Hamiripo babiri abasiani nibo Hamiripo, Olweni (Nyembi) nibo abalwanga abatabonaBasembe olwohuba lubatula mu Ruambwa nibamenya e Busembe, naye abaduma nende abadde babalanga bati, Abasembe ba Lununi abasembera hu Nyanja, mani nibo abatabona BADDE.

Kagenda siyabona bilayi dawe, ohuta hu mwana muyere obwami naye nga omuhulundu mudaala Kagenda yachaaka ohuyirimbana nende Ngweno Lununi, siemawo Kagenda nibakabana engombe chia lata wabwe nibakabuhana. Esiakera Kagenda natakerama edaala lya simwana nohuduhira obwami, ngina yali nasikoko. Handi Lwande yalama Ngweno Lununi. Naye Omwana womuhasi wa nasikoko yahaba okuhulundu mu hwibulwa, sanyala ohuhola emisiro chiedaala elyo. Yahaba omwana muyere ni ngina yecha nolukalakasa oyo niye ohola emisiro.

EYEE LYAKERA HWACHIA EBUNYALA NEBUSONGA

Amayee akakera nihukwa Bunyala nende Busonga, Amaye kano kali 3.

Omuganda nende Omusebe no Mumia.

OMUGANDA: Mundaalo cye Ekaka abaganda baseta abasamia, mani abandu be Ekaka beruha bakwa e Bunyolo nende e Busonga. Omwami mu Nyala yaali NGIRA nende simwana **OYOLO** nende **KUNDU.**

ODUNGA MUHAYO niye owabona Ekaka nabandu baye, mani Odunga yasaba Ekaka achie owaye e Buhayo amenyeyo, hulwo Ojuno nga Ojuno mululu muno, nga Odunga abasa ati Ekaka nanecha nende Odunga yecha ohumulasanira. Ekaka nabandu baye nibatula e Bunyala nende e Busonga, naye abola banga? E'ngombe e Bunyala haba sibachenda chiosi dawe ohumalaho Busonga nibo abandu be Ekaka badeha, lubola e Buhayo Odunga yasangalira muno Ekaka, mani abandu b'Odungo bachaka ohubuku-la abahasi babandu b'Ekaka ababoneha bulayi naye nga bola abakuba sibanya ohuba nende sibabola dawe. Abandu b'Ekaka bahola namaani omwami wabwe nga omundu wo Dunga abulamo. Abasiani bachia eyiri Odunga nibabola bati, esyalo siefwe sil-angwa MADOOLA NGOMBE mani ewe niwosayo engombe chiawo chino oba onaba ebilayi muno. Nisio esiakera basikuliha MADOLA NGOMBE niwosayo musialo esio ne nibahama eyati chibiri nga badaha Odunga abakobose musialo siabwe. E Butenge nisyo esifo sibalangaga MADOOLA NGOMBE.

Bulano Odunga yakobosa abasamia musialo siabwe, Odunga namenya mukina ne Ekaka amenya ewaye yiyatula nga Odunga yamenya nende Ojuno mukina olwohuba Ojuno yali

omululu nga amulinda eyiri abasuku baye. Odunga namenyere Mukina nabahaye baye, nabahasi babahayo bayabukulanga hubasamia nibabatula nibababola hubamwekwe babatalangaho. Huba muwabwo abas   amia bahola muno amaani. Bulano abandu abo bachaaka ohwekanyirisanga Odunga nga sibanyireho bati babangula nibali ewabwe; nga bamanyire bati Odunga niyo omwene obunyala. Odunga yaboola ati, lubahafunye ...

Odungo yasingira ohulwana nabasamia abahasi bakobole hu bahayo. Odunga ya-boola Ojune kenda husete abandu bengirire abandu baye. Ojune yaboola ati ese om-wami ndi omulwaye, chiaho nabandu bandi nga yekadia atio. Odunga yaseta bahuy-ana nendebasamia. Odunga aseta mahoma ohunguula batabona abahasi, abene bahasi sisinyaliha ohututusaho ano abahasi, olwo eye nirikwao. Odunga Siawola niye asseta omundu wo'mundu. Odunga yatula mudaala nadabadaba abolera Ojune nende Ekaka hu Ekaka nabola Odunga ati basamia mbakamisie bahayire ewabwe bafunyeyo e Buha-yo hu Odunga nafunyayo e Buhayo hu Odunga nata hu Ojune esulubbi ati sindahabo-lere Ojune yahaya ohunjira amakoha yakera

Odianga yetta omundu wange. Odunga luyafunyayo e Buhayo yabola ati Ojune oyo yesi ahaya ohufa, mani yatuma Odido Omunyanga ati ewe niwe omanyire ohuken-da esiro, ndaha ochie onjitire Ojune ndahahube omuhasi mani Odido yacha esiro Ojune

nakona naye niboola husiriwa esiolukoba baduhira nabakali mani batema okusala oku-
leyi boola hulukoba bambuhiraho bengira mukati nabandu bo Odido beyacia nabo. Buli
mundu yaholanga lulwali lwayamba lwenyumba cha Ojune bamanye bati alia no, Ojune
huyali nga akonere naye omwana yenyala hubuliri bwa Ojune naye Ojune aboola ati, simunyaho omuhasi ono yanyinyalireho omwana ni bulano abasuku bemonya nibalinda,
nga bamanyire mwali ni mukota Ojune akoterwe, ne endoolo ohumuyira ni bahwesa olwiki kaala nibasingirira nibafunaka efumo nisidira obusacha, nibamba batulira humu-
sola kula nibachia ohwekisa musino nibawulira bati, Afwire nibayira embosi Odunga
yasangala muno naberesa Odido Habisinya omuhasi.

• • • • • • • •

9

LWANDE WESONGA

SINO SITUNDU SICHAKA NENDE OHWIBULANUWA KOTI HWACIRIRA

Olwande lwo lupapula 8

BWIRE NAANGAGA WA WANDERA

NAFUNYA
NAMAKANGALA

Haaba siyebula omwana, niyeebula sihwanyala ohumuduhana

SIONGONGO WA EMBAAYA

NAKIROYA
NAKOLI

■ Nekesa Natabona, sihwecha hwanyala ohuduhana ebimutulaho.
Siongongo wa Siongongo

SIONGONGO WA SIONGONGO

NASICHONGI

Yakerama muha Abner Mayende Sombi, niyebulamo omusiani
Yafa: omuhana niye oliwo. Sihwanyala ohuduhana ametta kaaye

NGWENO LUNUNI

NAHAYO

Hakwe
Wamira
Mboko

HAKWE WA NGWENO LUNUNI

NAKWANGA
NASUBO

Ngweno Odibya.
Ouma Fuhi

NGWENO ODIBYA WA HAKWE

OUMA FUHI WA HAKWE

NASONGA
NAMUDDE

Ngweno Okiya
Were Odaari

NGWENO OKIYA WA OUMA FUHI

Bano sihwanyala ohuduhana embosi chibatulaho dawe

WERE ADAARI WA OUMA FUHI

Bano sihwanyala ohuduhana embosi chibatulaho dawe

OMWIHA WA WERE ODAARI

Bano sihwanyala ohuduhana embosi chibatulaho

Olwande lwo lupapula 9

WAMIRA WA NGWENO LUNUNI

NAMULEMBO

Obinda Otambula

OBINDE OTAAMBULA

Yaboola ati SIMUMBULAANGA DAWE MWAHA WULIRE
OBWAMI NIBUBINDA. (Ohwo nikhwo Ohwatula erita erio).

OBINDE OTAAMBULA

BWIBO — Omanyi Aucha

NAMULUMBA — Ekaka

OMANYI AUCHA WA OBINDA OTAAMBULA

NALUKADA — Ochieno Mugola
Ngweno Rabwori

OCHIENO MUGOOLA WA OMANYO AUCHA

NASUBO — Omanyo Mbogo
Ogaando

NAMAKANGALA — Ogoola

ABAHASI BA NGWENO LUNUNI NABANA BAYE

01. Nanyanga — Lwande II
02. Nahone — Ogoola
03. Namudde (Esibeyo) — Namiripo
Olwenyi (Nyembi)
04. Namangale — Waida
Mudubwa
Ngweno Kanga
05. Namakangala — Lwande Omolo
06. Nehere — Sombi
07. Nasonga — Naade
Ngweno Mudamalo
08. Namiripo — Awori Nahooli
09. Neroba — Lwande Magongolo
10. Nahayo — ■ Hakwe
Wamira
Mboko

Olwande lwo lupapula 10

OMANYO MBOGO WA OCHIENO MUGOOLA

NALIALI — Philipo Opio
NAMUYEE — Shem Ouma
NABIRONGA — Richard Ongamo
NAMIRIPO — Musumba
NANYANGA — Musungu
Sindano

PHILLIP OPIO

Omanyo Mbogo

OMANYO OGAANDO WA OCHIENO MUGOOLA

NAHAALA — Omanyo wa Omanyo Ogaando
NAMAINDI — Ochieno
Omanyo

NGWENO RABWORI WA OBINDA OTAMBULA

NAMENYA — Otyola Odaaro

12

OTYOLA ODAARO WA NGWENO RABWORI

NAMAINDI	Lwemba
	Obinda
NAMAINDI II	Yowana Walwala
	Abudasio Hatende
NALALA	Antonio Guloba
NAJABI I	Magero nende Ezekieli Opio
NAJABI II	Gasipabo Walala
	Morris Onganga
	Benard Barasa
NAKUHU	Edward Ekaka
NAWOONGA	Francis Ekaka (Oganga)
	Agaitano Ouma
	Joseph Juma
NADIANGA	Obinda Munyausi
NAMONI	Romano Ouma

LWEMBA WA OTYOLA ODAARO
Sihwaduhana ebindi

OBINDA WA OTYOLA ODAARO

NAKUHU	Onyago
	Wanyama
NAMWAGISA	Okiya

Olwande lwo lupapula 11

YOWANA WALWALA WA OTYOLA

NABAHOLO	Otyola
	Ngweno
	Namaindi
	Were
	Nalwenge
NAMUKUBA	Wangira
NMUDDE	Okuku
	Nahwanga

ABUDASIO HATENDE WA OTYOLA

NAPOWA	Charles Otyola
	Ben Namaindi
NAHULO	Wanyama

CHARLES OTYOLA WA OBUDASIO

NANYIMARO	?
NAMUNAPA	?

ANTONIO GULOBA WA OTYOLA

NAMULUNDU	Mangeni
	Oguttu
	John

MANGENI WA ANTANIO GULOBA

NAHABI	Sihwanyala ohuduhana ebimutulaho

MAGERO OTYOLA

NAKATIKO
Otyola Makoha
Okinyo Joseph Wandera

OTYOLA MAKOHA WA MAGERO

NAMULUMBA
NABULINDO
Otyola

EZEKIEL OPIYO WA OTYOLA

NAMAKANGALA
Ochieno

GASPARO WALALA WA OTYOLA

NAHUMIE
Ouma
Christopher Otyola
Taabu
Were
Okochi
Obinda
Jaja

MORRIS ONGANGO WA OTYOLA

NASUBO
Okochi
NAMWALIRA
Ngweno

Olwande lwo lupapula 12

LUGUNDA WA MUMBO

NEGEMBE
Odiambo
Luseni Juma

NASUBO I
Maloba
NASUBO II
Sigangale
NAMULEMBO
Wanyama

ODIAMBO WA LUGUNDA

NAMAGWE
Samuel Wandera
Wanyama Muchudde

LUSENI JUMA WA LUGUNDA

NAMWAYA
Petero Lugunda
Paul Lugunda
Muchudde
Ouma

SIGANGALE WA LUGUNDA

NEBERE
Charles Majoni
Humpress Barasa

WANYAMA WA LUGUNDA

NAMENYA
Sunday
Muchudde

MALOBA WA LUGUNDA

NAMUNYALA
Sunday
Mulima (Yafa)

WAMIRA NGWENO LUNUNI

NAMULUNDU
Muhemba

MUHEMBA WA WAMIRA

NAKIROYA
Ondayo
Embalwa

NAMANGALE
Omiya

NAMULEMBO
Ochieno

ONDAYO WA MUHEMBA

NALIALI
Muhemba
Dakayo

NAMIRIPO
Okumu
Bwaku

Olwande lwo lupapula 13

MUHEMBA WA MACHIO SIRINGO

NEHOBA
Sihwaduhana ehuwa limutulaho

NAMUDUMA
Wanyama
John Machio
Odimbe
Ogoola

NACHAKI
Taaka

DAKAYO WA MACHIO SIRINGO

NAMAHIA
Ondayo

OKUMU WA MACHIO SIRINGO

NABONGO
?

BWAKU WA MACHIO SIRINGO

EMBALWA WA MUHEMBA

NAMWINI
Uma
Namulundu

NALWENGE
Adika

NASUBO
Ogumba
Ekaka

UMA WA EMBALWA
Sihwaduhana ebimutulaho

NAMULUNDU WA EMBALWA

NAMWINI
Muhemba Njoroge

MUHEMBA WA NAMULUNDU

NALWENGE   Sihwaduhana ebimutulaho
NAMBANJA   Ouma
   Mbalwa
   Makoha

ADIKA WA MBALWA

NABONGO   Matias Nagafa
NSIWE   Mbalwa
   Nalwenge
NALIALI   Michael Makoha

MATIAS NAGAFWA WA ADIKA

NASIBWIHA   Oundo
   Adika

MBALWA WA ADIKA

NAHATUBA   Onyango
NAJABI   Ojiambo

Olwande lwo lupapula 14

OUMA WA EKAKA

Sihwaduhana ebimutulaho

OKUMU WA EKAKA

NAMANGALE   Bwire
NASINYAMA   Sihwakana embosi chimudiraho

OMIYA WA MUHEMBA

NANGWANGA   Ojiambo, Kwereho
NANJOSI   Ongeri
NABOOLI   Abdulia
NAMWINI   Olando

KWEREHO WA OMIYA

NAMUHOFWE   Kezironi Mugeni
NAHWANGA   Manda

KEZIRONI MUGENI WA KWEREHO

NAMUYEE   Odwori
   Onyango
   Wanyama
   Naam
NALIALI   Wycliffe Bwire
   Yosia Ekaka
   Moses Onyango
   Naande
NAMULUMBA   James Egessa
   Muhemba

MANDA WA KWEREHO
NAMAINDI
Nasonga
Juma

ONGERI WA OMIYA
Sihwakana ebimudiraho

ABDALLA WA OMIYA
NALIALI · Oguttu
NAMUHOFWE · Juma
NALIALI II · Owaka
NAMUBACHI · Barasa

OGUTU WA ABDALLA
Yesi sihwakana ebimudiraho

JUMA WA ABDALLA
NAHONE
Egessa
Kilo
Mbalwa

OLANDO WA OMIYA
NAKIROYA
Cornal Onyango
Okochi
Wamira
Egessa
Ouma

CORNAL ONYANGO WA OLANDO
NAMULUNDU
Sihwakana ebimudiraho

OKOCHI WA OLANDO
NAJABI
Olando
Eli

EGESSA WA OLANDO
NANYINEKI
 Sihwanyala ohuduhana embosi cimudiraho

OUMA WA OLANDO
NANYINEKI
Sihwanyala ohuduhana embosi cimudiraho

MUGENI WA OLANDO
NAMBANJA
Sihwanyala ohuduhana embosi cimudiraho

Olwande lwo lupapula 15

WAMIRA WA NGWENO LUNUNI
NAMAKANGALA
Okino

OKINO WA WAMIRA
NABAHOLO
Namulaha

NAMULAHA WA OKINO

NAHULO
Ngweno Pampa
Pamba

NGWENO NAMULAHA

NAKUHU
Pamba
Oundo

PAMBA WA NGWENO

NAMANGALE
Tambiti

OUNDO WA NGWENO
Sihwanyala ohuduhana embosi cimudiraho

NGWENO LUNUNI
Mboko

MBOKO WA NGWENO LUNUNI

NAKIROYA
Gombe
Dubasa
Nasenye

GOMBE WA MBOKO

NASONGA
NAMUDIBA
NAMUMULI
Ojiambo Maramba
Nababa
Ngweno

OJIAMBO MARAMBA WA GOMBE
Sihwanyala ohuduhana embosi cimudiraho

NABABA WA GOMBE

NAKUHU
Sanduku

SANDUKU WA NABABA

NABURI
Fwogo
Wandera Ganja
Okumu Ngweno

NABURI
Bwire Obwogo

FWOGO WA SANDUKU

NAHABEKA
Bwire
Sunday

WANDERA WA SANDUKU

NASIHUNE
Ochieno
Bwire

NALALA
Mangeni
Wafula
Wandera Wesonga

NGWENO LUNUNI

NAMIRIPO   Awori Nahooli

AWORI NAHOOLI WA NGWENO LUNUNI

NASONGA   Wamachode
                 Wamira

WAMACHODE WA AWORI NAHOOLI

NANGAYO   Ngweno
NAMAYAYI   Balongo
                 Okuku,
                 Muyanga

NGWENO WA MACHODE

NAMULEMBO   Kosima Galande

KOSIMA GALANDE WA NGWENO

Sihwakana Enono Ogutu

Olwande lwo lupapula 16

OKUKU WA MACHODE

NASONGA   Okochi
NAPUNYI   Wafula Abduheri
NASIBIKA   Wafwa
                 Ogoola
NAPUNYI II   Wanyama
                 Ausi Balongo
NAMWANGA   Magero

OKOCHI WA OKUKU

NAMUHULA   John Namayai
                 Ogondo
                 Ouma

MUYANGA WA MACHODE

                 Yafaa Nasiri Ohukeka

BALONGO WA MACHODE

NAHONE   Yolamu Masaba
                 Alex Wanyama

YOLAMU MASABA WA BALONGO

NAMAKANGALA   Difasi Ouma
NASIBIKA   Duncan Egesa
                 Hamphress Mugeni
                 Julias Wafula
                 Geofrey
NAMUTENDE   Wa Machodde

	DIFASI OUMA WA YOLAMU MASABA
NASUBO	Biita
	Sikuku

	EGESA WA YOLAMU MASABA
NAMULUNDU	Bwire Bogere
	Bwire Balongo

WAMIRA WA OWORI
Odende

NEROBA

NGWENO LUNUNI
Lwande Magongolo
Siboneha enyumba yino yeeyambania hu hamiripo nga yifanana nga aba Namuddu, naye siboneha bosi bali nende nguhwa wabwe, Neroba muha Ngweno Lununi, nibabere balangwa Namudde (Abasembe) niba Naroba omuhasi yali omumataki

Olwande lwo lupapula 17

NAMULOBA   Mudenyo

MUDENYO WA LWANDE MAGONGOLO

NABONGO I	Adundo
NAHASOHO	Adera
NAMBANJA	Ofwiho
NABONGO II	Mulindo

ADUNDO WA MUDENYO

NALIALI	Magongolo II
	Were Ojango

ADERA WA MUDENYO

Sihwaduhana Enono   Magongolo Adera

MAGONGOLO ADERA WA ADERA

NANJUKU	Ojiambo
	Muchere

MUCHERE WA MAGONGOLO

NABUKO   Sihwanyala ohuduhana ebimutulaho

OJIAMBO WA MAGONGOLO

NAKUNA   Ehudu

OFWIHO WA MUDENYO File 17

NALALA	Osobolo
	Mandu

OSOBOLO WA OFWIHO

NAJABI	Barasa
	Wandera
NAFWOFOYO	Odunga

MANDU WA OFWIHO

NASUBO   Ochieno
            Obuyu
            Sihaha

MULINDO WA OFWIHO

NALALA   Ochieno

NGWENO LUNUNI WA LWANDE WESONGA

NANYANGA   Lwande
            Lwande
            Awori – Lwo

LWANDE WA NGWENO LUNUNI

Sihwaduhana Enono   Awori Lwo*

AWORI WA LWANDE
Odinga

ODINGA WA AWORI
Siminyu (Ochooko)

NGWENO LUNUNI I
Ogoola

Olwande lwo lupapula 18

MUMBO WA WAMIRA

NABIANGU   Muchudde
             Luganda
NAMALELE   Wamira
             Biriko
             Kasaaka

MUCHUDDE WA MUMBO

NABUKAKI I   Mulima
NABAKHO   Grado Ogooha
NAMATOTE   Nikola Ofwejja
NAKUHU   Oyola
NAMUDAIRWA   Wanyama Odongo
NABUKAKI II   Opeke
                Konna
NACWERE   Barasa
NEBERE   Raphael Musumba

MULIMA WA MUCHUDDE

NADENGE   Wanyama Ogooyo
                Joseph Omuya, Sindano
NAMUNYEKERA   Ganynya
                Ogaara

GRADO OGOOHA WA MUCHUDDE

NABONWE · Alexender Luduba
Simion
Peter
Sephiel Lugunda
Adiriano
Slivano Apondi
Paul

NIKOLA OFWEJJA WA MUCHUDDE

NAHULO · Mulima Mumbo
Stephano Mangeni
NABUKAKI · Peter Muchudde
Grado Ogoha
Ojiambo Lugundu
NAMASIKE · Emanuel Muchudde
Grado Ogooha
Ojiambo Lugunda
NATINGORIAT · Odongo Gweno Mulema
Okello Ngweno Lununi

RAPHAEL MUSUMBA WA MACHUDDE

NANYFWA · Peter Ouma
Charles Mutesa
NALALA · John Were
ADETI · Moses Ouma
Manuel Ogutu

Olwande lwo lupapula 19

OUMA WA EMBALWA

Sihwaduhana ebibatulaho

NAMULUNDU WA EMBALWA

NAMWINI · Muhemba Njoroge

MUHEMBA WA NAMULUNDU

NALWENGE · ?
NAMBANJA · Ouma
Mbalwa
Makoha

ADIKA WA MBALWA

NABONGO · Matiasi Nagafwa
Mbalwa
NASIWE · Nalwenge
NALALA · Michael Makoha

MATIAS NAGAFWA WA ADIKA

NASIBWIHA · Oundo
Adika

MBALWA WA ADIKA

NAHATUBA	Onyango
NAJABI	Ojiambo

NALWENGE WA ADIKA

ADETI	Judge
NASIE	Majimbo
	Ojiambo
	Ouma
NAKIROYA	Taifa
NEIBIRA(KUMAM)	Juliasi Mbalwa
NASIROL	Ojiambo Adika, nende Wafula Siminyu
NAMUMA	Ouma Kabwere
	Mbakulo Obondo
	Odwori
NATIKOKO	Buyoka Hatete
NAKURUKU	Godfrey Nehabi
	Barasa Mwenge

MICHAEL MUHEMBA WA ADIKA

NAKIROYA	Machio
	Nalwenge
	Nahulo

OGUMBA WA EMBALWA

NAMAINDI	Grado Makoha

GRADO MAKOHA WA OGUMBA

	Rojasi Wafula
	Donald Lwoma
	Fred Ouma
	Sailas Namulumba
NANKIMA	Julias Embalwa
NAMUKUBA	Ben Ogumba
	Michael Mayiga

EKAKA WA EMBALWA

NALALA	Ourna
	Okumu
	Taabu
	Oundo

Olwande lwo lupapula 20

OKOCHI ONGANGO

NAMUDUMBA	?

BENARD BARASA WA OTYOLA

NAMUHULA	Juma Otyola
	Ouli

EDWARD EKAKA WA OTYOLA

NAMUDDE	Peter Otyola
	Ouma

PETER OTYOLA WA EDWARD EKAKA

NAMUDAIRWA Sihwanyala ohuduhana ebihiraho awo

FRANCIS EKAKA WA OGANGA WA OTYOLA

NAHULO Sihwaduhana ebingi

AGAITANO OUMA WA OTYOLA

NABONWE Taabu

? **JOSEPH JUMA WA OTYOLA**

? **OBINDA MUNYAUSI WA OTYOLA**

ROMAN OUMA WA OTYOLA

NAJABI Odibia Otyola
Nandunga
Okello

EKAKA WA OBINDA OTAMBULA

NASONGA Ouma Muhaha
NASUBO Onyango
NAMAKANGAL Obbondo
NAMULUNDU Masorea Ekaka

OUMA MUHAHA WA EKAKA

ONGANGO WA EKAKA

NAHASOHO Leuben Siriebo
NABONGO Atanas Ekaka
NAHONE Charles Obbare
NAMBANJA Eriakimu Obinda
NAMULUNDU Masorea Ekaka
NAMAKANGALA Leston Sikala

REUBEN SIRIEBO WA ONGANGO

NACHAKI Humphress Wanyama

ATANASI EKAKA WA ONGANGO

BWIBO David Ongango
Francis Barasa
Michael Wangira
Ekaka Odwori

DAVID ONGANGO WA ATANASI EKAKA

NATIKOKO Edwirin Ekaka

FRANCIS BARASA WA ATANASI EKAKA

NALANGO Lanald Ekaka

MICHAEL WANGIRA WA ATANASI EKAKA

NAHUMACHI James

EKAKA ODWORI WA ATANASI EKAKA

CHARLES OBBARE WA ONGANGO

ADETI
NAFUNYA

Abahana Bongone.
Ekaka (Makanika)
Nahone
Odwori
John

EKAKA MAKANIKA WA CHARLES OBBARE

NAMUKOBE

Obote
Jogoo
Kilo
Siriebo

NAHONE WA CHARLES OBBARE

NAMULUNDU

Mugeni
Barasa

ODWORI WA OBBARE

NALIALI

Mugeni

JOHN SIRIEBO WA CHARLES OBBARE

NAMULUNDU

Wandera
Siriebo

OBINDA ERIAKIMU WA ONGANGO

NAMUDUMA

Omuhana Yengene. Sihwaduhana ebimutulaho

EKAKA MASORE WA ONGANGO

Siyaleha omundu dawe

LASTON SIKALALA WA ONGANGO

OBONDO WA EKAKA

OCHIENGI NASIKAYE

NANYIWALO

Chore Abwayo nende Omanyo

CHORE ABWOYO WA OCHIENGI NASIKAYE

OMANYO WA OCHIENGI NASIKAYE

OGOOLA WA NGWENO LUNUNI 2

NALALA

Mbulu
Wandefu
Muniala
Sibala

MBULU WA OGOOLA

NABONWE

Ngweno Sigiria
Siganga
Ogoola II

NGWENO SIGIRIA WA MBULU

NABUKAKI

Eria Ochieno
Ogoola Ongeke

ERIA OCHIENO WA NGWENO

NAMIRIPO
NACHAKI I

Zablon Wanyama
Yonasani Mbulu
Amulamu Makoha
Daudi Odedo
Ojiambo Gideon Ngweno
Salomon Okelo
■ Ester Natabona.

NACHAKI II

Mangeni
Samuel Wanyama
Wycliffe Wafula
Wandera

NACHAKI III

Richard Egessa (Ngweno)
Samuel Mangeni
Onyango

NAJABI I

Wafula
Bwire

NAJABI II

Daudi Ngweno (Bwire)
Fredrick Wandera
Siminyu

NAJABI III

Aggrey Okuku
Paul Sitanga

ZABULONI WANYAMA WA ERIA OCHYENO

NAMUDIBYA
NAMUNYORO

Onyango
Baguma

BAGUMA WA ZEBLONI WANYAMA

NAMUMAYI

YONASANI MBULU WA ERIA OCHIENO

NAMUKOBE

Peter (Masiga) Ogoola
Geofrey Onyango

MAKOHA AMULAMU WA ERIA OCHIENO

NAFUKA

Wanyama
Wandera

DAUDI ODEDO WA ERIA OCHIENO

Ngweno

OJIAMBO GIDION WA ERIA OCHIENO

NAMUNYANKOLE   Bwire
Wandera

SALOMON OKELLO WA ERIA OCHIENO

NAMUSIGE   Okumu
Egesa

SAMUEL WANYAMA WA ERIA OCHIENO

NANYANGA   Ngweno

Olwande lwo lupapula 23

WYCLIFFE WAFULA WA ERIA OCHIENO

NAMUNYEKERA   Ogoola

WANDERA WA ERIA OCHIENO

NADONGO   Ngweno

RICHARD EGESA WA ERIA OCHIENO

Daudi
Mugeni

SAMUEL MANGENI WA ERIA OCHIENO

NASIRWA

DAUDI NGWENO WA ERIA OCHIENO

NALALA   Sitanga
Ngweno
Zakalia

FREDRICK WANDERA WA ERIA OCHIENO

NADONGO   Ngweno

AGGREY OKUMU WA ERIA OCHIENO

?   Ngweno
Sihwanyola enono y angina Ngweno

OGOOLA WA NGWENO

NABBIANGU   -

MBULU WA OGOOLA

NABONWE   Sitanga Obwaso
NABUKAKI   Yosia Wafula
NASIEMA   Yosamu Egesa
Yolamu Okumu
NACHAKI   Wanyama
NAMUPODI   Osinya
NAMUFUTA   Onyango

YOSIYA WAFULA WA SITANGA

NAMALA   Charles Mugeni
               G. Williamu Ojiambo
NAMBOKO   Peter Juma
NAMUMAYI   Michael Wandera
               Stephin Muhongo
               Wilber Bwire
               Daudi Ouma
               Benard Businge
               Simion Sanya
NACHONGA   Mugende Sitanga
NAMUSIHO   Mbulu

MICHAEL WANDERA WA WAFULA

NAKUHU   Geofrey Sunday

YOSAMU EGESA WA SITANGA

NACHAKI   Samuel Wanyama
               Aggrey Ojiambo
               James Oundo
               George Mangeni
NAMULAKA   Opio
NAMUTENDE   Odongo
               Wandera
NAMUNYEKERA   Opio
               Mangeni

Olwande lwo lupapula 24

AGGREY OJIAMBO WAS YOSAMU EGESA

?   Daudi Nantongo

JAMES OUNDO WA YOSAMU EGESA

NAMUTENDE   Rogers yafwa

GEORGE MANGENI WA YOSAMU EGESA

NABUKAKI   Taabu
               Richard Wandera

YOLAMU OKUMU WA SITANGA

NAKOOLI   Bwire
               Mangeni
               Wafula

BWIRE WA YOLAMU OKUMU

MANGENI WA YOLAMU OKUMU

WAFULA WA YOLAMU OKUMU

OSINYA WA SITANGA

NALALA WA MUKISA

MBULU HENERY

NGWENO LUNUNI

NAMANGALE | Waida

WAIDA WA NGWENO LUNUNI
Mudubwa
Ngweno Konga
Osinya

MUDUBWA WA WAIDA
Osinya
Peter Lwande
Eriya Achiengi

NASUBO

NGWENO KANGA WA WAIDA
Mbuya
Waida II

MBUYA WA NGWENO KANGA
Waida
Odimo

NAPUNYI

WAIDA MBUYA
Isirael Wafula
Daniel Achieno
Peter Mbuya

NALALA
NAMULUNDU
NAMUSOGA

ISIRAEL WAFULA WA WAIDA MBUYA
Julias Machio
Egessa

Olwande lwo lupapula 25

JULIAS MACHIO WA ISIRAEL WAFULA

EGESSA WA ISIRAEL WAFULA

NAMAINDI

DANIEL ACHIENO WA WAIDA
Charles Hamala

PETER MBUYA WA WAIDA

NAKUHU

JONATHAN OUCHO WA MBUYA
Nasubo

NAMANYI

DAUDI OKUKU WA MBUYA
Wanyama
Waida

NALIALI

29

ODIMO WA MBUYA
Livingston Oucho

LIVINGSTON OUCHO = ODIMO

NAMUTENDE
(Onyango) Wycliffe Mbuya
Ogutu

WYCLIFFE MBUYA WA LIVINGSTON OUCHO

NABONWE
NADIGO
Moses Odimo
Waida
Daudi Wafula

NABONGO
-

NAMANYI
OGUTU WA LIVINGSTON OUCHO
-

WAIDA II WA NGWENO KANGA

NAHAYO
Ibulaim Bwire
Erisa Ndiira

NAMASIRO
Yoweri Wandera
Dani Mujugga

IBULAIMU BWIRE WA WAIDA

NAMULEMESI
NAMAYINDI
Magero
NAMUDDE
Wafula
Ogutu

MAGERO WA IBULAIMU BWIRE

NAMULEMESI
Mangeni
NAMUKOBE
-

NABOOLI
WAFULA WA IBULAIMU BWIRE
Mbuya

Olwande lwo lupapula 26

OGUTU WA IBULAIMU BWIRE

NABUKAKI
Okumu

ERISA NDIIRA WA WAIDA

NAMAYINDI
Ali Wandera
Ojiambo Ndiira

NAJABI
Wanyama Ndiira

ALI WANDERA WA ERISA NDIIRA

OJIAMBO WA ERISA NDIIRA

WANYAMA WA ERISA NDIIRA

YOWERI WANDERA WA WAIDA

NALIALI Jackson Ouma

John Ogutu

NALIALI Albert Ojiambo

Barasa

NAMANYI Justin Wafula

JACKSON OUMA WA YOWERI WANDERA

ADETI Bwire

Mareki

Moses

NAMAHANJA Ouma

Olwande lwo lupapula 26

JOHN OGUTTU WA YOWERI WANDERA

NAMASES Monday

ALBERT OJIAMBO WA YOWERI WANDERA

NAHULO Wandera

BARASA WA YOWERI WANDERA

NAMULUNDU Bwire

JUSTIN WAFULA WA YOWERI WANDERA

NAMIRIPO Barasa

Justo

OSINYA WA MUDUBWA

NASICHONGI Peter Lwande

Eriya Achiengi

PETER LWANDE WA OSINYA

NAHOOLI William Ojiambo

Wasike

Wandera

Barasa

NAMWANGA Ochieno

WILLIAM OJIAMBO WA PETER LWANDE

NAJABI Mangeni (*see Below*)

Bwire

Wafula

Okumu

NACHIMO Bwire Simion

Amosi Egessa

Siminyu

Mahobbe

31

MANGENI WA WILLIAM OJIAMBO

NALIALI
Oundo

BWIRE WA WILLIAM OJIAMBO

NAMAKANGALA

WAFULA WA WILLIAM OJIAMBO

NAMANYI

WASIKE WA PETER LWANDE

NALIALI
Friday
Charles

WANDERA WA PETER LWANDE

NAMUSOGA
Geofrey Wanyama
Jimy

OCHIENO WA PETER LWANDE

NEKHOBA

ERIA ACHIENGI WA OSINYA

NALALA
Ofwiri
Mudubwa
NAMULUNDU
Pop Opio

OFWIRI WA ERIYA ACHIENGI

OPIO WA ERIA ACHIENGI

NASICHONGI
-

MUKKA WA NGWENO KANGA

WAIDA WA MBUYA

NAMUDUMA
Samuel Musigo

SAMUEL MUSIGO

NASICHONGI
Absolom Ojiambo
Firimon Okello
NAMUDAI
Tito Waida
John Wanyama
Aggrey Oundo

TITO WAIDA

ADETI
Nimrod Mbuya
Amulam Waida
Paul Wafula
Aggrey Oundo
Daudi Were

NGWENO LUNUNI

NAHERE
Sombi

SOMBI

NAMULEMBO
Obaala

OBAALA WA SOMBI

NALUKADA
Jinga

NASIMALWA
Obwora

Ngweno

NAHAYO
Lwande

JINGA WA OBAALA

NAKOOLI
Ojiambo

NAMANGALE
Kuchihi

OJIAMBO KINDA

NAMULUNDU
Livingstone Wanyama

Olwoochi

Ojwangi

WANYAMA – OJIAMBO

NAHONE
Livingstone Bwire

Lubega Jinga

Ouma

KUCHIHI JINGA

NAKWERI
Onyango Were

NACHAKI
Wafula Jinga

OLWOCHI OJIAMBO

NABULINDO
Godfrey Bwire

Geofrey Okumu

OJWANGI OJIAMBO

NALALA

OBWORA OBAALA

NAJABI
Halogo

HALOGO OBWORA

NAFWOFWOYO
Firipo Obaala

NAMULEMBO
Musa Magaga

Jackson Musembe

NABONWE
Were Chabugwe

NAKOOLI
Zabuloni Himbiri

Yoweri Halogo II

FIRIPO OBAALA WA HALOGO

NAHONE   Yosia Ojiambo
                  Nuwa Masirubu
                  Daniel Okello
                  Bulasio Obaala

NAHONE II   Juma
                  Ojiambo
                  Wafula
                  Barasa
                  Ouma

YOSIA OJIAMBO WA FIRIPO OBAALA

NAMUBASIRA   Jimbi
                  Lwande

NAHULO   Wafula
                  Pamba
                  Ouma

Olwande lwo lupapula 29

NUWA MASIRUBU WA FIRIPO OBAALA

NAMUFUTA   Wanyama
                  Bwire
                  Mayende

DANIEL OKELLO WA FIRIPO OBAALA

?   Paska
?   Ojiambo
?   Bogere

BULASIO OBAALA WA FIRIPO OBAALA

NAKWATI   Wandera
                  Amigo
                  Nahone

MUSA MAGAGA WA HALOGO

NAPUNYI   Wanyama
                  Ouma

NASERA   Nasimalwa
                  Majoni

WANYAMA WA MUSA MAGAGA

NANDEKIA

OUMA WA MUSA MAGAGA

NABWALA   Musa Magaga
NAMAKANGALA   Musa Magaga

NASIMALWA WA MUSA MAGAGA

NAMAKANGALA

34

MAJONI WA MUSA MAGAGA

NABWIBO   Musa Stephin

            Musa Magaga

NABURI

Olwande lwo lupapula 30

JACKSON MUSUMBA WA HALOGO

NEBEERE   Livingstone Halogo

            Obwora

            Mugeni

            Obaala

            Makoha (Sibaki)

NAMBANJA   Egesa

LIVINGSTONE HALOGO WA MUSUMBA

ADETI

OBWORA WA JACKSON MUSUMBA

NAMBANJA   Charles Bwire

            Stephin Oundo

            Francis Mangeni

            Kenneth Sunday

MANGENI WA JACKSON MUSUMBA

NAMULUNDU   Jackson Musumba

NAMUTES   Easter Kulaba

NAKOMOLO   Ojiambo

            Ouma

OBAALA WA JACKSON MUSUMBA

NANYIBOMI   Ojiambo

            Musa Ojiambo

            Egesa

NABOOLI   Bwire

MAKOHA WA JACKSON MUSUMBA

HAMIRIPO

EGESSA WA JACKSON MUSUMBA

NABOOLI   Manuel Musumba

            Moses (Musa)

WERE CHABUGWE WA JACKSON MUSUMBA

NAMUFUTA   Ojiambo

NAMANYAMA   Ojiambo

            Obwora nende Wafula

ZEBULONI HIMBIRI WA HALOGO

NANYIBOMI	Samuel Juma Halogo
	Najabi
	Wangira
	Barasa
NAHONE	Musa Magaga
	Obaala

Olwande lwo lupapula 31

NAMULUNDU	Egessa
	Sidialo
	Ojiambo
	Oyonjo

SAMUEL JUMA HIMBIRI

NAMENYA	James Sumba
	Wilson Mangeni
	Hamphress Sunday
	Wafula Juma

NAJABI HIMBIRI

NAHONE	Bwire Najabi
	Wanyama
	Charles Najabi

YOWERE WA HALOGO

NAMWANDIRA	Ogutu
	Wafula
	Sunday Bosi bafwa:
	Nakooli
	Were

LWANDE OBALA

NAMAINDI	Samuel Sombi II
NAJABI	Jacob Omondi
Hamiripo	Daniel Donga
NACHAKI	Salimu Wandera

SAMUEL SOMBI II

NABONWE	Abner Mayende
	George Ouma
NAMUDDE	Zedekia Wandera
	Wilson Mangeni
	Tito Sombi (Onyango)
Nakooli	Anderoa Ngdege
	John Rabongo

AMBER MAYENDE – SOMBI

NASICHONGI	. . . . .

36

GEORGE OUMA – SOMBI

NAMULINDA

Bwire (Obaala)
Onyango (Sombi)
Ojiambo
Mangeni
Wandera
Okumu

Olwande lwo lupapula 32

NAMULANGIRA

Lwande Wilberforce
Robert Sombi

ZEDEKIYA WANDERA – SOMBI

NAMBANJA
NAMULUNDU

Aggrey Obaala (Sombi)
Patrick Lwande
Fred Sombi
Jackson Lwande
Aggrey Obaala

NAMUKEMO
NADIDI
NAMURARAKA

Wilson Lwande
Bernard Wafula
Samuel Sombi
Wilber Ngweno Muloma
David Makoha

NAMULUNDU II

Godfrey
Bon
Moses Bwire

AGGREY OBAALA – ZEDEKIA WANDERA

NAMUKEMO

. . . . .

RABONGO JAMES BWIRE Z. WANDERA

NAKAROKO
NAMUKOBE

Henery Nambanja
. . . . .

PATRICK LWANDE – ZEDEKIA WANDERA

NAMUDAIRWA

Samuel Sombi

WILSON MANGENI WA SOMBI

NAMULUNDU I

Henery Onyango
Geofrey Bwire
Samuel Sombi

NAMULUNDU II

Livingstone Ouma
Robert Lwande
Walter Master Bwire
Benjamin Omenya

NAMUFUTA

Wycliffe Namudde
Backley Obbala Ojiambo

HENERY ONYANGO WA WILSON MANGENI

NADRUBA

Leonard Wafula

GEOFREY BWIRE WA WILSON MANGENI

NANDEKIYA

. . . . .

37

Olwande lwo lupapula 33

TITO (SOMBI) ONYANGO WA SOMBI

NAMUSONGE   Samuel Sombi
NALIALI   Carmasky Kubindi
    Zedekiea Hadudu
    Stanely Sombi

ANDEREYA NDOGE WA SOMBI

NAKWERI   Dakari Obaala
    Were
    Ojiambo
NAJABI   Samweri Sombi
    Andere Egessa
    Abneri Stephen

JOHN RABONGO WA SOMBI

JACOBO OMONDI WA LWANDE

NAMULEMBO   Yokana Lwande
    Samuel Wandera
    Jackson Ngweno
NABAHOLO   Edward Sombi
NASONGA I   Isaao Oduba
NASONGA II   Joram Musumba

YOKANA LWANDE WA JOCOB OMONDI

NAMENYA   Alex Onyango

ALEX ONYANGO WA YOKANA LWANDE

NAMIRIPO   Omondi

SAMUEL WANDERA WA JOCOB OMONDI

NABONGO   (Sindamanya)
    Patrick Bwire
NAJABI   Shadrack Barasa
    Geofrey Omondi
    Benard Ouma

JACKSON NGWENO WA JOCOB OMONDI

NAMUTORO   Ojiambo
    Bwire
    Fred
    Omondi

EDWARD SOMBI WA JACOBO OMONDI

NAMWAYA   Tom Okello
    Tambiti
NAMULUNDU   Ouma

Olwande lwo lupapula 34

TOM OKELLO WA EDWARD SOMBI

ADETI

TAMBITI EDWARD SOMBI

NALALA
NAMUGANDA   Maadi

ISAAC ODUBA WA JACOBO OMONDI
NAMUBUPI   Lwande
                Najabi
                Sombi

LWANDE WA ISAAC ODUBA
NABURI

NAJABI WA ODUBA OMONDI
NASIRISI   Stephen Omondi

SOMBI WA ISAAC ODUBA

NGWENO LUNUNI WA LWANDE WESONGA
NASONGA II   Banga

BANGA WA NGWENO LUNUNI
NAMAINDI   Ombole
                Embaaya
                Ngweno Dambakana
                Odooli
ODWAKO
OMBOOLE WA BANGA

EMBAAYA WA BANGA
NAHWAKU   Mbasiro
                Mulehe
                Siongongo
MBASIRO WA EMBAAYA

MULEHE WA EMBAAYA
NALIALI   ■ Akumu Natabona,
                ■ Nerima Natabona,
                ■ Guloba Natabona,
                ■ Natabona – erita lyakotera hulupapula
                Muchanji Naggaga,
                Wandera Banana

WANDERA BANANA WA MULEHE
NALALA   Stephin Mangeni
                Bwiro Naangaga

STEPHIN MANGENI OWA WANDERA BANANA
NAMUTENDE   Nangaga
                Bwire
                Masiga

Olwande lwo lupapula 35

HAMIRIPO WA NGWENO LUNUNI

NAMANGALE

Lwande
Namudde
Musebule
Ngweno Donga

LWANDE WA HAMIRIPO

?

Opio
Agwanda

OPIO WA LWANDE

NABONGO

Sembo Madara

SEMBO MADARA WA OPIO

NAMUDUMA

Yowaba Okuku
Disimasi Tanga
Baturumayo Nabongo

YOWABA OKUKU WA SEMBO MADARA

NAMAKANGALA I
NAMAKANGAL II

Jacob Okumu

NADUKAKI

Odwori

JACOB OKUMU – YOWANA OKUKU

NANYIBURA

Samu – Masuko
Robert Dely
Lita Tanga

DISMAS TANGA, SEMEO MADARA, NAMULUMBA

BATULUMAYO NABONGO – S. MADARA

NACHONGA

Ogutu
Joseph (Namude)

NALWENGE

Onyango
Monday

NAMUDDE WA HAMIRIPO

NABONGO

Sikala Agula.

SIKALA AGULA WA NAMUDDE

NALIALI

Odongo Sihawa
Were

NAMULUNDU

Sikala Oyoda

ODONGO SIHAWA – ONGOLI

NANYANGA

Wycliffe Namudde

Olwande lwo lupapula 36

Opada

NAJABI

David Ouma

INYASI WERE WA SIKALA OYODA

NAMUSIHO Atanasi Sikala

ATANASI SIKALA WA INYASI WERE

NASUBO Wandera
Ojiambo
Makoha Nyasi
Nyasaga
Bwire
Nyasi

WANDERA WA ATANASI SIKALA

NAMWALIRA Fredrick Wafula
Atanasi Ojiambo
NASIHUNE Tanasi Makoha
NAHULO

WERE WA SIKALA AGULA

NAMULUNDU Otengo
Yakerama Namulundu yali owa simwana huniyebula Otengo

OTENGO WA WERE OMUSIANI WA SIKALA

NANYINEKI Wilbrondo Okumu

WILBRONDO OKUMU WA OTENGO

NAJABI Onyango
Wafula (Yafwa)
Ojiambo
Wandera
Barasa
NAMUTIMBA Wanyama
Sanya
Mugeni
Barasa

ONYANGO WA WILBRONDO OKUMU

NAMUDDE Peter Masiga
John Wanyama

WAFULA WA WILBRONDO OKUMU

NAMUDEPI Wandera

OJIAMBO WA WILBRONDO OKUMU

NAMUDDE Bernard Mugeni
Denesi Oguttu
Godfrey Bwire
NAMUMALI Barasa Wilbrondo Okumu

41

Olwande lwo lupapula 37

ONGOLI WA ODONGO SIHANA
WANYAMA WA ONGOLI

NAHABI   Barasa
Ouma
Bwire

ODONGO WA ONGOLI

NAHONE   Okumu
Ojiambo
Gasino Mangeni (Yafwa)

NAMAINDI   Egessa
Orida Bubolu

NAHOBA   Bukalu
Sibiya nende Lumboti

ODWORI ONGOLI WA NAGWANGA

OCHOCHI WA ONGOLI

WERE WA SIKALA ADISI

SIKALA OYODA

SIKALA ADISI

NAMUDIBA WA ATIKO SIKALA (ADIS)

ATIKO SIKALA (ADISI)

NACHAKI   Ogutu
Mangeni
Juma
Wandera

NAHONE   Opada (Okumu)
David Ouma
Wanyama
Darasa Oundo
Ogutu Atiko

NAHAMENGE   Bwire
Ouma
Opio
Mangeni

NABAHOLO   Richard Ojiambo
Charles
James Wandera

NABAHOLO II   Lazalo
Ohasa
Isaac Barasa

Olwande lwo lupapula 38

WANYAMA WA OKUMU

NAPUNYI   Charles Ochieno

42

NAMUKOBE

MUSEMBULE WA HAMIRIPO
Ngweno Nabulayi

NALALA

NGWENO NABULAYI WA HAMIRIPO
Walungoli
Olunjala
Onyuni

NATIKOKO

WALUNGOLI WA NGWENO ARIADA OLUNJALU
Eria Omwene

NAJABI

ERIA OMWENE WA OLUNJALU
Stanely Asumanga

NAYIYE

STANELY ASUMANGA WA ERIA OMWENE
Richard Ojiambo
Yovani Mangeni

RICHARD OJIAMBO WA STANELY ASUMANGA

NALALA

ONYUNI WA NGWENO NABULAYI
Paulo Ngweno
Seperia Nyegenye (Abbanga)

NAHONE

NASIENYA

PAULO NGWENO WA ONYUNI
Eriazali Ouma
James Musumba (Yafwa)
Mangeni
Wafula
Wanyama

NAMUDUMA
NAMULANDA

ERIAZALI OUMA WA PAULO NGWENO

NAMULOBA

NAHULO
NASAKAMU

JAMES MUSUMBA WA PAULO NGWENO
Wandera
Jason
Matinda
Sanya
Sanya
James Musumba

NABONWE

MANGENI WA PAULO NGWENO
Patrick Egessa

NANYIRIMI
NASUBO

FREDRICK BWIRE WA PAULO NGWENO

Vincent Wandera

DISANI WAFULA WA PAULO NGWENO

NALIALI

ERINEYO WANYAMA WA PAULO NGWENO

NAYIYE
Juma
Wafula

SEPERIA NYEGENYE WA ABBANGA

NAMUHOOKOSI
Wilfred Ochieno
NAMANGALE
Walter Onyango

WILFRED OCHIENO WA SEPERIA NYEGENYE

NASIRWA
Stephen

WILFRED OCHIENO WA NYEGENYE

NGWENO DONGA WA HAMIRIPO

OJWANGI WA NGWENO DONGA

ADETI
Balongo

NEHOBA
Onyigi
Ojanji
Ngweno B.

BALONGO WA OJWANGI

NACHAKI
Wandera Balongo
Patrick Bbala (Yafwa)
Obbamba Balongo
NAHABI
Firikis Orembo (Yafwa)
Adeti (Yafwa)
Ouma Balongo

WANDERA WA BALONGO

NABONWE
Makoha Lungasa
NAMWINI
John Bwire
Mangeni Wandera

MAKOHA LUNGASA WA WANDERA

NANYANGA
NAMUDDE
Bwire Wandera

PATRICK BBALA WA BALONGO

NABONWE
John Okanya
NAKIROYA
Patrick Pamba
NAMUKOBE
Ouma
Godfrey
Ojwangi
Albert Ojiambo
Anthony Wandera

NAMIRIPO

OBETE WA ONYIGI
John Wandera
Alex Mangeni

NAHAYO

MARIKO MAKANDA WA YOWANA OGWANGI
Barasa (ABUHERE)

NAKUHU
NAMULEMBO

BARASA WA MARIKO MAKANDA
David Juma
Idi Barasa
Nyongesa Barasa

NAMANYI

WANJALA WA ONYIGI
Bodi
Abangi (Yafwa)
Maloba (Yafwa)
Onyango

NATIKOKO

Ojiambo

NACHWERE

BODI WA WANJALA
Wandera Bodi
Bwire Bodi

ABANGI WA WANJALA

NEBERE

ONYANGO WA WANJALA
Masiga

NAMUKOBE

OKAARA WA ONYIGI
Okochi
Masiga

NAMANGALE
NADEKE

OKOCHI WA OKAARA
Juma Onyigi

Olwande lwo lupapula 41

NAMUTALA

JOHN OKONYA WA PATRICK BBALA
Barasa (Balongo)
Okumu Okanya
Balongo Okanya

NANGAYO

OBBAMBA WA BALONGO
■ Banatabona 3

NAMUJALA

FILIKISI OREMBO WA BALONGO
Wangalwa

NASONGA
NAKOMOLO

WANGALWA WA FILIKISI OREMBO
Okuku
Bubolu
Fitaleo Osinya

45

FITALEO OSINYA WA WANGALWA

NALALA   Masinde
          Baati

ASEBE WA BALONGO

NASUBO   Bwire
          Okoowa

OUMA WA BALONGO

NAMUTENDE Geofrey Okochi
           Ojiambo
NAHABI   Cornel Bwire
           Mangeni
           Gusino
           Bwire

GEOFREY BWIRE WA OUMA

NEKERERE   Vicent Sanya
           Thomas Barasa

OJIAMBO WA OUMA

NAMUKONO   Ogutu

ONYIGI WA OJWANGI

NAHABI   Yowana Ojwangi
             Obete
NACHIMO I   Wanjala (andeme)
NAMUDAIRW   Okaara
NACHIMO II   Juma

YOWANA OJWANGI WA ONYIGI

NASUBO   Mariko Makanda
           Mbanico Obete

Olwande lwo lupapula 42

MARIKO MAKANDA WA YOWANA OJWANGI

NABAYO   Barasa (Abuhere)

BARASA WA MARIKO MAKANDA

WANJALA WA ONYIGI

NAMANYI   Boodi
           Abangi (Yafwa)
           Maloba (Yafwa)
           Onyango
NATIKOKO   Ojiambo

BOODI WA WANJALA

NAHWASI   Wandera Boodi
           Bwire Boodi

OKAARA WA ONYIGI

NAMANGALE
NADEKE

Juma Onyigi

Olwande lwo lupapula 43

OLWENI NYEMBI WA NGWENO LUNUNI

NALIALI
NASONGA I
NASONGA II
NALALA

Owori Habocha
Siduwa Owori
SIDUWA
Sidubo

BABOCHA WA OLWENYI NYEMBI

Nimurodi Ndongi

OWORI WA OLWENYI NYEMBI

Joel Ariada

SIDUBO WA OLWENYI NYEMBI

Ojiambo Agaaya

SIDUBO WA OLWENYI NYEMBI

Tainor Hakerwe
Abner Ekudu

OLWENYI NYEMBI WA NGWENO LUNUNI

NACHAKI

Sunu
Okweyo

NALIALI

Habocha

SANU WA OLWENYI NYEMBI

Morris Onyango
Nanel Wanyama

OKWENYO WA NGWENO LUNUNI

Ogana
Wambete

HABOCHA WA NGWENO LUNUNI

HABOCHA WA OLWENYI NYEBI

NALALA

Ndongi
Otiende

NDONGI WA HABOCHA

NAJABI

Obocho

OBOCHO WA NDONGI

NAMANGALE

Nimrod Ndongi

47

NIMROD NDONGI

NANJOSI
Booker Ndongi
Apolo Ndongi
Joshua Sigondi Ndongi
Patrick Jogoo
Emmanuel Banda

BOOKER NDONGI WA NIMROD NDONGI
Sigondi
Toti
Ezekiel Odonya

APOLO NDONGI WA NIMROD NDONGI

NAMENY
Nimrod Ndongi
Were

OTIENDE WA OLWENYI

NABURI
Bakanya
Chabiri (Chabiri luyafwa babekawo Bakanya)

BAKANYA WA OTIENDE

NAWOONGA
Hadera
Habuu (Hadera luyafwa babekawo Habuu)

HADERA WA BAKANYA

NANYIBOMI
Sigondi (Choroko)

Olwande lwo lupapula 44

NASONGA OWORI WA OLWENYI NYEMBI

NAMULUMBA
Opala

OPALA WA NASONGA OWORI

NAMANGALE
Wamalwa

WAMALWA WA OPALA

NABUKAKI
NAHASOHO
George Musumba
Wandera

OWORI II WA OPALA

NABONGO
NAKOOLI
Sibabale
Joel Ariada Mangoli

SIBABALE WA OWORI II

NAHULO
Odwori

ODWORI WA SIBABALE

NASONGA

JOEL ARIADA (MANGOLI) WA OWORI

NALALA
Jackson Ochieno
Joshua Wandera (Duncan)

JACKSON OCHIENO WA JOEL ARIADA

NAMUDDE
ADETI

Albert Owori
David Ojiambo (Kaka)

JOSHUA WANDERA (DUNCAN) WA JOEL ARIADA

NALALA
NASONGA II

Olweni Nyembi

OLWENI NYEMBI
Siduwa

SIDUWA WA OLWENYI NYEMBI

NAMUNAPA

Omuhehe

OMUHEHE WA SIDUWA

NAMAKANGALA
NAMANGALE

Zefania Agaaya
Zadoki Ouma (Ranyosi)

ZEFANIA AGAAYA WA OMUHEHE

NAMUMA

Cornel Malingu
Patrick Ojiambo

CORNEL MALINGU WA ZEFANIA AGAAYA

NAMENYA

John Omuhehe
Egessa Oburra

JOHN OMUHEHE WA CORNEL MALINGU

NAMUKOBE

Malingu (Abbara) nende (Tajiri Mawaya)

PATRICK OJIAMBO WA ZEFANIA AGAAYA

NAFWOFWOYO

Mafwamba
Agaaya

MAFWAMBA WA PATRICK OJIAMBO

NAJABI

ZADOKI OUMA WA OMUHEHE

NALALA

Wanyama
Wandera
Wafula

Olwande lwo lupapula 45

WANYAMA WA ZADOKI OUMA

NALYALI

Ndongi

WANDERA WA ZADOKI OUMA

NAHONE

Robert

WAFULA WA ZADOKI OUMA

NAMUSONGE

Ndongi

OLWENYI NYEMBI WA NGWENO LUNUNI

NALALA

Sidubo

SIDUBO WA OLENYI NYEMBI

NABWALA
NACHAKI

Ndoro

NDORO WA SIDUBO

NABAHOLO

Buluma

BULUMA WA NDORO

NABULE
NAHONE

Taidor Hakerwe

Alfunzi Nabwala

TAIDOR HAKERWE WA BULUMA

NAKOOLI II

Alex Oundo

Wilson Okello

Oundo Hakerwe

NAKOOLI I
NANJOSI

Nabwala

Bubolu

ALEX OUNDO WA TAIDRO HAKERWE

NALYALI

Wafula

Mangeni

ALFUNZI NABWALA WA BULUMA

NAMANGALE

Clement Wanyande

Okumu Nabwala

Sidubo Nabwala

NACHAKI WA NYANDE WA SIDUBO

NAMAYAYI

Siyaleha mundu musacha.

Oundo niye owafira mumaye e Tanganyika, nalehawo Omusiani –
Halengo Nomuhana Akumu; ngina Gideon Wanyama

NAHERE MATA DANIEL

NAMUDAIRWA
NEHOBA
NABULINDO

Siboche

Namukooli

Okuku (Ohaba)

Olwande lwo lupapula 46

NABONGO

Buluma

Dadi

■ Banatabona babiri – sihwaduhana ameta

NAMAINDI

■ Addea Natabona

■ Auma Samia Natabona

OUNDO WA WANYANDE

NAJABI

Yebula Opuli Halango

Manu Oundo yafwira mu mayee ake Tanganyika mu 1914.

DANIEL MATA WANYANDE

NAMBOKO

Yawawo nachya eBunyala erya nali nende enda ya Mata, niyebulayo omwana Achoaka. Namboko yachia erya hulwembaliha, hulwohuba Mata yali akerame Leah Ongoola (Odeywa), Siboche nafwire.

NAMENYA LEAH
ONGOOLA ODEYWA

Yali muha Siboche. Siboche yafwa niyebule naye abana babiri, omuhana nende omusiani. Omuhana niye:

■ Ofwamba Natabona

Omusiani niye MULIRO

Abo nibo abaali abaana ba Siboche.

Mata niyakerama yebulamo abana 8.

■ Abo 8 bosi bali Banatabona

olunyuma niyebula abasyani 2, nibo bano:

ABNERI EKUDU

YEKOYADA MBUNDA. Nibo abekala enda.

ABUNERI EKUDU WA DANIEL MATA

NAHABUKA I
NAHABUKA II

Reubeni Namenya
Jophiter Okumu
Julius Onyango
Samuel Baker Bwire

NAGENI

Eridadi Ongoola
Wilberforce Ekudu Bwire
David Wafula
Benard Wandera

NALYALI

Jophiter (Yefusa) Ouma

REUBENI NAMENYA WA ABUNERI EKUDU

NADONGO

Wilber Bwire

ERIDADI ONGOOLA WA ABUNERI EKUDU

NACHAKI

Moses Namenya

JULIUS ONYANGO WA ABUNERI EKUDU

NAMUKULWA (NEREKE)

WILBERFORCE EKUDU WA ABUNERI EKUDU

NABAHOLO

DAVID WAFULA WA ABUNERI EKUDU

NACHAKI

2

BENARD WANDERA WA ABUNERI EKUDU

NALYALI

Wilber Bwire

YEKOYADA MBUNDA WA MATA

NACHONGA
Benya Bwire
Michael Wanyande
Okello
Ojiambo

NASIYEE
Charles Mata Wandera
Lauben Leah Ojiambo
Godfrey Ouma (Singuba)

NAHIBE
Dickson Ngweno (Mugaluka)
Samuel Sidubo
Daniel (Acid) Mayende
Joseph Ndiaba
Nuwa Namenya

Olwande lwo lupapula 47

BENYA BWIRE WA YEKOYADA MBUNDA

NACHAKI
Ronald Ojiambo
Yona Mbunda

MICHAEL WANYANDE WA YOKOYADA MBUNDA

NANKIMA
Fred Wanyande

CHARLES MATA WANDERA WA YOKOYADA MBUNDA

NAHBWI
Buleyan Masiga
Timoth Mukisa
Andrew

LABANI LEAH OJIAMBO WA YOKOYADA MBUNDA

NABYANGU

GODFREY OUMA WA YOKOYADA MBUNDA

NAGEMI
Levi Mbunda

JORAM WAFULA WA DANIEL MATA

NASIYEE
Stephen Mulehe
Namukooli
George Ojiambo
Godfrey Were Ojiambo
Joseph Ogutu
Julius Wanyama (Nalyali)

NAMUSOGA
William Egessa
David Oundo

STEPHEN MULEHE WA JORAN WAFULA

NAMUDIRA
Eli Mata (Chubbani),
Emmanuel Oguttu
James Ojiambo

JOSEPH OGUTO WA JORAM WAFULA

OWEFUMBE
NAMAGANDA
Daniel Raymond Mata

NAMAGANDA

GODFREY WERE WA JORAM WAFULA
Livingstone Were

NAPUNYI

SIBOCHE WA WANYANDE
Stefano Okiya

NAMANGALE

SITEFANO OKIYA WA SIBOCHE
Davidi Odunga
Clement Ojiambo (Obbimbo)

NADONGO

CLEMENT OJIAMBO (OBBIMBO)

NAHERE

NAMUKOOLI WA WANYANDE
Burocho. Burocho yatula ano hale mu 1918 nachira musyalo sya
Tanganyika, nohwola esiha sino sihumanyire nga lwali.

NAMUDDE

OKUKU (OHABA) WA WANYANDE
Peter Egessa
Anderea Sidubo

NEBERE

PETER EGESSA WA OKUKU (OHABA)
Yebula, Banatabona bongene

NAMANGALE

ANDEREA SIDUBO WA OKUKU (OHABA)
Akello Wanyande
Moyi

NALYALI

SIPEMI WA SIDUBO
Oduba

NASITWOKI

ODUBA WA SIPEMI
Wasiguli

NAMAKANGALA

WASIGULI WA ODUBA
Wamalwa

Olwande lwo lupapula 48

NAMUTENDE

WAMALWA WA WASIGULI
Pantaleo Wanyama

NAIDI
NAMAKANJA

PANTALEO WANYAMA WA WAMALWA
Luka Egessa
Mangeni
Wafula
Ngolobe

Olwande lwo lupapula 49

NACHAKI

OLWENYI NYEMBI
Sunu
Okwenyo
Ondero

SUNU WA OLENYI NYEMBO

NANYANGA

Nangenge
Onyango Sigoma
Obongooya

NANGENGE WA SUNU

NASUBO

Hadoke
Ngweno Dwaara
Odwooli

HADOKE WA NANGENGE

NANYANGA

Nabbaya
Petero Obwaso
Enosi Onyango

PETERO OBWASO WA HADOKE

NAMUHOOKOSI

Banatabona 3

ENOSI ONYANGO WA HADOKE

NASIHUNE

Samuel Wanyama
David Mangeni

SAMUEL WANYAMA WA ENOSI ONYANGO

NAMUGWERE

Allan Wanyama
Enosi Wanyama

NAMUGANDA

Waiswa Wanyama
Kato
Nabangi
Hadoke

DAVID MANGENI WA ENOSI ONYANGO

NASICHONGI
NASONGA

Enosi Onyango
George Wangira

NGWENO DWAARA WA NANGENGE

NAKIROYA

Olowo Obbando
Morris Onyango
Francis Adenya

OLOWO OBBANDA WA NGWENO DWAARA

NAJABI
NABUKA

Ngweno J.
Wanyama

NGWENO II WO OLOWO OBBANDO

NABUKA

Wanyama

MORRIS ONYANGO WA NGWENO DWAARA

Olwande lwo lupapula 50

HILLARY BONIFACE NGWENO

OMUSUNGU? ENONO

Banatabona (2)

ANTHONY ONYANGO WA MORRIS ONYANGO

NAMUDDE
Patrick Ngweno
Henrey Muluka
Justin Namwanga
Archileus Sidda
■ Regina Adikinyi Natabona

ARCHILEUS OUNDO WA MORRIS ONYANGO

NAMUGABO (Munyole)
Stephen Oundo
Charles Oundo
Joseph
■ Banatabona Babiri

OMUGANDA
Morris Oundo
Junior Oundo

FRANCIS ADENYA WA NGWENO DWAARA

NAMULUMBA
Black Wandera
Syaalo

BLACK WANDERA WA FRANCIS ADENYA

NABULAGAYE

ODWOOLI WA NGWENO

NAMANGALE
Stephin Ogono
Were Odwooli

NAKOOLO
Mikairi Ngweno
Manuel Wanyama

NASONGA
Sotoka

STEPHIN OGONO WA ODWOOLI

ADETI
Wilfred Okumu
Mudina
Jackson Ouma
David Wanyama
Clement Kilo

WILFRED OKUMU WA OGONO

NAHONE
Wanyama
Ngweno
Richard Barasa Buluma

NASUBO
Samson Wandera
Fred Sanya
Moses Okumu

MUDINA WA STEPHIN OGONO

NABONWE
Sam Wandera
Eriya Bwire

OSINYA WA STEPHIN OGONO
David Ogono
Silas Onyango

WERE ODWOOLI WA ODWOOLI
NAMUSIHO Wandera
NASINYA Muzee

WANDERA WA WERE ODWOOLI
NGEMI . . . . .

Olwande lwo lupapula 51

MUZEE WA WERE ODWOOLI
NAMAYERO Maloba Odwooli
Fred Bwire

MANUEL WANYAMA WA ODWOOLI
NASIHUNE Enosi Onyango Luyafwa, Manuel Wanyama nakerama
NASIHUNE niyebula,
Wilson Oguttu
Stephin Wafula
Kwoba
Oundo

WILSON OGUTTU WA MANUEL WANYAMA
NAMUTESO

STEPHIN WAFULA WA MANUEL WANYAMA
NALALA Oliver

WILLIAM KWOBA WA MANUEL WANYAMA
NAMUSOGA . . . . .

OUNDO WA MANUEL WANYAMA
NALALA . . . . .

OKWENYO WA LWENI NYEMBI
NABONGO Oguna
Olowo

OGUNA WA OKWENYO
NALYALI Zablon Wambete
George Asumanga

ZABLON WAMBETE WA OGUNA
NANYILALO Wilson Oguna (Okumu)
Yokana Egessa
NAMENYA ■ Banatabona 4

WILSON OGUNA (OKUMU) WA ZABLON WAMBETE

NABURI — Ongudi
Wandera
Maliro

NAMUHOOKOSI — ■ Natabona mulala yengene

YOKANA EGESSA WA ZABLON WAMBETE

NANYANGA — Ojiambo Egessa
Wandera Egessa

NAMUKOBE — . . . . .

ASUMANGA WA OGUNA

NAJABI — Onyango

ONYANGO WA ASUMANGA

NAMUTESO — Moses Wandera
. . . . . — . . . . .

NACHINI WA OLWENYI NYEMBI

NACHAKI II — . . . . .
NANYANGA — Ouma Olyeddo
Nachimi luyafwa Omijjo nakerama Nanyanga, niyebulamo
Matayo Matalo

OUMA ORIEDDO WA NACHINI

NAJABI — Bubolu

Olwande lwo lupapula 52

BUBOLU WA OUMA ORYEDDO

NANYANGA — Nachini II
Hadoke II

NACHINI II WA BUBOLU

NAMUMACHI — Kenneth Bwire
Dev Wafula
Milton Barasa
Vicent Tibbita
Maklin Wandera

OMUJJO WA NACHINI

NANYANGA — Matayo Matalo

MATAYO MATALO WA OMUJJO

NAJABI — John Owori
Zablon Kitari
Jackson Onyango

OWORI WA MATAYO MATALO

NAMULEMBO — Patrick Ouma
Walter Magambo
Nelson Bwire

NAMANGALE — Bwire

JACKSON ONYANGO WA MATAYO MATALO

NASIMALWA

Geofrey Onyango
Peter Onyango
Fred Onyango
Wandera

Olwande lwo lupapula 53
Olwande lwo lupapula 54

NGWENO HADU MAHOLA

NAMUTAMBA

Namutamba yaali omuhasi wa Awori Nahooli.
Abe BANDA, badaha Lwande abaabe abandu bachye babahonye
eyee, nga ABASIBIKA baali badaha ohuseta enono ya
BAHOOLI, balasane nabo, hu BAHOOLI nibecha eyiri Lwande
Wesonga, nibamusaba ababe abandu bachye babahonye. Naye
abandu ba Lwande nibaboola bati hwenya omuhana wundi,
olwohuba omuhana mulala sanyala ohwidisa amabanga Kabandu,
hubulano ABAHOOLI nibameda omuhana oyo NAMUTAMBA.

LWANDE WESONGA WA LWANDE BIRUNGO NAMUDU

(NAMUTAMBA) NGWENO MAHOLA

NGWENO MAHOLA WA LWANDE WESONGA

NABONWE

Bwobo
Mulyaha

NALALA

Lwande II

NAMULWANI

Ojwanga Obinda

NABONWE II

Masaba Ngundira (Osinjo)

NASIBWOCHI

Mutika
Ngweno
Sisera

BWOBO WA NGWENO MAHOLA

NAMAKANGALA

Ochwinga

OCHWINGA WA BWOBO

NEHOBA I

Oyula Wandera

NEHOBA II

Nambudye
Henrey Mangeni
Okwomi
Mukaga

OYULA WANDERA WA OCHWINGA

NALALA

Olowo
Thomas Ouma

NANYANGA

Ojiambo
Odundo

NASERA

Orabi

NAMBUDYE WA OCHWINGA

NABONGO   Ochwinga
NALALA   Nyabbola
           Siganda

OKWOMI WA OCHWINGA

NALALA   Oyula yamukerama huniyebulamo Ojiambo

SIGANDA WA NAMBUDYE

NANYANGA   Amosi Egondi
           Yolamu Hasibante

YOLAMU HASIBANTE WA SIGANDA

NAHULO   Charles Onyango

PASCAL ONYANGO

NABUKAKI   Mukaga
           Owori
           Siganda

MULYAHA WA NGWENO MAHOLA

NABONG   Andrew Nyanja
           Omolo
           Luduba

Olwande lwo lupapula 55

ANDREW NYANJA WA MULYAHA

NAMULUMBA   Okuku
NASUBO   James Ogoola
NALWENGE   William Odera
              Barnabba Masinde
              Yovani Wafula
              Nathanael Ouma
NAMAKANGALA   Chillo
              Wanyama
              Wangalwa nende Omala
NASUBO   Mulyaha
              Lwande
NAMENYA   Bwire

JAMES OGOOLA WA ANDREW NYANJA

NAMULUNDU   Vicent Lugendo
            Wilberbad Sifuna
            Silvester Bwire
            Patrick Gozza
            Okumu
NASIBAYI   Wandera

WILLIAM ODERA WA ANDREW NYANJA

NAMULOBA   Moses Ouma
            Daudi Wanyama
            Salomon Mangeni

BARNABBA MASINDE WA ANDREW NYANJA

NAHAABI Wandera

YOVANI WAFULA WA ANDREW NYANJA

NANGOHO Joseph Bwire
NASINYAMA Henery Ojiambo

NATHANAEL OUMA WA ANDREW NYANJA

MUTANZANIA George Opio
Charles Odongo
James Okello
Stephin Hamala

OMOLLO WA MULYAHA

ERIEZA LWANDE

ERIEZA LWANDE WA OMOLLO

NAMUTALA Edward Wasike
Albert Siminyu
Paulo Nyegenye

OSOBO WA .....

NANYIBOMI Bwire

Olwande lwo lupapula 56

CHILLO WA ANDREW NYANJA
Wanyama
Wangalwa

WANGALWA WA ANDREW NYANJA

NADONGO Nyanja

OMALA WA ANDREW NYANJA

NANGOHO Ogutu
Namulu
Masiga

VINCENT LWANDE WA .....

NAMUGANDA
NALALA

LWANDE II WA NGWENO MAHOLLA

LWANDE MULYAHA WA LWANDE II
Dangi

DANGI WA LWANDE MULYAHA

NASUBO Lwande

60

LWANDE WA DANGI

NAKOOLI
Yowasi Buluma
Erukana Wandera
Yolamu Mabbachi
Dan Were

YOWASI BULUMA WA LWANDE

NALIALI
Living Wanyama
Gidioni Bwire
Dickson Magero

ERUKANA WANDERA WA LWANDE

NAMULUNDU
Oundo

YOLAMU MABBACHI WA LWANDE

NANYANGA
Richard Egessa
Aggrey Lwande
Williamu Wandera
Henery Namalwa

MULYAHA WA LWANDE

NALYALI
Fransisco Ojiambo
Rowrence Wanyama

AGGREY LWANDE WA YOLAMU MABBACHI

NABAHO
Nafwa
Egessa
Nabuyiya
Maritino Otyola
Eriezali Guloba

Olwande lwo lupapula 57

EGESSA WA AGGREY LWANDE

NAMUKOBE

DANGI WA LWANDE

NAMAKANGALA

JEREMIAH NGWENO WA . . . . .

NAMAINDI
Absolom Masinde
Peter Egessa

ALONI ADIKA WA . . . . .

NAMUKUBA
Bwire

NGWENO MAHOLLA WA LWANDE WESONGA

NAMULWANI
Ojwangi

OJWANGI WA NGWENO MAHOLA

NABAHO
Wandera
Omwichango

61

WANDERA WA OJWANGI

NAMANGALE

Achoode
Ogaando
Penda
Ongango

PENDA WA WANDERA

ONGANGO WA WANDERA
Dangali

OMWICHANGO WA OJWANGI

NEHOBA

Boloki

BOLOKI WA OMWICHANGO

NAFWOFWOYO

Okambo
Makaada
Serwano Obanda

NAMUKUBA

Pantaleo Boloki

MAKAADA WA BOLOKI

NAPUNYI

Manuel Ojwangi

MANUEL OJWANGI WA MAKAADA

NAKUHU
NAMAKANGALA I

Muluka
Ojwangi Boloki
Obanda

NAMAKANGALA II
NAMADI

Makaada
Gablier Onyango

SERWANO OBBANDA WA BOLOKI

NAMUSIHO
NABONGO

Benjamin Machio (Chango Machyo W'Obanda)
Akisoferi Maloba
Ojiambo
Makoha

Olwande lwo lupapula 58

NAMUDDE

Onyango
Egessa

BENJAMIN MACHIO WA OBANDA

NANGANDA

Andrew Chango (Omwichango)
Peter Obanda (Dr)
Armstrong Wejuli
Boloki
Ngweno
- Susan Nafula Natabona
- Addis Nekesa Natabona
- Ada Nabwire Natabona
- Hope Nasubo Natabona
- Edith Nabwire Natabona (Mukoko)
- Catherine Ajambo Natabona

AKISOFERI MALOBA WA OBANDA

NANJOSI
NADECHO   Obbanda

OJIAMBO WA SERWNO OBANDA

NAMANGALE   Amuria
Willy Ojiambo
Magume
Obbanda

MAKOHA WA SERWNO OBANDA

?   Mwichango
?   Obbanda

Olwande lwo lupapula 59

BATALEO BOLOKI WA BOLOKI

NASUBO II   Malingu
Bwire
NAPUNYI   Opondo
Mugeni
NASUBO II   Mangeni
Obbanda

MALINGU WA PANTALEO BOLOKI

NAKURUKU   Boloki

OPONDO WA PANTALEO BOLOKI

NAMULUNDU

MANGENI WA PANTALEO BOLOKI

Olwande lwo lupapula 60

NGWENO MAHOLLA WA LWANDE WESONGA

NABONWE   Masaba

MASABA WA NGWENO MAHOLA

Ngundira (Osinjo)

NGUNDIRA (OSIJJO) WA MASABA

NAMAINDI   Bujubo
Mwanga
Indoro
NADWANGI   Zefania Okumu
Edward Owori
Ongomo

ZEFANIA OKUMU WA NGUNDIRA

NASUBO II   Wandera
Mika Bwire
Okello
NAHULO   Ojwangi
NASUBO II   Ouma

EDWARD OWORI WA NGUNDIRA OSIJJO

NANYANGA Wycliffe Oundo

WERE WA .....

? Asango

Onyango

Odungo

NGUNDIRA

? Bati yaali nende ebyayo ebingi, naye bamuletera ebyayo ebindi
bati yayenge, naye yaboola ati, ese omwene nda ..... nga hu
Ngundira chyango echi mbula onanjayire, nihwo ohwatula erita
NGUNDIRA, erita niye OSINJO.

NGWENE MAHOLA WA LWANDEWESONGA

Masaba

MASABA WA NGWENO MAHOLA

? Awori

Ogaanga

Onyango Hatera

Onyango Odyonga

AWORI WA MASABA

Lwande

Gwato

Mugenya

Odunga

Olwande lwo lupapula 61

DANIEL WANJALA

NAMUKUBA Nakasio Egessa

ODUNGA WA MUGENYA

NANDAKO I Lwande

Awori

NACHWERE Lwande

NANDAKO II Mugenya

NACHAKI I Ouma

NACHAKI II Lwande (Monday)

Mayende

AWORI II ODUNGA

NANKIMA Nanyanga

LWANDE WA ODUNGA

NACHAKI Mugenya

64

MUGENYA WA ODUNGA

NADAARE Ojiambo
Bisse
Samba
Daniel Wanjala
Ojuku

DANIEL WANJALA WA MUGENYA

NAMUKOBE I Mukaga
Were
Okello
NANYANGA Wilson Nayaala
Bwire
Barasa
Ojiambo
NAMULUNDU Onyango
NATIKOKO Egessa
NAMUKOBE II Okumu
Wafula
Wandera

MUKAGA WA DANIEL WANJALA

NAMAINDI Wanyama (Were)

WILSON NEYAALA WA DANIEL WANJALA

NAJABI Toyota
Wabwire
Daniel Wanjala
Mangeni

Olwande lwo lupapula 62

AWORI WA MASABA

NAMANGALE Slvanus Wangalwa
Cosma Gwato
William Sikaala
NAMUDDE Andrea Ogooya

SLYVANUS WANGALWA WA AWORI

NAMULUCHA John Wafula
Fredrick Bwire
Vincent Opio

NELSON ODONGO

NANYANGA Andrew Bwire
Gedi Sangalo
John Wanyama

CORNEL OKELLO

NASINYAMA
NAHABI Wanyama

65

JOHN WAFULA WA SILYVANUS WANGALWA

KABALEGA
Wanyama
Onyango
Ouma
Wandera

FREDRICK BWIRE WA SILYVANUS WANGALWA

ADETI
Sanya
Wandera
Barasa

NAYINGANI
Opio
Okello

NAMUTENDE
Joseph
Ogutu

VINCENT OPIO WA SILYVANUS WANGALWA
Awori nende Osbon

CORNEL OKELLO WA SILYVANUS WANGALWA

NASUBO
Denes Sunday
Sam Baras

WILLIAM SIKAALA WA AWORI

NAMANGALE
Anderea Ogooya
Jared Wandera

NALALA
George Bubolu
Joshua Ogutu

NGWENO MAHOLA WA LWANDE WESONGA

NASIBWOCHI
Mutika

MUTIKA WA NGWENO MAHOLA

MUTIKA WA NGWENO MAHOLA
Wanga
Enaali
Kadaka

Olwande lwo lupapula 63

ENAALI WA MUTIKA
Fudiembe

FUDIEMBE WA ENAALI

NALIALI
Musa Fudiembe

MUSA FUDIEMBE WA FUDIEMBE

NANYANGA	Yosiya Gusinja
	James Okinda
NAMULUNDU	Enosi Otika
	Jonathan Ouma
	Mangeni
	Buchunju
NAMUKOMBE	Erieza Muganda
	Garisom Wandera
NAMULUNDU	Abisayi Wanyama
NAMUYEE	Daudi Ouma

YOSIA GUSINJA WA MUSA FUDIEMBE

NASIBIKA	Wafula
	Wanyama
NASIMALWA	Wandera
	Patrick Ouma
NAMURWA I	Ojiambo
	Bwire
MAMURWA II	Mugeni
	Bwire
	Mangeni

JAMES OKIND WA MUSA FUDIEMBE

NAHABI I	Alupakusadi Machyo
	Wanyama
NAHABI II	Barasa
	Martin Musa Fudiembe

ENOSI OTIKA WA MUSA FUDIEMBE

NANGAYO	Egessa

YONASANI OUMA WA MUSA FUDIEMBE

	Musisi
	Mutika

Olwande lwo lupapula 64

WANYAMA WA DANIEL BULUMA

NACHAKI	Muganda

WAFULA WA DANIEL BULUMA

NACHAKI	Daniel Buluma

OKOMBA WA MUGANDA

NAMULWAANI	Eridadi Ouma
	Okumu
NAKIROYA	Wangira
NAMAKANGALA	Osinya wa Eridadi
	Odwori

DANI NALEBE WA MUGANDA

NYARUWA
Kadaka
Muganda
Judh Wanga
Ochoola

DAUDI OUMA WA MUGANDA

NAYIGAGA
Wafula
Muganda
Musa Wandera

NGWENO MAHOLA WA LWANDE WESONGA

NAMULWANI
Ngweno Sisera

NGWENO SISERA WA NGWENO MAHOLA

NAHUMACHI
Hamala Halanga
Makuda

HAMALA HALANGA WA NGWENO

SISERA

NAMANGALE
Obwora

OBWORA WA HAMALA HALANGA

NAMAINDI
Agoola
Odieso

NACHONGA
Zakaliya Osolo

ODIESO WA OBWORA

NABONGO
Wasike

WASIKE WA ODIESO

NAHASOHO I
Juma

NAHASOHO II
Okochi
Obwora
Okochi (?)
Ogutu
Odwori

Olwande lwo lupapula 65

[ERITA   LYASANGUHAWO]

NASUBO I
George Hamala
Richard Ngweno
Wilson Ogana
Edward Namangale Agoola
Samuel Makuda
Christopher Nachonga
Eriudi Odwori

NASUBO II
Wycliffe Ouma
Fred Osolo

NAMULEMBO
Isaac Obwora
Nachonga Opio
Okello
Namwonja

OGUTU WA ZAKALIIA OSOLO
Odieso
Geofrey Ogutu
Hamala

GEORGE HAMALA WA ZAKALIIA OSOLO
NAMACHOLE
Situma
Charles Bwana
Tom Mulongo
NEHOBA
Nathan Hamala
Aludda
Poter Henrey Hamala

RICHARD NGWENO WA ZAKALIA OSOLO
Joshua Osolo

WILSON OGAANA WA ZAKALIA OSOLO
Daniel Auma
James Ogaana
Peter Ogaana
Tom Osolo
Fred Ogaana

ERASTO OBWORA WA MAKOHA LUNGASA
NASINYAMA
John Makoha

JOHN MAKOHA WA ERASTO OBWARA
NAMIMBIRI
Jackson Osolo
Francis Makoha
Bendicto Obwara
Ochiengi Mayu
Radero
Idemba

WALTER MAKUDA WA ZAKALIA OSOLO
Evan Wandera
Dolifis Wandera

FRED NGWENO WA…
Keneth Ngweno
Anthony Ngweno

MARUDA WA NGWENO SISERA
NAMANGALE

Olwande lwo lupapula 66

MBALWA WA …
NAMANGALE
Paulino Omedda
Ogaale
Okuku

PAULINO OMEDDA WA MBALWA

NASINYAMA   Alfred Sisera

OUMA WA MAKUDA

NABONGO   Ezekiel Makuda
Onyango
Ochiengi
Wandera
NANYFWA   Zablon Wanyama
Benjamin Ahenda

EZEKIEL MAKUDA WA OUMA

NAMUDDE   Samuel Makuda
NAMUHOMA   Ouma
NASONGA   Ochieno
NAMAKANGALA   Ouma

OCHIENGI WA OUMA

NAMULUMBA   Ouma

ZABLON WANYAMA WA OUMA

NAMAINDI I
NAMAINDI II
NACHAKI   Ngweno
Makuda

BENJAMIN AHENDA WA OUMA

NABURI   Ouma
NAMAKWE   Ouma

NGWENO SISERA WA NGWENO MAHOLA

NAMULEMBO   Halanga

HALANGA WA NGWENO SISERA

Olunjalu

OLUNJALU WA HALANGA

NAMAYERO   Nicodemu Ngweno

NICODEMU NGWENO WA OLUNJALU

NAHOOLI   Ngweno

APIO WA HALANGA

NALALA   Nangweri
Ngweno (Alego)

ERASITO OBWARA WA MAKOHA

NASIMANYA   John Makoha
            Walter Makuda
            Fred Ngweno Lununi
NABORO   Patrick Ojiambo
            Vilian Edbang Makoha

Olwande lwo lupapula 67

NAMUMULI   Enosi Ochiengi
NACHAKI   Godfrey Osodo
            Luka Stephin Opio

MAKUDA WA NGWENO SISERA

NAMBANJA   Munyuwalo
            Makoha
NASONGA   Mbalwa
NAMANGALE   Ouma

MAKOHA WA MAKUDA

NAMANGALE   Ouma luyafwa, Makoha yakerama muha simwana, niyebulamo
            Makuda Obbara
NADIBBONYO   Buluma˙
            Ohaba
NAMAINDI I   Jacob Bwire
NAMAINDI II   Jeremiah Wandera
            Ombunga
            Obwora luyafwa Makoha Lugasa yakerama, Nachonga muha
            Erasto Obwora, niyebulamu Erasto Obwora

BULUMA WA MAKOHA

NALALA   Jastas Namanyi
            Wawuya

JASTAS NAMANYI WA BULUMA

NAHULO   Ojiambo

OHABA WA MAKOHA LUNGASA

NACHONGA   Solomon Makoha

SOLOMON WA OHABA BARASA

            Ochiengi
            Makuda
            Makuda
            Nafwa
            Sihaba

JACOB BWIRE WA MAKOHA

NABURI   Julias Obwora
            Israel Onyango

JULIAS OBWORA

            Egessa

EGESSA WA JULIAS OBWORA

NABYANGU

JEREMIAH WANDERA WA MAKOHA

ADETI

Augustino Omondi

Wycliffe Makoha

Silvester Ochiengi

AUGUSTINO OMONDI WA JEREMIAH WANDERA

NASUBO

William Omondi

WYCLIFFE MAKOHA WA JEREMIAH WANDERA

?

Juma

OMBUNGA WA MAKOHA LUNGASA

Washington Juma

Albert Okumu

Olwande lwo lupapula 68

Aggrey Tabu

Ojwangi

WASHINGTON JUMA WA OMBUNGA

Ogoola

Odwori

LWANDE BIRUNGO WA NGWENO

NABONGO

Lwande Wesonga

LWANDE WESONGA WA LWANDE BIRUNGO

NAMUDU

Lwande Mulyamboka

LWANDE MULYAMBOKA WA LWANDE WESONGA

Wangoho Rafwaki I

WANGOHO RAFWAKI IWA LWANDE MULYAMBKA

NASIBIKA

Mukongo

MUKONGO WA WANGOHO RAFWAKI I

NAMAGANDA

Wanjala

NACWERE

Wangoho Pendo II

WANJALA WA MUKONGO

NAPUNYI

Oduyo

Hayingu

Wangoho III

ODUYO WA WANJALA

NAMYINDI

Romano Gusino

Macial Doloko

NALWENGE

Longinus

Ouma

John Ogema

Macial Doloko

ROMANO GUSINO WA ODUYO

NAMUSIHO   Domiano Ouma

LONGINUS OGOHA WA ODUYO

NASUBO   Ogoola
John Ogema
Clement Mboko
Patrick Okumu

JOHN OGEMA

NABULINDO   Charles Wanjala
NAGWE   Joseph Oduyo
BABULINDO   Luberuto Malingu
Patrick Mugeni
Morris Gusino
Fred Makoha
NEHAMA   Robert Taabu

ROMANO GUSINO

ADETI   Patrick Ouma
Ogoola
Oduyo
Tambiti
Mbolu
NAMUBACHI   Bubolu
NABURI   John Wandera
NAMUTALA   Fred Ochiengi
Godfrey Obbanda

OMIANO OUMA WA ROMANO GUSINO

NAHULO   Oduyo
Kabuli

Olwande lwo lupapula 69
LWANDE WESONGA WA LWANDE BIRUNGO

NAMUDU   Lwande Mulyamboka
NABILYACHO   Odemi

ODEMI WA LWANDE MULYAMBOKA

?   Muhula
?   Odomi

MUHULA WA ODEMI

NASUBO I   Wanyande
NASUBO II   Ngweno (Osiyo)
NABBONYO   Ongenge

WANYANDE WA MUHULA

NACHONGA I   Haluba
NACHONGA II   Petero Nabahunya

PETERO NABAHUNYA WA WANYANDE

NAKUHU   Joseph Wandera

NAKIROYA   Nabbangi

Ouma

NGWENO (OSIYO) WA MUHULA

NAJABI   Asumanga

Wilson Wangalwa

Sengori

WILSON WANGALWA WA NGWENO (OSIYO)

NACHWERE   Wandera

Mangeni

Ouma

Onyango

ONGENGE WA MUHULA

NACHIMO   Yeremiah Ochimi

Okello

Ajongo

YEREMIAH OCHIMI WA ONGENGE

NANJAYA   Mikaya Namangale

Mesusera Muhula

OKELO WA ONGENGE

Meyo

Muhula

MIKAYA NAMANGALE WA YEREMIAH OCHIMI

NAWONGA   James Ongenge

NAMUDEMO   Ochimi

Daglas Muhula

MESUSERA MUHULA WA YEREMIAH OCHIMI

NAMUDAIRWA   Wandera

Muhula

NAKOYI   Ongenge

Ochimi

Okumu

NAMANYI   Barasa

OJONGO WA ONGENGE

NAKEWA   Odomi

Nasanael Ouma

Olwande lwo lupapula 70

NASANAEL OUMA WA OJONGO

Abbangi

Oke`llo

ODEMI WA ODEMI

Mayende

Ogulo

OKUMU WA ODEMI

NALUKADA	Ajango yakeram muha simwana
NAKIROYA	Matayo Odemi

MATAY ODEMI WA ODEMI

NACHWERE	Onyango
	Ngweno Osiyo
NAHABI	Obbakiro

Olwande lwo lupapula 71
Olwande lwo lupapula 72

WESONGA WA LWANDE MULUNGO.
KAGENDA "AMALAKULI KA NEHAMA"
OMALA WA KAGENDA

ABAHASI BA KAGENDA

NABWALA	Omala
	Sichimi
NANGOMA	Waecha Ofumbuha
NANJOWA	Muhachi
	Ngundira

OMALA WA KAGENDA

NAKUHU	Lwande

LWANDE WA OMALA

NABONGO	Ndumwa
NASINYAMA	Achiengi
NAMANGALE I	Okuku
NAMANGALE II	Malibo

NDUMWA WA LWANDE

NAMENYA	Ochaso
NALALA	Olijjo
NAMENYA	Ohuya

OCHASO WA NDUMWA

NAHABI	Gwayya
NAHABI	Yafesi Namenya
NAHABI	Kosea Jungo
LA KERI NAMBUBI	Charles Oundo
NAHABI	Ignatio Mudambo
	Ignatio Mudambo
	Ndumwa Orobe
	Ohuya
	Odanga

■ Apoto Ekingi, Natabona, wuno Mukoko, yatwibulira abewa bano: Ochaso, nende Onyoba.
■ Esesa Nadoli, Natabona, wuno Mukoko, yebula abewa beffe bano: Abuner Buluma, Namenya, Lekoboam Onyango, Amanda Nabwire.
■ Ajwang Natabona, wuno Mukoko, yebula abewa beffe bano: Owino, Ochieno nende Aoko.

75

OLIJJO WA NDUMWA

NAHABI	Stephin Ndumwa
NAMUKUBA	Mutanda
	Nonga
NACHAKI I	Wafula
NACHAKI II	Omala
NACHAKI III	WILSON OPIO
NACHAKI IV	Yovan Makoha
NACHAKI V	Yonasani Godan

STEPHIN NDUMWA WA OLIJJO

NABIANGU	Mangoli
NACHAKI I	Budaha
NACHAKI II	Ndumwa

BUDAHA WA STEPHEN NDUMWA

NASUBO

Olwande lwo lupapula 73

OMALA
MAKOHA OSOGGO

NASIBIINGI	Ayimbi
	Omaala
NAMUHUMWA	Ogula
TEREZA OKOOLA	Alfred Bwire
	Pascal Ouma
	John Ogutu
	Manuel Mangeni

ALFRED BWIRE WA MAKOHA OSOGGO

NABURI	Okochi Bwire
	Julias Juma
	Majoni
	Peter Mayende
NASERA	Jophiter Barasa
	Moses Onyango

PASCAL OUMA WA OGEMBA OSOGGO

NALALA	Musumba Ouma
	Patrick Lumumba

JOHN OGUTU WA MAKOHA OSOGGO

NASIKAANI	Ouma
	Ogemba
	Teresa
	Sitabi

MANUEL MANGENI WA MAKOHA OSOGGO

NAHULO	Francico Ogemba

OGEMBA WA KUBADI

NAMANGALE	Mangeni Ogemba

MANGENI WA OGEMBA

NANYIREMI Stanely Wanyama
Wilber Bwire

STANELY WANYAMA WA MANGENI

NASITWOKI Mukaga Wanyama
Friday Wanyama
Odembo Wanyama

BWIRE WILBER WA MANGENI

NAMULUNDU Robert Wangira

End
Olwande lwo lupapula 74

TEFIRO WAFULA WA OLIJJO

NAMAINDI Erisa Mangeni
NAMINDI Ochaso

ERISA MANGENI WA TEFIRO WAFULA

NAHASOHO Juma Wafula
Wilson Opio
NAMAKANGALA Olijjo
Omala
Wafula
Nahulo
Okumu

JUMA WA ERISA MANGENI

NAMUTENDE
NAMAKANGALA

ALFRED OMALA WA OLIJJO

NAMUFUTA
NAKALYOKO Bwire
NAKALYOKO Ochieno
NAKALYOKO Kagenda
NAKALYOKO Okumu

OCHIENO WA ALFRED OMALA

NAPUNYI

NONGA WA OLIJJO

NEHOBA Achwada

WILSON OPIO WA OLIJJO

NAMAKANGALA I Olijjo
NAMAKANGALA II Wafula
NAMAKANGALA III Okuku
NAMAKANGALA IV Nahulo
NALWENGE I Ouma
NALWENGE II Wandera
NAMAKANGALA V Majoni
NAMAKANGALA VI Osaamo
NAMAKANGALA VII Musumba

OLIJJO WA WILSON OPIO

NAMULUNDU   Simon
Birungi
Junior

NAMUGANDA
NAMUNYANKOLE

Olwande lwo lupapula 75

WAFULA WA WILSON OPIO

NAFWOFWOYO

YOVAN MAKOHA WA OLIJJO

NAPUNYI   Mayindi
NAPUNYI   Ouma
NAPUNYI   Wandera
NAKOOLI   Majoni
Obote (named after the first Prime Minister of Uganda)
Sajja
Opondo
Nabuya
NAMAYOGA   Okello
Makaanda Ojiambo

OUMA WA YOVAN MAKOHA

NAHULO   Amosi
Jamy
Mukisa

YONASANI GADAN WA OLIJJO

NAMAKANGALA
NAMUFUTA   Samuel Oundo
NASONGA   Omala
NAMAKANGALA   Aringo

YAFESI NAMENYA WA OCHASO

NAMAINDI   Wandera

CHARLES OUNDO WA OCHASO

MIRABU AGUTU NAJABI Wanyama
Wafula Ochaso
NAMAKANGALA   Mugeni
Ochaso
■ Constance Nabwire, Natabona, Mukoko
■ M. Auma Natabona, Mukoko
■ Ruth Osinya, Natabona Mukoko
■ Flo Hadudu, Natabona Mukoko
■ Betty Mugeni, Natabona, Mukoko
HENDERIKA MASIGA   OjamboWandera
■ Nafa Natabona, Mukoko
■ Sunday Natabona, Mukoko

NEKESA
AIDA   ■ Agnes Nabwire Natabona, Mukoko
■ Irene Dina Natabona, Mukoko
NAMENYA   Bwire

KOSEA JUNGE WA OCHASO
Bbita
Charles
Edward Wandera
■ Faisi Natabona, Mukoko
■ Esther Natabona, Mukoko

IGNATYO MUDAMBA WA OCHASO
NAMAINDI   Tanga

WANYAMA WA CHARLES OUNDO
NANYIHODO

Olwande lwo lupapula 76

ACHIENGI WA LWANDE
NAMULEMBO   Gaunya Oguro
NAMULEMBO   Ohwango
NAMULEMBO   Okuku Nalibbo
NAMULEMBO   Okuku Ngendo

GAUNYA OGURO WA ACHIENGI
NABUNJE   Ombale
Ochiengi Okaalo
Barasa Oguru
Peter Kadimba
NALWENGE   Pantaleo Wandera
Juma Lucas
NAJABI   C. Lwande Agunga Kengo

OHWANGO WA ACHIENGI
NAMUSIHO   Mugonda
Omala
Wandera

OKUKU MALIBBO WA ACHIENGI
NAJABI   Oundo
Abbele Yosamu Wanyama
Aimbi
Clement Lwande Oguro
Semeyo Ochiengi
Pantaleo Oguro
John Omala

OHUYAA OHONJO WA NDUMWA
NALUBANGA   Oheto
Okumu Nakubo

OHETO WA OHUYAA
Omala Lwande

OKUMU NAKURO WA OHUYAA

NABULINDO

ERINEYO KATA WA OGEMBA

NAHASOHO
Wandera
Ouma
Bwire
Mange`ni

Olwande lwo lupapula 77

WANDERA WA ERINEYO KATA

NAMULUNDU
Oguma wa Kata

OGUMA WA ERINEYO KATA

MAGO, ARE
Banatabona 3

OGEMBA WA ACHIENGI

NACHONGA
Kubadi
Nduku

KUBADI WA OGEMBA

NANYIFWA
NAMUDDE
Okello Mayunga
Ogemba II
Oundo
Wafwa

OGEMBA II WA KUBADI

NAMANGALE
Kata
John Osaalo
Augustino Okello

JOHN OSAALO WA OGEMBA II

NAMANYI
Obukya Makoha

AUGUSTINO OKELLO WA OGEMBA II

NAMUFUTA
Ouma
Opio

OUNDO WA KUBADI

NACHAKI
NAMIRIPO
NAJABI
Omala
Okello
Wandera

OMALA WA OUNDO

NAJABI I   Bendicto Wangalwa
NAJABI II   Anyango (Wanyama)
Stephin Wandera
Albert Okumu
Stephen Barasa
Milton Ojiambo
NAHASOHO   Alex Juma
Wilson Mangeni
NAKOOLO   Ouma
Bendicto
NEWUNJE   Wilber Egessa
Stepheni Ouma
NAMAKWA   Wafula
Sanya

ANYANGO (WANYAMA) WA OMALA

NAMUKUBA   Robert

STEPHIN WANDERA WA OMALA

NAMUMALI   Leonald Wandera
Moses

Olwande lwo lupapula 78

ALEX JUMA WA OMALA

NEBERE   Patrick Bwire
Ouma
Oundo

WILSON MANGENI WA OMALA

NAMALELE   Wandera (Solo)
Godfrey Bwire

WANDERA WA OUNDO

NAMWAYA   Kubadi
Oundo
Wafula
Peter Ouma
Hagai
Godfrey

OSAALO WA MAYUNGA WA KUBEDI

NANYIFWA   Okuku Rabwogi
Makoha Sogo

OKUKU RABWOGI WA OSAALO

OHETO WA OHUTAA
Edward Ouma
Wasike

MAKOHA SOGO WA OSAALO WA MAYUNGA

NAMULU

Ayimbi
Omala

AYIMBI WA MAKOHA

NAMBASI

Aggrey Musungu
Peter Ouma
Joseph Majimbo
Clement Lwande

AGGREY MUSUNGU WA AYIMBI

NAKOMOLO

PETER OUMA WA AYIMBI

NAMUKOMO

Elijah Peter

OMALA WA MAKOHA

NAJABI

Milton Taabu Omala
Wilson Mangeni

MILTON TAABU OMALA WA OMALA WA MAKOHA

NAHASOHO

Benard Sanya
Wilber Ojiambo
Geofrey Onyango

OMALA WA KAGENDA

Onyobo
Ogemba

ONYOBO WA OMALA WA KAGENDA

Nahaland

NAHALANDA WA ONYOBO WA OMALA

NAPUNYI

Julias Wangalwa
Ouma (Pusi)

Olwande lwo lupapula 79

JULIAS WANGALWA WA NAHALANDA

NASIYE
NAJABI

Ogutu
Wandera

OUMA PUSI WA NAHALANDA

NABYANGU
NAMENYA

Jackson Mangeni
Wandera
Wanyama
Juma

WANDERA WA OUMA (PUSI)

NEHUNYE

Wafula
David

WANYAMA WA OUMA (PUSI)

NATONGI
Mugeni
Leonald Ouma
George Wanyama

JUMA WA OUMA (PUSI)
Onyango
Dani Ouma
James

LWANDE WESONGA

NEHAMA
Kagenda

KAGENDA WA LWANDE WESONGA

NABWALA
Omala
Sichimi

NANGOMA
Wanga Ofumbuha

NANJOWA
Muhachi
Ngundira

WANGA OFUMBUHA WA KAGENDA

NACHAKI
Ogaara
Obbiero
Sichimi

NAHONE
Syawola

NAMULEMBO
Ogaara
Sichimi
Emuli

NANJOWA
Muhachi

OGAARA WA WANGA OFUMBUHA

NAHASOHO
Michael Okuruma
Edward Mugeni
Disani Okello
James Mukaga

OBIERO WA WANGA OFUMBUHA

NABWALA
Hamonye
Ouma Osodyo

HAMONYE WA OBIERO
Muhenye
Nasibu Obiero

EMULI WA WANGA OFUMBUHA

NAMUDDE
Hamonye

NAMIRIPO
Muhadda

NASUBO OBBIERO WA HAMONYE

NANGANDA
William Nachoyee

WILLIAM NACHOYEE WA NASUBO OBERO

NAMWALIRA   Okuku
Ouma
Wafula

NALWENGE   Ouma

SYAWOLA WA WANGA OFUMBUHA

NAHULO   Odyanga
Mukuhu

NADEKE   Ongwe

ODYANGA WA WANGA OFUMBIHA

NAJUNWA   Orodi
NAMULUNDU   Bwonya
NAMAINDI   Ongodde

ORODI WA ODYANGA

NASIBAYI   John Ngwabe
Erisa Onyanga II

NAMUKUBA   Mangeni
NAMULUNDU   Okuku

JOHN NGWABE WA ORODI (MAWAA)

NANDEKE   Orodi II

ONYANGA II WA ORODI (MAWAA)

NALALA   CMP (Williamu Ouma)
Wycliffe Orodi
Samson Kwoba
Osinya

MANGENI WA ORODI (MAWAA)

NAMUDDE
NAMUHOMA   Sunday

SUNDAY WA MANGENI WA ORODI (MAWAA)
Wankya

ONGWE WA SYAWOLA

NABAHOLO   Ohereho
Wanga

OHEREHO WA ONGWE

NAMULUNDU   Bwoya
Daudi Magunda

DAUDI MAGUNDA

NAMUDDE I   Bwonya luyafwa Daudi Magunda nakerama NAMUDDE I,
niyebulamu:
Wilson Nahulo
Livingston Ohebero

WILSON NAHULO WA DAUDI MAGUNDA

NALALA
Simon Wandera
Patrick Odwori

LIVINGSTON OHEBERO WA DAUDI MAGUND

NAMENYA
Livingston Ohebero
NAMURWA
Odianga
Stephin Onyango
Moses Owori

Olwande lwo lupapula 81

NAMULEMBO
Juma Ohebero
Mangeni Ohebero
NAJABI
Okochi Ohebero

WANGA WA ONGWE

NAMWENGE
Barasa
Agaitano Mulyedi

BARABARA WA WANGA

NANYANGA
Julias (Humber) Ouma
Andrew (Magero) Wanga

JULIAS (HUMBER) OUMA

NANGWE
?
NAKIROYA
Bwire
Mugeni
Egessa
Benard Wandera

AGAITANO MULYEDI WA WANGA

NAHABI
Agaitano Mulyedi yakerama Nahabi, niyebulamo:
Wanjala
NANYANGA
"Barabara yamukerama muha Barabara mwanangina,
Huniyebulamo Barabara nende Wanjala"

SICHIMI WA WANGA OFUMBUHA

?
Dibondo
Ogaara ll
Mungweno
Paul Musungu
Zakalia Sibero
Daali

DIBONDO WA SICHIMI

NASIHUNE
Batolomayo Bwire
Samuel Wandera
NAHASOHO
Eriakim Mahondo

BATOLOMAYO BWIRE WA DIBONDO

NAHONE
George Mulucha
Gilbert Bwire

GEORGE MULUCHA WA BATOLOMAYO BWIRE

NAMUHOKOSI   Majaliwa

Batolomayo Bwire

GILBERT BWIRE WA BATOLOMAYO BWIRE

NAMIRIPO   Batolomayo Bwire

OGAARA II WA SICHIMI

NAHASOHO   Edward Mugeni

James Bwire

Disani Okello

ANDREW (MAGERO) WANGA WA BARABARA

NAMUDDE   Bosco

Wanyama

NABAKOOLWE   John Mangeni

David Bwire

Egessa

Olwande lwo lupapula 82

NALWENGE   Yowana Mujabi

NALUKAADA   Alexander Wanga

NAMULEMBO   Silvester Ochieno

Christian

YOWANA MUJABI WA TAIDOR NGUNDIRA

Benard Mujabi

Boniface Owino Mujabi

Peter Mujabi

Michael Mujabi

Okello Mujabi

ALEXANDER WANGA WA TAIDOR NGUNDIRA

NAMULEMBO   Michael Omondi

Walter Ojwangi

MORRIS OGANI ODOOL

ADETI   Fredrick Barasa

Paul Ogani

ADETI II   Odwori Ogani

Vicent Owino

WANGA OFUMBUHA

NANJOWA   Muhachi

MUHACHI WA WANGA OFUMBUHA

NAHULO   Oheto

ADETI   Mulayaa

NAKOOLI HAUNWA

OHETO WA MUHACHI

NABONGO
Obbiero

OBBIERO WOHETO

NAMULEMBO
Oheto II

Ouma

HAUNWA WA MUHACHI

NABONGO
Obbiero

Kagenda

OBBIERO WA HAUNWA

NAMAINDI
Gawunya

BADUNI
Ngabi

NABUKAKI
Magero

GAWUNYA WOBBIERO

NASIWE
Okochi

NAMBENGERE
Kanoti

Oligo

MULAYAA WA MUHACHI

ADETI
Oligo

Ongala

OLIGO WA MULAYAA

NABONWE
Oduki

Ombogo

MUGENI WA OLIGO

ONGALA WA MULAYAA

NAKUHU
Ojwangi

Osinya

NAMUNYEKERA
Ouma

Olwande lwo lupapula 83

BOSCO WA ANDREW (MAGERO) WANGA

NAMUSOGA
Eric Ivan

NAKIROYA
Denes

WYCLIFFE ORODI WA ERISA ODYANGA

NAMULUNDU
Jack Laban

NACHAKI
Dauso Bwire (Ongodde)

Fred Orodi

SAMUEL WANDERA WA DIBONDO

NANYANGA
Stephin Bwire

NAMAKANGALA
Dibondo

NAHONE
Geofrey Oundo

George Mulucha

Aggrey Bwire

ERIAKIM NAHONDO WA DIBONDO

NAMWAYA
Wycliffe Mulucha
Henery Bwire
Sanyu Mungweno

NAMULEZI
NAHONE
Ojiambo
Omaajjo

MUGWENO WA DIBONDO

NASIYE
Zakaliya Sibeero
Paul Musungu

ZAKALIYA SIBEERO WA MUNGWENO

NAMULUNDU
Wilson Ouma

PAUL MUSUNGU WA ZAKALIYA SIBEERO

NAMULUNDU
Absolom Magaga
Ignatiyo Wafula

DALLI WA SICHIMI

NAFWOFWOYO
Masinde
Yokosafati Musumba
Gideon Wandera

ANDEREA DALLI III

NAKIROYA
Jackson Ojiambo
Charles Ouma
Humphreys Onyango
George Wafula

NABUKAKI
Livingston Mugeni
Richard Mukaga
Stephin Wandera
Robert Mangeni

OMOLO WA WANGA OFUMBUHA

NANYANGA
Omolo
Suduhu
Odooli

OMOLO WA OMOLO WA WANGA OFUMBUHA

NAMENYA
Domas Were
Taidor Ngundira
Augustino Were

AUGUSTINO WERE WA OMOLO

NAMAYERO
Clement Odooli
Cornel Odipo
Boniface Nachona
Paul Were
Alfred Were

NAMULEMBO
Henry Were

BUKEKO WA NGUNDIRA

NACHONGA
Omijja

OMIJJA WA BUKEKO

Ngweno

Bukeko II

NEHOBA II
Muniala

NGWENO WA OMUJJA

NASUBO
Gaunya

Omijja Abala

GAUNYA WA NGWENO

NAMULEMBO
Omijja Kerereyo

Bubolu Agakan

Ngweno Tumbo

Joshua Musungu

■ Nabwire Natabona

■ Foronica Natabona

NABAHOLO
Odwori Tinga

Petero Omwilo

■ Felesita Natabona (Omukoko) – yadeha mu Baburi

■ Regina Natabona (Omukoko) – yadeha mu Badde yebula:

Egesa

Barasa

Tabu

ODWORI TINGA WA GAUNYA

NAMUDDE
Taabu

BUKEKO II WA OKIJJA

NASUBO
Osinya Pamba

OSINYA PAMBA WA BUKEKO II

Nanyibomi

Nambisa Bulasio Ouma

PETRO OMWILO WA GAUNYA

NAMULEMBO
Egesa

Oguttu

Were

Barasa

OMIJJA KEREREYO WA GAUNYA

NAMUNYEKERA

NAMUMULI

Tomasi Ngweno

Odwori Hasuhiri

Adwoli Gaunya

Yalo Omijja

Nakudi

NASIHUNE

BUBOLU AGAKAN WA GAUNYA

NACHAKI

Saverio Ouma
■ Harriet Night (Nabwire) Natabona
■ Rose Acheno Natabona

NAMUDDE

Masiga
Jackimu

NAMULANDA

NGWENO TUMBO WA GAUNYA

NAMUMULI

Papa Ngweno
Sebuya Ngweno

NADIMO
NAMAKANGALA

Joshua
Sanya Tumbo
■ Foronica Natabona (Omukoko) sihwaduhana yiyadeha, naye
Yebula abewa beffe bano:
Francis Ogoti
Francis Obayo
Donati

ODWORI TINGA WA GAUNYA

NAMUDDE

Taabu

JOSHUA MUSUNGU WA GAUNYA

NAMUDDE

Perusi Auma Natabona (Omukoko), yadeha mu Bajabi, yebula:
Makoha
Oganyo
Musungu
Nakoyo
■ Nafula Natabona (Omukoko), yadeha e Buhulo yebula:
Ouma Obura

NAMUDAYIRWA

Odwori Tinga

ODWORI TINGA WA JOSHUA MUSUNGU

NAMUDDE

Wilberforce Taabu

BUKEKO II WA OKIJJA

NALIALI I
NALIALI 2
NASUBO

Ibrahim Ololo
Wanjala
Osinya Pamba

IBRAHIM OLOLO WA BUKEKO II

NAJABI
NAMWENGE

Misisera Oloo
■ Teresa Apondi Natabona, (Omukoko) yadeha e Bupunyi.
Yebula:
Omuya
Taabu
Atonio Ngonga
Bindicto Oguttu

NAMATTE

ATONIO NGONGA WA IBRAHIM OLOLO

NAMANGALE I

Saverio Sanya
■ Winfred Awino Natabona
■ Adikinyi Natabona
Benna

NANYIHODO

Benard Bwire
Godfrey Wanyama
Peter Wafula
Andrew Masiga

BENDICTO OGUTTU WA IBRAHIM OLOLO

NAMANGALE

Ibrahim Ouma
Pamela Anyango

NAMATTE

Nyikola Ogesa
Benya Odwori
■ Fulumena Natabona (Omukoko), yadeha mu Bachaki yebula
omwiwa weffe wuno:
Muchalia
■ Aguttu Natabona, sihwaduhana ebimutulaho

NYIKOLA OGESA WA BENDICTO OGUTTU

NASONGA

Paul Ouma Namatte
Jophitor Maloba
Joseph Bwire

BENNYA ODWORI WA BENDICTO OGUTTU

NAMIRIPO

Dickson Bwire
Ololo
■ Penina Anyango Natabona

NAPUNYI

James Okumu
Sanya
Patrick Oguttu

NAMAYINDI

Peter Chadiha
Antony
Wanyama

MISISERA OLOO WA IBRAHIM OLOLO

NAMUKUBA

Edward Mugeni
■ Connie Nabwire Natabona
■ Josophine Nafula Natabona
■ Teresa Agutu Natabona
■ Clare Sunday Natabona
■ Harriemti Matama Natabona

WANJALA WA BUKEKO II WA OMIJJA

NAMIRIPO
NALALA

Nisani Ogwabe
Achiengi

NISANI OGWABE WA WANJALA WA BUKEKO

NAKOLI
Hitula
John Onyango

JOHN ONYANGO WA NISANI OGWABE

NASUBO
■ Ajambo Natabona
■ Nabwire Natabona
Osinya Pamba
Godfrey Onyango

NAMULINDA
Peter Wanyama
■ Nasirumbi Natabona
■ Naight Natabona

OSINYA PAMBA WA JOHN ONYANGO

NAMBISA I
Bulasio Ouma
■ Nekesa Natabona (Mukoko) yadehera Abajabi

BULASIO OUMA OWA OSINYA PAMBA

NASONGA
Majoni
Jackson Nambisa
Sowedi Osinya
■ Leunida Taaka Natabona
■ Rose Aguttu Natabona
■ Rose Oundo Nataboma

MUNIALA WO OMIJJA

NAMULEMBO
Opedda
Obwege

OBWEGE WA MINIALA WO OMIJJA

NAHABOCHA
■ Kuucha Natabona (Mukoko), yadeha e Buliali.
Yebula Bwire.
■ Achola Nora Akuku Natabona (Mukoko) yadeha e Bukiroya.
Yebula omusoliri mula yengene. Akuku yafwa omwana nasisiri
Mulwesi. Simwana nende owoluya nibo abamuhusa. Omusiani
bamulanga bati JUSTICE JAMES MUNAGE OGOOLA. Yakeka
omuhaye yibalanga baati Florence Nightingale (Naiti) Ogoola,
(omuhana wo mwenengo Wandera). Omuhaye, wuno yatwibulira
abecuhulu ba Batabona bano:
Apollo Benjamin Munange Ogoola,
Katherine Nora Natabona (Nata) Ogoola,
Angela Florence Muzaki (Zaki) Ogoola,
Jacqueline Taaka Ogoola,
Margaret Madangu Ogoola, Hope Adongo Chamaruth (Tamaruth)
Nahabocha
Ogoola, wuno bamukuliha enguliho ya nguhwangene hulwande
lwa ngina erita lya Chamruth or Tamaruth.

OPEDDA WA MUNIALA

NALWENGE
Muniala
Odongo
■ Nabwire Spana Natabona

NACHAKI
Nyegenye

NAKWEDDE
Phillimon Bubolu
■ Anyango Natabona (Mukoko) yadeha mu Bakuhu.
Yebula abewa batabona bano:
Muniala
Nabwire

NAHABOCHA
Nyangweso
(Wuno, Oppeda yakerama.
James Barasa
Omuhasi
■ Jonorosa Anyango Natabona omukoko
wa mwanangina
yibalanganga bati Obwege)

PHILLIMON BUBOLU WA OPEDDA

NAHAYO
■ Corolyne Bubolu Natabona
■ Dorine Bubolu Natabona

OMUGANDA I
Opedda wa Bubolu
OMUGAND II

NYEGENYE WO OPEDDA

NAMANGASA
Antony Muniala
Obichu Nyegenye
Were Nyegenye
Hagondi Nyegenye
Omiyinga Nyenye
Ouma

NAMANGALE
Taabu
■ Jesca Amboyi Natabona

NAMAKANGALA
Mwamad Opedda
Makin Nyegenye
Atuya
Ndugu

NYANGWESO WO OPPEDA

NAMUPODI
■ Nabwire Natabona

NACHAKI
Muniala

ODONGO WA OPEDDA WA MUNIALA

NAHAYO
Zabroni Obwolo

ZABRONI OBWOLO WA ODONGO

NALIALI
Okochi
Juma
Wandera
Muniala
Kongorasi
Fredrick Nyongesa

OKOCHI WA ZABRONI OBWOLO

NASWA   Baraza

WANDERA WA ZABRONI OBWOLO

NAJABI   Sunday Obwolo
Benard Okumu
Richard Ouma
Moses Okuku
Meddi (Okochi)

FREDRICK NYONGESA WA ZABRONI OBWOLO

NACHAKI   Barasa
Mwana

NAMUSWA
NAMWAYA

MUNIALA WA ZABRONI OBWOLO

NAMENYA   Sunday
Were
Boloki
Akura

KONGORASI WA ZABRONI OBWOLO

HAGONDI NYEGENYE WA NYEGENYE WO OPEDDA

NAHABI   Omijja Hagondi
Hantono
Omijja
Okombo

OMIJJA WA HAGONDI WA NYEGENYE WO OPEDDA

NAMENYA   Wilber Bwire
Robert Wanyama
Odongo
Okello

JAMES BARASA WA OPEDDA

NASITWOKI   ■ Nalwire Natabona

MUNIALA WA OPEDDA

NANYIMODDO   ■ Nabwire Natabona

ODONGO WA OPEDDA

NAHOLI   Muniala (Botswana)
Sunday (Austraria)
Odongo
Opedda

OSINYA PAMBA WA BUKEKO II WA OMIJJA

Nanyibomi
Nambisa Bulasio Ouma

MUNIALA WA BUKEKO II

LWANDE

LWANDE WA MUNIALA KAGENDA II

KAGENDA II WA LWANDE
Nadebu Bwonya
Buluma (Musamia)

BULUMA WA KAGENDA II
Yowana Hafulu

YOWANA HAFULU WA BULUMA
Elias Mujucfa

NALALA
BUKEKO II WA OMIJJA
Wanjala
Ololo

OLOLO WA BUKEKO II
NAJABI   Mususera Olowo
NAMATE   Nikola Ogessa
                     Benjamin (Benya) Odwori
NAMWENGE   Anthony Ngonga
                     Bendicto Ngweno

?
NIKOLA OGESSA WA OLOLO
Ouma Paul Namatte

NAMULEMBO
MUNIALA WA OMIJJA
Obwege
Hagondi

NAMAINDI
NAMULEMBO   Hagondi
                    Opeda

OBWENGE WA MUNIALA
Odongo

ZABRONI OBWOLO
NAMULEMBO?   Hagondi
                    Opedda

NAHAYO
ODONGO OBWENGE.
Zabroni Obwolo

ZABRONI OBWOLO WA OBWENGE

NALYALI
Okochi
Wilson Wandera
James Muniala
Fredrick Nyongesa
Naming Kaisofasi
Kongorasi

OKOCHI WA ZABRONI OBWOLO

NASWA
Baraza

WANDERA WA ZABRONI OBWOLO

NAJABI
Sunday Obwolo
Okumu Benard
Richard Ouma
Moses Okuku
Meddi

FREDRICK NYONGESA

NACHAKI
Barasa
Mwana

NAMUSWA
NAMWAYA

JAMES MUNIALA

NAMENYA
Sunday
Were
Boloki
Akura

KONGORASI

HAGONDI WA OBWENGE

NAHABI
Patrick Omijja Hagondi
Hontono
Omijja
Okombo

OMIJJA WA HAGONDI

NAMENYA
Wilber Bwire
Robert Wanyama
Odongo
Okello

Olwande lwo lupapula 85

ODUKI WA OLIGO

NADEKE	Mengo Okigo
	Ogoola Oduki
	Wandera Oduki
	Juma Oduki
NAMAINDI	Onyango Oduki
	Juma Oduki II
	Ogutu Oduki
	Oundo Oduki
NAMAINDI II	Okelo Oduki
	Oundo Oduki
	Gawunya Oduki
	Ojiambo Oduki

MBOGO WA OLIGO

NABONGO	Ochiengi
	Sikuku
	Akumu
	Nekesa
NADEKE	Nabboro
	Muhachi
NAMUNYEKERA	Oriero Gawunya

MUGENI WA OLIGO

LWANDE WA WESONGA

NEHAMA	Kagenda
NANJOWA	Ngundira wa Kagenda
NASONGA I	Bukeko
NASONGA II	Dikidi
NAMULUCHA	Kubengi
NALUKADA	Mboyo

KUBENGI WA NGUNDIRA

NAHULO	Gasundi
	Mbakulo
NAMUDDE I	Owori
NAMUDDE II	Nambakwa

Olwande lwo lupapula 86

YONASANI NGWABE WA BUKEKO III

NAKOLI	Hitler
	Onyango

OMIJJA ABBALA WA NGWENO

NAHASOHO	■ Natabona mulala yengene

NGUNDIRA WA KAGENDA

NASONGA II	Dikidi

DIKIDI WA NGUNDIRA

NALYALI	Namwiwa
	Agaaro
NANYIBONI	Lusimbo

97

NAMWIWA WA DIKIDI

NABONGO — Ouma Nyaroya

OUMA NYAROYA WA NAMWIWA

NAKAALA
NAMANGASA — Aroni Omondi
Oulo
Stephin Omochi
Dikidi
Petero Wandera
NAPUNYI — Toas Mubbachi
Juma
Simon Nasude

ARONI OMONDI WA OUMA NYAROYA

NAMIRIPO — Ngundira
Peter Nanwiwa

PETER NAMWIWA ARONI OMONDI

NAMUNYEKERA

CALASTO SUMBA WA WAMBUDO

NANGAYO
NAKOOLI — Ojiambo

STEPHIN OMOCHI WA OUMA

COMULUS (NGUNDIRA) WANDERA

NEHOBA — Were
NAKOOLI — Charles Omondi
Opio
Odongo
Mukaga

PETERO WANDERA WA OUMA

COMULUS (NGUNDIRA) WANDERA

NASUBO — Ouma
Egessa
Stephin Omochi

OGAARO WA NAMWIWA

LUSIMBO WA DIKIDI

NAHULO — Ogengo
NAMWALIRA — Oduyu

OGENGO WA LUSIMBO

NASIWE — Kuucha
NABOOLI — Juma
NASUBO — Iginatio Ogutu
John Wandera

KUUCHA WA OGENGO

NABONGO   Francis Wanyama

FRANCIS WANYAMA WA KUUCHA

IGINATIO OGUTU WA OGENGO

NAMENYA   George Maloba
NALIALI   Jackson Okumu
           Richard Odwori
           Milton Ogengo
           Patrick Oduyu
           Stephin Kuucha (Fredrick)

Olwande lwo lupapula 87

GEORGE MALOBA WA IGINATIO OGUTU

JACKSON OKUMU WA IGINATIO OGUTU

MUTULA WA DIKIDI

NAHASOHO   Wambudo
            Ngundira Ondyedye

WAMBUDO WA MUTULA

NGUNDIRA ONDYEDYE WA MUTULA

NEYINDA   Abuneri Omunya

ABUNERI OMUNYA WA ONDYEDYE

NALALA   Joramu Egondi
          ■ Makoha Natabona yaali omukoko yafa
NAJABI

GASUNDI WA KUBENGI

NAMANGALE   Orubo

ORUBO WA GASUNDI

NASIMALWA   Buya

BUUYA WA ORUBO

NABONGO   Gidion Odiedo
NAMBANJA   Wandera
NALWENGE   Ojiambo
            Mubbachi
            Juma
            Onyango
NAHEMBA   Lucas Onjalo

99

GIDEON ODIEBO WA BUUYA

NASONGA	Josophati Odwori
	Charles Ochieno
	Edward Ogoola
NABUKAKI I	Joseph Nyongesa
	Joseph Ohito
NABUKAKI II	George Wandera
NASONGA II	Apola Obbala
	Andrew Obbala
	Charles Juma
	Fredrick Omondi
NAPUNYI	Williamu Owino
NASONGA III	Ojiambo

Olwande lwo lupapula 88

OJIAMBO WA BUUYA

NAPUNYI	Ochiengi
	Okochi

NABACHI WA BUUYA

NASONGA	Buuya
	Odwori

JUMA WA BUUYA

NANYNEKI	Orubo
	Nadede
	Okite

ONYANGO WA BUUYA

NAPUNYI	Buuya
	Otika
	Obbala I
	Obbala II

LUCAS ONJALO WA BUUYA

NANYIMARO	Odenga
	Okumu
	Nomuhana
NAMAKANGALA	Buuya
	Cotton

ODENGA WA LUCAS ONJALO NGUNDIRA WA BUUYA
Buuya

LWANDE OMUNYISA WA ...

NASONGA	Oyaaga
	Otiro
NAMAINDI	Kwereho
NABONGO	Wanjala

OYAAGA WA LWANDE OMUNYISA
Opondo
Ogutu

NAMUDDE

OTIRO WA LWANDE OMUNYISA
Yokana Kadima

YOKANA KADIMA WA OTIRO

NAJABI

MESO WA OWORI
Comlus Wandera

NADEKE I
NEHOBA

COMULUS WANDERA WA MESO
Cornel Ojiambo
Onyango
Keya Ochiengi

NADEKE II

Osuwo nende Odwori

NABUKAKI

CORNEL OJIAMBO COMULUS WANDERA
Omondi
Ochieno
Meja
Ojwangi

NAMAINDI

ONYANGO WA COMULUS WANDERA
Furango
James
Omooro
Peter Ochiengi

Olwande lwo lupapula 89

NAPUNYI

KEYA WA COMULUS WANDERA
Ombare
Mejja

NAPUNYI

OCHIENGI WA COMULUS WANDERA
Ochieno
Fredrick Odwori
Wandera

NAMAINDI

OSUWO WA COMULUS WANDERA
Ouma

NABOOLI
NAJABI

CHWALA WA OWORI
Clement Were
Oundo

NASIREKU

CLEMENT WERE WA CHWALA
Ochiengi

NAMUNAPA

COMULUS WANDERA
Kubengi
Inginia

101

ABWOKA WA OWORI

NABONGA I   James Odwori
             Ouma
             Kubengi
NADEKE   Joseph
             Nicola
NABONGO II   Daudi Buluma
NAMUDUMA   Owori

JAMES ODWORI WA ABWOKA WA OWORI

NABURI   Ochiengi
             Pius

KUBENGI WA ABWOKA WA OWORI

NASONGA   Baras
             Ojiambo
             Pius Okongo

JOSEPH WA ABWOKA WA OWORI

MERELE   Abwoka
             Wandera

DAUDI BULUMA WA OWORI

NABURI   Anyesi
             Wandera
             Mugubi
             Jengo
NAFUNYU   Tinga
             Namwenge
             Idi

ANYESI WA DAUDI BULUMA
Daudi Romy

WANDERA WA DAUDI BULUMA

NABURI   Nikola
             Daudi

Olwande lwo lupapula 90

BULUMA WA OWORI

NAJABI   Kanoti Odwori
             Owori Raminya
NAGWANGA   Pius Onyango
             Mahulo
NAJABI II   Okechi

KANOTI ODWORI WA BULUMA

NASIMALWA   Oyaanga
             Makanga
             Ramisi

OWORI RAMINYA WA BULUMA

NAHULO
Okumu
Oundo
Onyango
Charles Odwori

PIUS ONYANGO WA BULUMA

NALUKADA
Grado Odoowo
Ndenga

NDENGA WA PIUS ONYANGO

NALALA
Ochieno
Bukeko L. Nasonga
Muniala
Naminjoo Ngundira

NGUNDIRA WA ARONI

NAMAKWE
Ouma
George

Olwande lwo lupapula 91

OKECHI WA PIUS ONYANGO

NANYANGA
Onyango
Egessa
Ochiengi

ONYANGO WA OKECHI WA PIUS ONYANGO

NAMAKANGALA
Buluma

LWANDE WESONGA WA LWANDE MULUNGO

NEHAMA
Kagenda

KAGENDA WA LWANDE WESONGA

NANJOWA
Ngundira

NGUNDIRA WA KAGENDA

NAMULUCHA
Kubengi

KUBENGI WA NGUNDIRA

NAHULO
Mbakulo

MBAKULO WA KUBENGI

NAHAALA

Ngundira II
Ochieno
■ Akumu Natabona ya dehera Abalundu
Yebula abewa beffe bano:
Mwolo
Walter Osinya

NAMAINDI

Ngema,
Dismasi Hagyo,
■ Okanya Natabona yadehera omu Byangu Wagabi
Okanya Natabona yebebula abewa beffe, naye wuno niye
yihwanyala ohumanyaho ebimudiraho:
James Machio Mbakulo owali mulala hub Senator abatangira mu
Government ya Jomo Kenyatta, Kenya luyaduhana ohwefuka
ohutula hu Great Britain.
■ Njaywe Natabona yadehera abakaangala, yebula Paulo Nyagui
(e Nambuku).

NAMUDDE

Magina
Mwabi
Mugoya

NACHAKI

Yeremia Masiga
Echibbi – Wuno sibamulomalomangaho – Siboneha mbwe anyala
ohuba niyafwa hale muno.
■ Achola Natabona yadehera Owori omusiani wa Magosolo, e
Butangasi.
Abana ba Achola Natabona:
Matiasi Ochieno
Ojiambo
Magero
Abewa abo bebula abecuhulu ba Batabona bano:
Matiasi Ochieno yebula:
Mbakulo
Tekela Nachaki
Ojiambo yebula:
Nachaki
Laisa
Ojiambo
Magero yebula:
Nangobe Nachaki
Hadudu
Nabwire
Nerima
Kuwucha.
Kuwucha yebula:
Joseph Bwire Mukwajo
Nafa Mbakulo (Obondo).

Joseph Bwire Mukwajo yebula:
Richard Baan Ochieng
Godfrey Bwire
Gorret Riaka
Florence Nasirumbi
Judith Auma
David Mangeni Okanya
Patrick Joseph Wandera
Andrew Ouma
Richard Baan Ochieng yebula:
Benard Ouma
Filix Ojiambo
John Wanyama
Dickens Barasa
Godfrey Bwire yebula:
Nicole Taaka
Gorret Riaka yebula:
Oliver
Rebecca
Simon
Florence Nasirumbi yebula:
Ivan Mugeni
Issac Bwire
Femiah Anyango
Fiona
Nafa Mbakulo (Obondo) wa Kuwucha yebula:
Jessica Anyango
Jessica Anyango yebula:
Gilbert Ouma
Gilbert Ouma yebula:
Cilisia Makoha. Abandi sihwanyala ohuduhana ebibatulaho.

NB: Bati Kubengi yaali omwicha wa simwana Nachaki.
Simwana Nachaki baali bamulanga bati Owori Dadi,
Omuchaki. Bati, Kubengi yachichanga ohumukeniyira koti
owasye yibakana oluyaali. Yecha yabona omuhana
omunyirifu handi nga Aboneha cbilayipo, yeca yamudaha
muno ohumukeka. Yecha yayirira simwana Nachaki
engombe cyosi chiyali nadahire. Naye Kubengi yemawo acya
ohulwana mu yee. Yabasa ati nakaluha huyemewo ahole
emidunga kwo huleta Nachaki koti omuhasi waye. Kubengi
yal-wananga muno amaaye, yaali amanyire ebidinyu bya
mayee. Natawawo ohucya ohulwana, yabolera omusiani waye
ati niwicuhira ndahaya ohukaluha okekanga Nachaki.
Esiehabi mbi luno luyacya ohulwana eyee nende Abateso
haba siyakaluha. Abateso ba mulasa efumu lyamudira esirifu
no mwoyo mani yafwa. Nisio esyatulaho Omusiani wa
Kubengi Mbakulo ohukeka Nachaki.

NGUNDIRA (II) WA MBAKULO MALAMBA

NASIMALWA Yusufu Nakuhu
NAHEMBA AKOCHI Yosiya Were (Butonya)
Garisom Ohonga
■ Asinasi Ngundira Natabona, yadehera aba Lala yebula:
Zewuliya Were
Ghadi Maloba
James Oduki
Getrude Sibabale
Abecuhulu beffe ba Asinasi Natabona sihwanyala ohuduhana
ebibatulaho.
NAHEMBA ANYANGO Obonyo

YUSUFU NAKUHU WA NGUNDIRA (II) MALAMBA

NAMULEMBO Jonathan Mbakulo
(Ayireni Oyaka) ■ Victoria Taka Natabona yadehera aba Mayindi
■ Faisi Nekesa Natabona yadehera aba Teso
■ Ludiya Agutu Natabona yadehera aba Miripo (siyebulayo
abana).
Abecuhulu beffe sihwanyala ohuduhana ebibatulaho.
NAHONE Yese Mugeni
Emanuel Wanyama
Saul Ouma
■ Edisa Onyonga Natabona yadehera a Balundu
■ Nabwire Natabona yadehera aba Mayindi
Sihwanyala ohuduhana ebihiraho awo.

JONATHAN MBAKULO WA YUSUFU NAKUHU

NAMUDDE (Leya) Ezekiel Kubengi
Jacob Ochieno
Saul Ngundira III
MBWAALI (Musoga) ■ Ajiambo Natabona yadehera aba Hone e Kenya
■ Anyango Natabona yadehera aba Miripo
NAMUDDE (Ester Abele) Steven Ngundira
Robert Oyaaka
Akisoferi Oundo
Yekonia Rojas Masiga
■ Alice Ohonga Natabona yadehera aba Mango
■ Nabwire (Night) Natabona yadehera aba Kiloya
MARIAMU ■ Saamanya Natabona yadeha e Buhayo mu Baguri
NAMAMBA
(Mutanzania mu ba Pare)
WANGABI (Muganda) Damulira Mbakulo
NAMAHYA Geofrey Ohonga (Bwire)
Edward Mbakulo

KUBENGI EZEKYERI WA JONATHAN MBAKULO

NAKOOLI

John Wandera
Joseph Ojiambo
John Bwire
Kaazi Kenneth Mbakulo
Nabwire (Night) – Natabona yali omukoko yadehera aba chonga;
■ Indra Natabona
■ Bhutto Natabona
■ Beti Natabona

Olwande lwo lupapula 92

JACOB OCHIENO WA JONATHAN MBAKULO

NACHAKI

Godfrey Ouma
Kaazi Mbakulo
■ Ajambo Natabona

NAMAINDI

Robert Ochieno mwana we simba
Omuhaye wuno ali nende abana bahana ameta haba sihwanyala
ohukaduhana.

SAUL NGUNDIRA WA JONATHAN MBAKULO

NYALUWO

Martin Ngudira,
■ Mulago Natabona adehera aba Lyali, erita sihwamanya.

DAMULIRA WA JONATHAN MBAKULO

NACHAKI

Joseph Wanyama G.W.

EMANUEL WANYAMA WA YUSUFU NAKUHU

NACHAKI

Ojiambo (Pururu)

ISAAC FAHIRI

NAMANGALE
NAMUKUBA
NASONGA

Jackson Ochieno
Stanely Mbakulo
Disani Mbakulo Bwire
Phillimon Wanyama

NEKEDERA

Gideon Oundo (Gasundi

YOSIA WERE KUBENGI BUTONYA WA NGUNDIRA II MALAMBA

NAMUDDE
(Agasa Nabwire)

Disani Onyango Mbakulo
■ Robina Agoola Natabona Agoola yadehera Ouma Heya omu
Mirippo
■ Robina Agoola Natabona yatwibulira abecuhulu bano:
Ochieno Heya
Wafula Heya
Namudde heya
Nambisa
Namiripo odehera aba Malenge
Akumu odehera aba Mayindi.

NAMULEMBO
(Auma)

George Kubengi
John Odongo
■ Nambisa Natabona yadehera Abamale
■ Akumu Natabona yadehera Abamaindi

DISANI ONYANGO MBAKULO WA YOSIA WERE

NADIMO I
(Erisabeth Nabwire)

Charles Ngundira Maalamba

NADIMO II
(Miria Anyango)

Godfrey Wandera Akochi
Julius Namudde
Patric Bwire (Namige)Mbakulo
Joshua Were Butonya
■ Grace Nafula Natabona yadehera Abalwenge
■ Harriet Nabwire Natabona yadehera Abafofoyo
■ Janet Namulundu Natabona yadehera Abamanyi

NASIENGERA
(Debora Taaka)

Disani Mbakulo yakerama omuhaye wuno, John Kadima Nafire.
Yebulamu:
■ Joan Maliza Kadima Natabona. Natabona wuno asiri mu
Somero.

CHARLES NGUNDIRA MAALAMBA
Emanuel Mbakulo
Wandeyi Mbakulo
Manuari Mbakulo
■ Dorika Namulundu Natabona
■ Akello Namudde Natabona
■ Davini Nadimu Natabona
■ Kasalina Mbakulo Natabona

GODFREY WANDERA AKOCHI

JULIUS NAMUDDE MBAKULO
Edward Kubengi
Nelson Mandela Mbakulo
Disani Mbakulo
Abahana:
■ Namudde Mbakulo Natabona yadeha musyalo sye Bugwere
■ Najabbi Mbakulo Natabona

PATRICK BWIRE (NAMIGE) MBAKULO
Tyson Bwire Mbakulo
Disani Manuari Mbakulo Abahana:
■ Nekesa Nadimo Natabona adeha musyalo sye Budola
■ Joan Kubengi Natabona adeha ebuhwama mu Badde.

JOSHUA WERE KUBENGI BUTONYA
■ Grace Nafula Natabona adehera Samuel Barasa omu Lwenge.
■ Grace Nafula Natabona yebula abewa babatabona bano:
Obasi,
Anthony Barasa,
Areni Barasa,
Mama Barasa,
Harriett Nabwire, adehera Paulo Nyanya omu Fowfowyo,
Mambo Sikoti Wafula
Janet Namulundu, adehera Ndabba Omumanyi yebula
Kadima Ndabba

GEORGE KUBENGI WA YOSIA WERE BUTONYA

NAMUYUMBU
Yosia Butonya
■ Auma Namulembo Natabona yadehera Abafofofyo

OMUMADDI/MWOYO
Jeremiah Masiga

OMUSOGA
Butonya Kubengi

(Agnesi Muha Kubengi)
Auma Namulembo

YOSIA BUTONYA WA GEORGE KUBENGI

JEREMIAH MASIGA WA GEORGE KUBENGI

BUTONYA KUBENGI WA GEORGE KUBENGI

JOHN ODONGO WA YOSIA WERE BUTONYA

NASIMBWA/MUGANDA
Kubengi Odongo
Yosia Were Butonya
■ **Auma Natabona** yadeha olwande lwe Mityana eyo

NASUHUNE
Stephen Ngundira

(Grace Ajiambo)
Dan
Godfrey Maloba
■ Kwawaho Boro Natabona yadehera Aba Lubanga abana bosi suhumanyire ametta kabwe. Nabandi abangi bahutanyalire ohuduhana amata.

NANYIBOMI
Ronard Ouma

YOSIA WERE BUTONYA WA JOHN ODONGO

STEPHEN NGUNDIRA WA JOHN ODONGO

DAN WA JOHN ODONGO

GODFREY MALOBA WA JOHN ODONGO

RONARD OUMA WA JOHN ODONGO

GRISOM OHONGA WA NGUNDIRA II MALAMBA

YOSSAMU OBONYO

RAMOGI /MUDAMA
Jacobo Egondi

(Alowo)
Edward Akochi
■ Ajiambo Natabona yadehera Farasiko Matenga omu Gasa
■ Ajiambo Natabona yebula omicuhulu mutabona wuno: Matenga
■ Ohonga Natabona (yadehera abanyole mani yecha yasiha).

JACOBO EGONDI WA YOSSAMU OBONYO
Alex Barasa
Ngundira

ALEX BARASA WA JACOB EGONDI WO OBONYO

NAKOOLI

Obonyo
Wandera
Butonya
Sida Barasa
■ Nakoli Barasa Natabona.
Abandi amatta sihukamanyire.

OBONYO WA ALEX BARASA

WANDERA WA ALEX BARASA

BUTONYA WA ALEX BARASA

SIDA BARASA WA ALEX BARAS WA JACOB EGONDI

EDWARD AKOCHI WA YOSSAMU OBONYO
Efumbi Akochi
Abandi ametta sihwanyala ohuduhana.

EFUMBO WA EDWARD AKOCHI
Atebula

OCHIENO WA MBAKULO WA KUBENGI

NAMUNYALA

Yosia Obbienyo
Yekoyada Ngundira
■ Elizabeth Agutu Natabona Omukoko, yadehera Abachaki
Elizabeth Agutu Natabona yebula abewa babatabona bano:
Joel Mayende
Patrick Okumu
Nora Mugeni – yadehera Disani Namude omu Suubo
Eseresi – yadehera aba Makoya
Debola – yadehera aba Suubo,
Ana Edisa Auma Okecha. Yebula abecuhulu beffe bano Natabona
Okecha nende Georgina
■ Ebiseri Taaka Natabona, Mukoko, yadehera Abaganda mu nono
yibalanga baati Abamamba. Yadehera Omwawule otangira mu
Samia Bugwe yibalanga bati Saulo Namuyenga nga yehala
musisala syekanisa ye Busia. Yatula e Buganda, Church
Missionary nibamutumire ohwicha eno ohusomesa edini.
Ebiseri Taaka Natabona yebula abewa babatabona bano:
Marikisiwa Kiberu
George Kigobe
Gayi Namuyenga
Yuniya Tebandeke
Mangalita Namuyenga
■ Janet Hadudu Natabona yadehera omudde Obakiro, bati
bamwenda esibeyo. Janet Hadudu Natabona yebula abewa ba
batabona bano:
Nabwire (Namudde) yadehera aba Suubo,
Hendrika Achieno (Namudde) yadeha e Bulyali

NAMANGALE   Isaac Fahiri
NAMUKUBA   Gideon Oundo

YOSIA OBBIENYO WA OCHIENO WA MBAKULO

NAMWINI

■ Erina Nanjala Natabona yadehera aBadde
Erina Nanjala Natabona yebula abewa beffe bano:
Magero Okumu
Mugeni (Namudde) adehera aba Depi,
Federesi Nabwire (Namudde) yadehera aBenge

YEKOYADA NGUNDIRA WA OCHIENO

NAMULEMBO

James Mbakulo
Edward Oguti (Yaafire 2015)
■ Esereya Nabwire Natabona, Mukoko yadehera aba Kuhu
■ Alice Anyango Natabona, Mukoko, yadehera aba Laala
■ Gladdys Agutu Natabona, Mukoko, yadehera aba Jaabi

JAMES MBAKULO WA YEKOYADA NGUNDIRA

NADONGO

Richard Kubengi
Wilber Ouma
Joel Barasa
■ Nabwire Natabona, Mukoko, yadehera aBalala
■ Taaka Natabona, Mukoko, yadehera aba Yeemba.

EDWARD OGUTI NGUNDIRA WA YEKOYADA

NAHONE
(Alimerida Hayoko)
NAMAKANGALA
(Jesika Nerima)

■ Edisa Namukangu Natabona, Mukoko, yadehera aba Subo

Charles Kubengi Mangeni
■ Florence Agutu Ochieno Natabona, Mukoko, yadehera aba Jabi
Florence Agutu Ochieno Natabona yebula abewa babatabona
bano:
Wafula Sayilasi
Mosesi Wafula
Kasalina Namulembe (Najabi)
Abandi sihumanyire ametta kabwe

RICHARD KUBENGI WA JAMES MBAKULO

WILBER OUMA WA JAMES MBAKULO YEKOYADA

JAMES BARASA WA JAMES MBAKULO YEKOYADA

CHARLES KUBENGI MANGENI WA E. OGUTI
■ Nabwire Ngundira Natabona Mangeni
■ Nahulo Natabona Mangeni
■ Namunyala Natabona Mangeni

ISAAC FAHIRI WA OCHIENO WA MBAKULO

NAMANGALE
NAMUKUBA?
NASONGA

Jackson Ochieno
Stanely Mbakulo (Yafwa)
Disani Mbakulo Bwire
Philimon Wanyama
■ Natabon yibenda esibeyo sya Karara Natabona wa Ngema wa
Mbakulo, e Buchaki owa Bendifasiyo Ombito omuchaki.

JACOB OCHIENO MASAHI

NEKEDERA

Gideon Oundo (Gasundi).
Bati simwana Gideon Oundo, niyafa Isaac Fahiri yakerama ngina huyebula Jackson Ochieno.

JACKSON OCHIENO WA ISAAC FAHIRI
Jackson Ochieno yafwa namalire ohukeka. (We do not have the names of his children)

STANELY MBAKULO WA ISAAC FAHIRI

?

Musa Mbakulo,
Benard Wafula,
Samuiri Ogula Mbakulo,
Humpheries Bwire,
Peter Oundo Ojiambo.
Abahana nibo bano:
■ Jane Anyango Natabona, Mukoko, yadehera aba Gemi,
■ Rose Auma Natabona, Mukoko, yadehera aba Gemi,
■ Beti Natabona
■ Juliet Natabona

DISANI MBAKULO BWIRE WA ISAAC FAHIRI

NAMULUNDU

Namangale Ohonga,
Martin Ochieno,
Isaaka Mugeni,
Rbert Kubengi,
Geofrey Ochieno,
Wilfred Wandera,
Marvin Mbakulo.
Abahana nibo bano:
■ Anetti Ajiambo Natabona
■ Proscovia Nabwire Natabona
■ Sharoni Nasirumbi Natabona
■ Robina Natabona
■ Shiba Namulembe Natabona.

PHILIMON WANYAMA WA ISAAC FAHIRI
Godfrey Osinya
Kwawaho Fahiri
Awubo Fahiri
Abahana nibo bano:
■ Nabwire Natabona, Mukoko, adeha muBadde
■ Mugeni Natabona, Mukoko, adeha e Budola
■ Jesica Auma Natabona, Mukoko, adehera Abachaki sihweculisa ammetta ka baana Adongo

GIDEON OUNDO WA GASUNDI WA MBAKULO
NALWENGE

Dr George Mbakulo Bwire Oundo
Frederick Okumu Oundo
Philips Kubengi Oundo
Francis Ojiambo
■ Ms Rose Akello Natabona, Mukoko, yebula abana bano, abewa ba Batabona.
Ms Nabwire
Charles Ouma
Edwin
Ms Nambi
Junior Wandera
Wandera.
■ Jennifer Anyango Natabona
■ Taaka Butonya Natabona
■ Pamela Nasirisi Natabona – abana bane. Ameta sibatuba dawe.

DR GEORGE MBAKULO BWIRE OUNDO
OMUGISU

OMUTESO -
Nakarimanyang'a
(Alice Achalata)

Capt. Robert Oundo
Bwire Oundo
Eric Sanya
■ Faisi Nekesa Oundo Natabona
Henry Kubengi Oundo

FRED OKUMU WA GIDEON OUNDO
NAMULUNDU

Arther Oundo
Phiona Oundo
NAMUDDE

Aba siani badatu – ametta sihwaduhana

PHILIPS KUBENGI OUNDO
OMUGANDA

Conrad Kubengi Oundo
■ Ms. Kubengi Oundo Natabona

FRANCIS OJIAMBO OUNDO
NAJIMARE

■ Hope Taaka Natabona – saali nomwana
■ Fortunate Ojambo Natabona – yebula omuhana yibalanga bati Mercy.
Sanya Ojambo

NGEMA WA MBAKULO
NAMUDDE
NASONGA

Wanjala
Ojiambo Budaha Ngema
■ Nerima Haduli Natabona, Mukoko, yadehera Abalala.Yebula omusiani mulala yibalanga bati Mangeni
■ Kalara Natabona, Mukoko, yadehera Bendefasio Ombito Omuchaki, yebula bano:
Victoria Nachaki
Auma
Barasa – Ombito yamuhusa

OJIAMBO BUDAHA WA NGEMA WA MBAKULO

NAMAKANGALA (Rose) Aggrey (Danyuha) Kubengi (Yaafa)
Ramathan Pusi Ojiambo
Richard Odwori Ojiambo,
Simon Ojiambo.
Bwire

NAMULEMBO Aliwo ba **Natabona** ba Namulembo haba sihumanyire ametta.
NAKIROYA Mugeni wa Ojiambo Budaha

AGGREY (DANYUHA) KUBENGI

RAMATHAN PUSI OJIAMBO

RICHARD ODWORI OJIAMBO
Mangeni

SIMON OJIAMBO

BWIRE OJIAMBO

WANJALA WA NGEMA WA MBAKULO

DISMASI HAGIO WA MBAKULO

NAKOOLI Gabriel Ochieno – yaali omuhongo muno mu East African Police.
(Police Inspector in King's Government, mubiha ebyo Uganda
yaali yisifukibwa nende United Kingdom or (GB)
Buluma Beyi

NACHAKI Siyebula omwana. Babola bati yaali omukumba.

GABRIEL ONYANGO OCHIENO

NAMULEMBO Peter Odwori
Okumu Mayembe
■ Auma Natabona, Mukoko, yadehera Abaheri mani yecha yaffa.

PETER ODWORI WA GABRIEL OCHIENO
Mbakulo wOdwori
■ Tina Kubengi Natabona, Mukoko, adehera aba Mayindi

OKUMU MAYEMBE WA GABRIEL OCHIENO
Ouma waMayembe
Yeremia Masiga Mukaga
Kubengi wa Mayembe
■ Ba Natabona baali 2 ameta sihwamanya.

MBAKULO WO DWORI WA PETER ODWORI

OUMA WA MAYEMBE

YEREMIA MASIGA MUKAGA WA MAYEMBE

KUBENGI WA MAYEMBE

BULUMA BEYI WA DISIMASI HAGIO WA MBAKULO

NAJABI
Onyango Beyi
Juma Beyi
Egessa Beyi
■ Taaka Natabona, Mukoko, yadehera Abamaindi

NAMULEMBO
Tabu Namulembo.
Buluma Beyi, yecha yakerama Namulembo muha Gabriel
Ochieno, hu yamwibulamo Tabu Namulembo.

ONYANGO WA BEYI

JUMA WA BEYI

EGESSA WA BEYI

TABU NAMULEMBO WA BEYI
Kubengi Tabu
Afura Tabu
Sweeti Tabu
■ Nekesa Natabona, Mukoko, adehera aba Kangaala abandu ba
Mutiki ebu Kuhu

MAGINA WA MBAKULO

NALALA
Colonio Luduba
■ Erina Anyango Natabona, Mukoko, yadehera Simion Wafubwa
Omusera.
■ Erina Anyango Natabona yebula omwana mulala yengene,
omwiwa wabatabona yibalanga bati:
Wilson Okwenje.
Wilson Okwenje yebula abecuhulu ba Batabona bano:
Joseph Okwenje
Nalala Okwenje
Natabona (Bona) Okwenje
Bathsheba (Sheba) Okwenje
Benoni Okwenje
■ Donatina Osinya Natabona, Mukoko, yadehera Abamaali.
Yebula abana naye sihwanyala ohuduhana ametta.

Olwande lwo lupapula 93

MWABI WA MBAKULO

NAMUKOBE
Stephano Wandera
Muchere Mwabi

ADETI
Thomas Ouma Mwabi
Joseph Ngundira III Mwabi
■ Taaka Natabona

NASUBO
 Jimmy Wanyama Mwabi

115

STEHPANO WANDERA MBAKULO WA MWABI
Kubengi
Ochieno
■ Nekesa Natabona, Mukoko, adehera aba Hokosi. Abana sihwabamanya.
■ Agutu Natabona, Mukoko, yadehera Abaduma. Mani sihwanyala ohuduhana omundu otubolera abana bano nende nihwakesaho lukaali muno handi muno

FRANCIS MUCHERE MWABI WA MWABI
Opio Muchere
Egesa
Mangeni wa Muchere Muchere yeca yakerama muha Stephin Wandera
Mbakulo namaalire ohufwa mani yecha Yamwuibulamo:
■ Agutu Natabona, Mukoko, yadehera aba Maceke
■ Adongo Natabona, Mukoko, yadehera aba Ngaale
■ Akello Natabona, Mukoko, yadehera Abadde
■ Hamala Natabona, Mukoko, yesi yadehera Abadde
■ Achola Natabona, Mukoko, yadehera aba Lyali
■ Taabu Natabona, Mukoko, yadehera Abadde
■ Nekesa Natabona, Mukoko, adehera aba Hokosi.
Ebyo nibyo byongene bihwanyala ohuduhana hu bakoko bano.

OPIO MUCHERE WA MUCHERE

MANGENI WA MUCHERE

NADIDI

NASIYE

JOSEPH (YUSUFU) NGUNDIRA III WA MWABI
Odongo
Wandera
■ Night Natabona, Mukoko, yadehera Abamulembo
Kadogo Ngundira
■ Apiyo Natabona, Mukoko, yadehera Abamulembo
■ Tono Natabona, Mukoko, yadehera Abalala
■ Rose Natabona, Mukoko, yadehera Abalundu
■ Lilly Natabona
■ Flora Natabona

NEHOBA
NAMULUNDU

JIMMY WANYAMA MWABI WA MWABI
■ Getu Nabwire Natabona, Mukoko, yadehera Abatende
Mangeni George
Bwire Mwabi
Wilson Makoha
■ Nekesa Natabona, Mukoko, yadehera Abamaindi
■ Taaka Natabona, Mukoko, yadehera Abahumachi

THOMAS OUMA MWABI WA MWABI

NAMUKUBA

Masiga

Juma

Charles Namulucha

- H. Nabwire Natabona, Mukoko, yadehera Abamaindi
- N. Nafula Natabona, Mukoko, yadehera Abahwana
- Sunday Natabona, Mukoko, yadehera Abafuta
- Friday Natabona, Mukoko, yadehera Abahokosi

NATIKOKO

- Nabwire Natabona, Mukoko, yadehera Abatesso

MASIGA WA THOMAS OUMA WA MWABI

JUMA WA THOMAS OUMA WA MWABI

NAMULUCHA WA THOMAS OUMA WA MWABI

GEORGE MANGENI WA JIMMY WANYAMA

BWIRE MWABI WA JIMMY WANYAMA

WILSON MAKOHA WA JIMMY WANYAMA

ODONGO WA YUSUFU NGUNDIRA III

WANDERA WA YUSUFU NGUNDIRA III

KADOGO NGUNDIRA WA YUSUFU NGUNDIRA III

KUBENGI WA STEPHIN NGUNDIRA

OCHIENO WA STEPHIN NGUNDIRA

YEREMIA MASIGA WA MBAKULO

NALALA
NAKOOLI

David Mbakulo
■ Faisi Nora Auma Makoha Natabona, Mukoko, yadehera
Christoper Crowther Makoha omusiani muhulundu wa Ezekiya
Wamurwa owali owe Saza lye Buhayo.
■ Faisi Natabona yebula abewa ba Batabona bano:
Benard Dindi
Pamela Okwara,
Peter Ghana Ongangi
Beatrice Ndubi (Nekesa)
Elizabeth Okhala (Mami)
Michael Naomi Okwara,
Simon Mukhwana,
Lydia Dindi,
Kenneth Madada,
Abraham Okoti,
Everline Irene Omodo,
Yeremia Josuah Masiga,
■ Mirika Machio Natabona yebula abewa babatabona bano:
Nabwire (Night) Kubengi Mutanda,
Richard Ibrahim Were,
Rose Masiga Ojwangí,
Benard Ochondo
Godfrey Kagenda Masiga,
Hamphrence (Hamphrey) Owori Masiga,
Faith Akello,
Edwin Opyo,
Winfred Adongo,
Milton Bwire,
■ Agasa Anyango Wanyama Natabona, Mukoko, yadehera
Bathlmew Wanyama.
■ Agasa Natabona yebula abewa babatabona bano:
Elizabeth Kubengi Auma,
Sunday Wanyama,
Wejuli Wanyama,
Friday Wanyama,
Margo Wanyama,
Bogere Wanyama,
Jerry Masiga Wanyama,
Abahana 3 bandi sihumanyire ameta kabwe.
■ Beti Masiga (Elizabeth R. Kakembo) Natabona, Mukoko,
yadehera Suleiman Ssenyonga Kakembo owe Njovu mu Buganda
Yebula abewa babatabona bano:
Adam T. Masiga Kakembo – Wuno yebula abecuhulu babatabona
bano: Bona (Natabona) S. Kakembo nende
Jago S. Kakembo.
Sanyu. N. Kakembo – wuno mwiwa wabatabona.

DAVID MBAKULO WA YEREMIA MASIGA

NAMUTENDE (Deborah)

Martin Luther Mbakulo
James Kubengi
■ Natabona, Mukoko, yadeha eBuhayo mu ba Guri
■ Natabona, Mukoko, yadehera aba Kiroya

118

MARTIN LUTHER MBAKULO WA DAVID MBAKULO

JAMES KUBENGI WA DAVID MBAKULO
Ali nabana naye siyeca yatubolera ameta kabana.

	OWORI WA KUBENGI
NANYINYA	Abwoka
	Buluma
NAJABI	Omingo
	Okello
NABONGO	Sicha
	Messo
	Achwala

	OMINGO WA OWORI
NASIYE	Raphael Owori
NAKOOLI	Oroma

	RAPHAEL OWORI WA OMINGO
NABURI	Barasa
	Odongo

	ODONGO WA RAPHAEL OWORI
NAMUDDE	Gilbert Ojiambo

	OROMA WA OMINGO
NAMULEMBO	Ogoola

	OKELLO WA OMINGO
NEBERE	Masudi
	Ouma
NAMENYA	Majanga
NEBERE II	Manuel Ojiambo

	MASUDI WA OKELLO
NAJABI	Okello

	MAJANGA WA OKELLO
NAHULO	Sunday
	Wandera

MANUEL OJIAMBO WA OKELLO

NADONGO   Hilary Bwire
    Peter Wafula
    Barasa
    Aginga
    Ogutu
    Ongunyi

SICHA WA OWORI

NAMULEMBO I   Oseno
    Opio
NASUMBA I   Juma
NAMULEMBO II   Abenda
NAMULEMBO III   Omondi
NASUMBA II   Wanyama
NAMUNAPA   Owori

OSENO WA SICHA

NAMULUMBA   Omondi
NAMUNAPA   Oworia

OPIO WA SICHA

NANYANGA   Obwora
    Kubengi
    Ochieno

JUMA WA SICHA

ADETI   Ogoola

NGUNDIRA WA KAGENDA

NAMULUCHA   **KUBENGI**

KUBENGI WA NGUNDIRA

NAMUDDE I   Nambakwa

NAMBAKWA WA KUBENGI

NAHULO   Ngundira
    Nambasi
    Ogessa

NGUNDIRA III WA NAMBAKWA

NABYANGU   Ngwabe
NACHAKI   Odongo Osewa
NAMAKANGALA   Kadima

NGWABE WA NGUNDIRA III

NASINYAMA   Kubengi III

ODONGO OSEWA WA NGUNDIRA III

NALIALI   Were Sande Osena

PETRO OKUMU WA NAMBASI

NAFOFOYO   Globa Egombe Bwire

NAMBASI WA NAMBAKWA

NAMBOOLI   Ayunga

Okumu

Olwande lwo lupapula 95

AYUNGA WA NAMBASI

NALALA   Okochi Oguttu

Mangeni

Ochiengi

NEHOBA   Okaro

Omujo

Ouma

Midi

Wafula

OGESSA WA NAMBAKWA

NAMULUNDU   Basirio Masiga

NABIANGU I   Pataleo Ngundira III

NABIANGU II   Magunia

Wanyama

Okumu

NAHASOKO   Osyeko

BASIRIO MASIGA WA OGESSA

NAMUKOBE   Barasa

Okochi

NAMULUMBA   Oguttu

Were

WANYAMA WA OGESSA

NAHULO   Ogessa II

NABULINDO   Mangeni

NAMUKEMO   Ogessa II

MAGUNIA WA OGESSA

NAMUGANDA   Odongo

Opio

OKUMU WA OGESSA

NAMANGALE   Bebi

Wafula

NEREKE   Bogere

KUBENGI WA NGUNDIRA

NAMUDDE II   Kagenda

KAGENDA II WA KUBENGI

NAMIRIPO   Ogaale
                    Bendicto Ochimi
                    ■ Ngundira Natabona, Mukoko, yadehera Abakooli
                    ■ Fulumera Mukodi Natabona, Mukoko, yadehera Abafuta
                    ■ Nambasi Natabona, Mukoko, yadehera Abakakangala
                    ■ Roda Anyango Natabona, Mukoko, yadehera Abakiroya
NAHASOHO   Albert Malejja
NASUSUNGWA   ■ Haddu Natabona, yadehera Abakiloya
NAMULUNDU   Aduoli
NAKWERI   ■ Apondi Natabona, Mukoko, yadehera Abalundu

OGALE WA KAGENDA II WA KUBENGI

NASONGA   Mesusera Muchanji
                    (Ogale yeca, yayira Nasonga, Buluma Beyi nahayire muhwebanga
                    e Jinja)
NAHABEKA   Gabriel Konna
                    Pateleo Ogutu
NAHASOHO   Erineo. Okuku
                    (Nahasoho yali mu ha Kagenda, Ogale yakerama bukerama
                    huyebula Erineo Okuku)
NAHONE   Juma
                    ■ Abwoka Natabona, Mukoko, yadehera Abajabi
                    ■ Auma Natabona, Mukoko, yadehera Abalundu

MESUSERA MUCHANJI WA OGALE

NAHASOHO   Siyali nomwana
NEHEMA   Kagenda III
                    Daddy
                    ■ Jobi Natabona sihwaduhana ebihiraho awo
                    ■ Anyango Natabona, Mukoko, yadehera Abalyali

KAGENDA II WA MESUSERA MUCHANJI

DADDY WA MESUSERA MUCHANJI

GABRIEL KONNA WA OGALE

NAHASOHO   Matias Wanyama
                    G. Sande
                    John Ojiambo
NAHONE   Bwire
                    Byasi
                    M.Oundo
NAMUGISU   Kagenda III
                    Ochimi
NEINDA   Kagenda III
NACHAKI   Ogale II

E. OKUKU ERINEO II WA OGALE

NASINYAMA

F. Wanyama
Changa
Kubengi II
Siminyu
Odenga

NEHAMA

Kagenda II

PATALEO OGUTU WA OGALE

NAMUKUBA

Wandera
Mugeni
Egessa
Ouma

NAHASOHO

Barasa
Bwire
Tabu
Ouma

JUMA WA OGALE

NAGEMI

Tito Ogale II

TITO OGALE II WA JUMA

ALBERT MALEJJA WA KAGENDA II

NAMUKUBA

Ojiambo
Okumu

OJIAMBO WA ALBERT MALEJJA

OKUMU WA ALBERT MALEJJA

BENDICTO OCHIMI WA KAKENDA II

NAMAMBA

Joseph Onyango

JOSEPH ONYANGO WA BENDICTO OCHIMI

ADUOLI WA KAGENDA II

WERE KUBENGI WA NGUNDIRA I

NEBERE

Mafulu

MAFULU WA KUBENGI

NACHAKI

Ohodo
Semeo Wandera

NAMAINDI
NAHASOHO

Ondato

- Ejulieri Akumu Natabona, Mukoko, yadehera Abakiroya
- Ezeri Achiengi Natabona, Mukoko, yadehera Ababoli
- Makoha Natabona, Mukoko, yadehera Abasisika
- Agutu Natabona, Mukoko, yadehera Abasiye
- Ajmagi Natabona, Mukoko, yadehera Abakiroya

OHODO WA MAFULU WA WERE KUBENGI

NAMUFUTA

Manuel Oundo
Peter Ouma

MANUEL OUNDO WA OHODO

NAMIRIPO

John Ojiambo (Yafwa)
Charles Kubengi
David Bwire Ejore
Henry Oguttu
- Nafula M. Natabona
- Oliver Nekesa Natabona
- Suzan Ajiambo Natabona

JOHN OJIAMBO WA MANUEL OUNDO

NALYALI

Charles Kubengi
Bwire Ejore
Bwire Oundo

BWIRE EJORE WA MANUEL OUNDO

OGUTU OUNDO WA MANUEL OUNDO

BWIRE WA MANUEL OUNDO

PETER OUMA WA OHODO

NAPUNYI

SEMEO WANDERA WA MAFULU WA WERE KUBENGI

NAMWINI

Barnaba Abwoka
Manase Wanyama
Joel Owori
- Obimbwa Natabona, Mukoko
- Natabona . . . . .

BARNARBA ABWOKA WA SEMEO WANDERA

NAKUHU
NASUBO

Charles Kubengi
Fred William Odira Abwoka
Wilberforce Wafula
George Robert Bwire
John Stephin Abwoka Ogaali
Wandera Abwoka Ogaali
Moses Georfrey Abwoka Ondato
■ Mary Ajiambo Natabona
■ Anna Nachaki Natabona
■ Midy Nabwire Natabona
■ Irene Nasirumbi Ogaali Natabona

CHARLES KUBENGI WA BARNABA ABWOKA

NAMIRIPO

Patrick Wanyama Kubengi

FRED WILLIAM ODIRA ABWOKA WA B. ABWOKA

ADETI

Allan Odira
Laban Ouma Odira
■ Joan Ajiambo Natabona
■ Lavenda Odira Natabona
■ Flavia Odira Natabona

WILBERFORCE WAFULA WA BARNABA ABWOKA

NANJAYA

Humphres Ivan Wafula
Bensi Bwire
■ Moreen Taaka Natabona
■ Auma Caroline Natabona
■ Mugeni Peninah Natabona
■ Lilian Ajiambo Natabona

GEORGE ROBERT BWIRE MAFULU

NAMBOLYA

Bryan George
Denis Mafulu
Edwine Abwoka
Derick Wandera
■ Charity Ajiambo Natabona

JOHN STEPHIN OGAALI WANDERA ABWOKA

NABUKAKI

Fred Wandera Mafulu Abwoka
Ojiambo Vincent Wandera

NAMUGANDA

Winni Namatovu Wandera

MANASE WANYAMA WA SEMEO WANDERA

NAMIRIPO

Richard Wafula
Dickson Sanya
Wilfred Sunday
Godfrey Bwire

RICHARD WAFULA WA MANASE WANYAMA

NALYALI

Martin

NAMUHOKOSI

DICKSON SANYA WA MANASE WANYAMA

WILFRED SUNDAY WA MANASE WANYAMA

GODFREY BWIRE WA MANASE WANYAMA

NAMUDANDU

JOEL OWORI WA SEMEO WANDERA
James Bwire
Sam Semeo Wandera

NAMWANDIRA

JAMES BWIRE WA JOEL OWORI
Harbert Kubengi
George

NAMUDANDU

HARBERT KUBENGI WA JAMES BWIRE

GEORGE WA JAMES BWIRE WA JOEL OWORI

NAMUFUTA

ONDAATO WA MAFULU WA WERE KUBENGI
Vincent Siminyu
Barasa Ondato

Olwande lwo lupapula 98

NAMUSOGA

BARASA WA ONDATO
Chyambi

NASISIKE

VINCENT SIMINYU WA ONDAATO
Samuel Mauko
Ndazi
■ Natocho Natabona
■ Esaza Natabona
■ Margaret Natabona
Sihari

NEGOMA

Ojiambo
Majezi
Okangana
Mubari
■ Auma Natabona
■ Tikabura Natabona

NAMAKANGALA

SAMUEL MAUKO WA VINCENT SIMINYU
Harrison
Kiliton

NANYANGA
NAMIRIPO

OJIAMBO WA VINCENT SIMINYU
Brian
Natocho
Tondwa
Boy
Okuku
Isaac

MAJEZI WA VINCENT SIMINYU

NAGOLYA
Zida
Tibita
Erumbi
■ Betty Natabona
Mbeye
Kene

HADONDI WA KUBENGI WA NGUNDIRA

NASIMALWA
Oduho
Nabongo
Guyoni

NASUBO
Hadondi
Onyango
Okwomi

ODUHO WA HADONDI WA WERE KUBENGI

NAMAKANGALA
Daudi Abwoka
Musa Abwoka

NAMUKUBA
Daniel Hadondi

NANDYEKIA
Bulasio Hadondi

NABONGO
Paul William Ouma

DAUDI ABWOKA WA ODUHO

NAMUBACHI
Suleiman Hadondi

NAMULUNDU
Charles Olumbe

NAMULEMBO
Jackson Wanyama

SULEIMAN HADONDI WA DAUDI ABWOKA

ADETI
Sunday Robert Abwoka

NABULINDO
Monday Abwoka Julius
Masiga Evan Ngundira
Nimrod Saando Bwire

NASIGABA I
Samuel (Kiiga) Onyango

NASIGABA II
Godfrey Ojiambo
Sanya

CHARLES OLUMBE WA DAUDI ABWOKA

NABWOLA (MUGUSHU) . . . . .

JACKSON ABWOKA WA DAUDI ABWOKA

NABYANGU
Frank Bwire
Fred Wafula
Desmond Wandera
Jimmy Wanyama

MUSA ABWOKA WA ODUHO
Yakerama muha Daudi Abwoka niyebulamo
Daudi Bwire Abwoka.

DAUDI BWIRE ABWOKA WA MUSA ABWOKA

NAMUDDE   Tito Wafula Abwoka
Victor Okumu
Timothy Bwire
Moses Eli Okido
Thomas Were

DANIEL HADONDI WA ODUHO

NAMULIRO   James Masiga Namukuba
Willy Were
Willingstone Daudi
Henry Ojiambo
NEREKE   Samuel Nasubo Hadondi
Godfrey Namukuba
Abwoka Bwire
NAHULO   Ronald Wandera
Robert Wanyama
Samuel Were
John Hadondi
Saanda
NAMACHEKE   Samuel Were
Kubengi

JAMES MASIGA NAMUKUBA WA DANIEL HADONDI

NAMULUNDU

WILLY WERE WA DANIEL HADONDI

SAMUEL NASUBO WA DANIEL HADONDI

NAMUDDE   Tobby Abwoka

LESTER JUMA GUYONI

NAKUHU   Collins Bwire Hadondi

WILLINGSTON BWIRE WA DANIEL HADONDI

NADONGO   George Mark Bwire N

BULASIO HADONDI WA ODUHO

NAMWINI   Stephin Bubolu
Were
Ojiambo
Ouma
Malingu
NAMUBACHI   Milton Egessa
David Bwire
Denes Odongo

STEPHIN BUBOLU WA BULASIO HADONDI

NAMAINDI   Bwire Odu
NAMUGANDA   Godfrey

PAUL WILLIAM OUMA WA ODUHO

NAMULISA Naphtal Mugeni Ouma
 Wycliffe Wandera Ouma
 Rachffe Onyango
 Harrison Wafula
 Kalori Okumu
NASALWA David Okello
 Godfrey Wanyama

Olwande lwo lupapula 100

NAPHTAL MUGENI OUMA WA PAUL W. OUMA

NAHASOHO Moses Opio
NAMAKANGALA Kubengi

WYCLIFFE WANDERA OUMA WA PAUL. W. OUMA

NAMUKIGA Junior Ngundira Nelson Sanya
NAMUGANDA Richard Hadondi
NANYIHODO Isaach Wandera

FRANCES RACHEFF ONYANGO WA PAUL WILLIAM OUMA

Musa Abwoka

WAFULA WA PAUL WILLIAM OUMA

David Okello
Keniddy

MBOYO WA NGUNDIRA WA KAGENDA

NANYIBOMMI Nambeddu
NASUBO I Obbino
NASUBO II Onyango
NAMULUMBA Sikwekwe
NAMAINDI Obbande
 ■ Nafwa Natabona Mukoko
NALIALI Omulo
 Odooli
 Ngundira
NASONGA Masinde Akadda

NAMBEDU WA MBOYO

NAHONE Daudi Ngundira wa Nambedu
NAMUDDE Saala Halobe

DAUDI NGUNDIRA WA NAMBEDU

NAMUYEMBA Michael Bubolu
NAMAKANGALA Enosi Ogaambo

MICHAEL BUBOLU WA DAUDI NGUNDIRA

NAMUYEMBA Ngundira James Wanyama
 Patrick Ojiambo
 David Bwire Ogaambo
 Moses Were

JAMES NGUNDIRA WANYAMA

NAHASOHO
Siketa
Mather
Mahande
- Morine Siketa Natabona
- Ajiambo Natabona
- Patricia Mahande Natabona

DAVID BWIRE OGAMBO

NANYANGA
Geoffrey Wandera Ogambo
Benard Ogambo
Denes Mukaga Ogambo
Eddy Barasa
Steven Ogambo
Philex Wafula
- Sharon Nafula Natabona
- Joan Masiga Natabona

GEOFFREY WANDERA

NACHAKI
James Bwire
- Metrine Auma Natabona

BENARD BWIRE OGAMBO

BWIBO
- Gift Auma Natabona

PATRIC OJIAMBO

NABORO
NAMAINDI
Bwire Ogambo
Ivan Ouma
Syrus Wandera
Dakan Wafula
- Irene Nabwire Natabona
- Catherine Makoha Natabona
- Sandra Nabwire Natabona
- Rukiya Charity Natabona

MOSES WERE

BWIBO
Domonic Afuna
Michoel Bubolu
Fuguson Babone

Olwande lwo lupapula 101

ENOSI OGAMBO WA DAUDI NGUNDIRA

NAMUPODI
John Taabu Mangeni Ogambo
Charles Bwire Ogambo
Joseph Onyango
David Ngundira Makoha Ogambo

NAKAMONDO
Geoffrey Masiga Ogambo
Jared Wanyama Ogambo
David Oundo Ogambo

NAYIRUNDI
(Omunyoro)
OMURASIA
Aboki Makoha
Benya Masahalya
Omusiani

JOHN TAABU MANGENI OGAMBO

NYONYI NYANGE
(Nakazibwe)
Eric

CHARLES BWIRE OGAMBO

MAMBA
(Nassuuna Justine)
Jessica Nabwire
Jazmin Nekesa

GEOFFREY MASIGA OGAMBO

NAKUMICHA (Mugishu)
NAKUNJA (Mugwe)
NAIRUNDU (Munyoro)
ENTE-CLAN (Muganda)
■ Doreen Nekesa Natabona
■ Brenda Ogambo Natabona
■ Sharon Nafula Natabona
■ Shiela Ogambo Natabona
Emanuel Ogambo
Elijah Ogambo
Hasheem Ogambo
Ethan Akram Ngundira
Hakeem Nambedu

JARED WANYAMA OGAMBO

NAMAINDI
Enosi Bwire
Saimon Wafula
Jonathan Ogambo

NAMUDDE
NAHONE
■ Natabona
■ Natabona
■ Natabona

NAYIYE
David Oundo Ogambo
Moses Ogambo
Michoel Okuku Ogambo

NAMUBUPI
NAMUGANDA
Solomon Ogambo
David Mugeni
Benjamin Bihemaso? Ogambo

NAHASOHO
NAMULUNDU
Christopher Ogambo
Dan Ogambo
Denes Wafula

JOSEPH ONYANGO

NABURI
NAJABI
NAMULEMBO
Leuben
Joweri Ngundira Ogambo
Inocent Mugeni Ogambo

OBBINO WA MBOYO

NAMAKANGALA
Okoko
Sigube
Nonga

NASONGA I
NASONGA II

Onyango yakerama muha Basulira yebula
■ Banatabona bahaaya – sihwakana ameta.

OKOKO WA OBBINO

NAMAINDI
Yakerama omuhasi wa Nonga. Hunamayindi yebula wuno:
Odongo Okoko

ODONGO WA OKOKO

ONYANGO WA MBOYO

NASONGA
Magina
Basulira

MAGINA WA ONYANGO WA MBOYO

NADIDI
Okello
Asiro

BUSULIRA WA ONYANGO WA MBOYO

NASIMALWA
Charles Barasa
Festo Serusa

SIKWEKWE WA MBOYO

NAMAKANGALA
NAHULO
Daudi Mudonga
Jones Were (Kenya)
Kagenda
Ngundira

DAUDI MUDONGA WA SIKWEKWE

NAMAYERO
Haba siyaleha musiani mani abahana
sibabatamu. Fesi sibatubolera ametta.

JONES WERE WA SIKWEKWE

NANGAYO
Ywana Sikwekwe
Joseph Onyango
Domiano Obworo
Nahulo
Omondi

OBBANDE WA MBOYO

NABONWE
NAMBENGERE
Ngundira Ogweyo
Mboyo
Suuli

NGUNDIRA OGWEYO WA OBBANDE WA MBOYO

NAMUKUBA
Nabasebe
Dani Okuku
Seuli
Otyo
Egessa
Lukiri Ngundira

Olwande lwo lupapula 102

MAKOHA BWIRE WA NGUNDIRA OGWEYO

NAMULUCHA
Ogutu
Olaago
Wanyama
Wandera

MBOYO WA OBBANDE

NAPUNYI	Anderea Wandera
NADIDI	Abahana – Banatabona
NASIBWAHI	Jackson Onyango
NANYIMARO	Guy Mboyo

NAFWA WA MBOYO

NAMULOBA	■ Yaleha ba Natabona Bongone

OMULO WA MBOYO

NAMANGALE	Bati yafwa hale natebula

AKADDA WA MBOYO (NASONGA)

NANYIMWOTI I	Okochi
NANYIMWOTI II	Yona Buluma Ngundira
NAHONE	Yawawo wamwe nafire

OMULOO WA MBOYO (HANDI)

NAMULUNDU	Mboyo yafwa asa
NASIMALWA	Ouma
NAMAKANGALA	Ngundira yakerama Namakangala hunamwibulamo: SAMUEL EGONDI

SAMUEL EGONDI WA OMULOO (NGUNDIRA)

NANYIBOMI	Peter Makoha
	Semu Omullo
NALIALI	Afaana yebula abahana bongone. Bati siyaleha musiani

SEMU OMULLO WA SAMUEL EGONDI

NAHASOHO	■ Banatabona 4

NAMBEDU

NAHABI	Yobu Namudde
	Erisa Ogambo
	Absolom Wandera

YOBU NAMUDDE WA SAALA

NASIMALWA	Adonia Onyango
	Henry Wandera
	Akisoferi Namunapa
	■ Eseza Natabona Mukoko. Yadeha ebuhayo.
NANJAYA	Anania Bwire

Olwande lwo lupapula 103

ADONIYA ONYANGO WA YOBU NAMUDDE

NAMAKANGALA	Ouma
	Nahabi
	Masahalya Ngundira
NAMANGALE	Yobu
	Ojiambo
	Ngundira
	Paul
	Sanya

ERISA OGAMBO WA SAALA

NANYIMWOTI III   Ouma

BUSULIRWA WA MBOYO

NASIMALWA   Onyango
Charles Baras (Bobbo)
Festo Sumba

KAGENDA I
Masinde

MASINDE WA KAGENDA I

NASONGA   Okuku

OKUKU WA MASINDE WA KAGENDA I

NAMUDDE   Ouma

OUMA WA OKUKU WA MASINDE

NAMULEMBO   Erieza Lwande

ERIEZA LWANDE WA OUMA

NAMUSIHO   Paruti Wandera
NAMACHEKE
NABONWE   Charles Onyango
Ouma
NAMUFUTA   Wanyama Lwande
Kagenda III
Odongo

PARUTI WANDERA WA ERIEZA LWANDE

NACHONGA   Lazaro Mugeni
Johnson Odwori
NABAHONO   Benard Obbanda
NAMIRIPO   Henry
NAMACHEKE
NASISINGWA

CHARLES ONYANGO WA PARUTI WANDERA

NALWETA   Ouma
Erieza Lwande II
NABWALASI   Wanyama

WANYAMA WA ERIEZA LWANDE

NEREKE   Moses Oguttu
Jonathan Mbakulo
NAMUNAPA   Kagenda III wa Erieza Lwande
NABONWE   Lwande

· · · · · · · · ·

ESITUNDU SYOHUDATU

EMBOSI CINDI

I   **DISANI MBAKULO II**

"Ese Nise Disani Mbakulo II wa Yosia Were Butonya, wa Ngundira Maalamba, wa Mbakulo, wa Kubengi, wa Ngundira, wa Kagenda. Ndehalaho nende baakuka Yeremiya Masiga, Semei Wandera, Yolamu Masaba nende Samuel Egondi nabandi abamboleranga olwibulo lwefwe ohutula hu sya Akuru. Sya Akuru wuno, yasikalayo mu Misiri (Egypt). Siboneha, omusiani waye Samia yakenda nabasye bongene.

Ndasomaho mumekero kaali nikaluwo. Ndachakira Lumino Primary School, Busia Integrated School, Kings College Budo. Ndasomera emirimo mu East African Posts and Tele-communication Central Training School Mbagathi, Nairobi nende mu East African Railways and Harbours Training School Nairobi.

Ndaholaho mu Posta nende mu Railways emirimo chikabuhane ohwola lundawuluha mu mwika 1987. Handi ndecha ndaholeraho Gavumenti yefwe yebitundu ohutula 2002 ohwola 2004. Handi ndiho huhahiho habakofu bo mu Lugala lwe Busia."

(Signed) Nise Disani J. W. Mbakulo

Disani Yahola muno handi muno ohufuka egali nende Edward Ogutti natafwa nga bakesaho ohu leta ametta ka beho beffe. Sibyali ebyangu habba. Olundi bali hubafukanga amagali hubacya e Buhunya ohukonya abeho beffe, becha bakwa mu mufurejje, bekeranaho na maggali kabwe. Omulongi niye owa honya baali baahafunihe amakumba. Esyo sisyabakayira ohuciririra no mulimo kwohukonya abebule beffe. Handi abandu bandi bakalanga bati becha ohuduhanamo essende enyingi sakira bahola emirimo ecyo lukali. Naye abo balichingi abadidi, handi nga sibabona esiciririra muhuwandika ebindu bitutulaho. Mani Disani Mbakulo, mwebasa muno handi muno handi muno humulimo kuyahola. Natali niye sindahanyalire ohwongeramo abandu bahira obungi bandongera hu Ekudu biyahola.

Omuyaku wundi owahonya lukali koti lu mbekeseho, niye Edwadi Ogutti. Yesi natafwa mu 2015, yaali amalire ohunyandikira biyenya muboleho handi nibyo bino.

135

II   NISE EDWARD OGUTTI

"Njibulwa Mulukongo Lwe Butenge

Mumuluha Kwe   Naluwire

Mugombolola ye   Lunyo

Baba niye Yekoyada Ngundira

Omusiani   wa Jakobo Ocheno

Omusiani   wa Mbakulo

    "   wa Kubengi

    "   wa Ngundira

    "   wa Kagenda

    "   wa Lwande

    "   wa Ngueno Mulema

    "   wa Tebino

    "   wa Lwande Omuliamboka

    "   wa Orubosioka

    "   wa Lali

    "   wa Musamia

    "   AKURU"

Ogutti yaholaho mu "Nyanza Textile"

Esyehabi mbi Ogutti, yecha obulwaye bwamuyingira mu mwaka 2015, yecha yafwa. Hwamwifwirwa lukali muno.

III   OUMA PAUL NAMATTE

Omwiho weffe wundi owahonya ohwongera hu ebindu bi Abner Ekudu biyatandika nga bidira hu lwibulo lwa Bukeko I niye wuno Ouma Paul Namatte. Ouma yesi bino nibyo biyawandika hu mwene.Ouma yesi bino nibyo biyawandika hu mwene.

"Ebindu bino bya Bukeko I biholebwe nende Ouma Paul Namatte wa Nyikola Egesa wo Ololo wa Bukeko II wo Omijja.
Ndabifuna khu bakuka bange bandakanawo handi ndabaasa nobwicha muno nabo nga Ololo wa Bukeko, Opeda wa Muniala, Osinya wa Bukeko nende Omijja wa Gaunya".

Ouma wuno, yesi abona eyaale. Disani Mbakulo niyamubola ohuhola omulimo kuno, yasingiriramo. Handi yecha yahola omulimu omulayi muno. Mani ndeca ndamuberesa oluyali oluhongo muno. Otyo muno kuka.

IV   ENOSI OGAMBO

Enosi Ogambo wuno mubeeresa oluyali oluhongo muno. Hulwohuba natali niyee nende omusyani wayee yibalanga bati Geoffrey Ogambo, esitabo sino sisyahanyalihe ohubawo. Ndecha ndamanya endi Abner Ekudu yaali naholere omulimo omuhongo muno handi muno ohudira hu hwibulanwa hweffe hwe saga lya Lwande Wesonga. Handi bambolera baati buli situndu syabechuhulu ba Lwande Wesonga, yatechangayo ekopi yebindu biyawandika, ngesiciririra mbwe omundu yesi mumoni eyo, yesi yahongereho. Ndateba abandu bandali nimanyire endi banyala ohuba nende epapula ecyo bamberese koti Abner Ekuddu yawandika, mu ohukonyeresa hwaye? Saaliwo owangaluhangamo. Nihandi, abahira obungi baali bamanyire mbwe, ese omulimo kwange muhulundu ebiha bino, nikwo okwohutusa e bitabo "Publisher". Ndecha ndabukanana nende mulala hu bandu ba Abner Ekuddu, ndateba ebindu bye Ekuddu biyaleha nyala ndaabifuna. Omusyani yangaluhamo ati yecha ohundetera ebindu ebyo. Nasiri bulano omusiani oyo asisiri hu ngira.

Naye, Geoffrey Ogambo luyawulira ati ndahanga ohuwandika olwibulo lweffe, yangaluhamo ati, "Masenge njicha ohulomaloma husimu nende Enosi ali nabyo ahuletere". Olunyuma, Geoffrey yecha yachia engo (Samia, Uganda). Niyabolera Enosi ati Masenge addaha ebindu byoli nabyo, Enosi siyebaasa haaba. Yamubereserawo, mani yandetera. Syekesa omwoyo mulayi kwabeho beffe bano. Baali nende ohubona ohwe EYAALE MUNO. Fesi abechuhulu ba Lwande Wesonga I, hubola hutu MUTYO MUNO HANDI MUNO. Mani sakira hwanyala ohuhola hubindu bino bihuholereho handi abandi bahakololose ebyahyama handi bongeraho.

ENOSI MACHIO OGAMBO

Enosi Ogambo yabola ati, bamwibula mu mwaka kwa 1942, hulukongo lwe Bulondani. Simwana baali bamulanga bati Daudi Ngundira, koti lu Abner Ekuddu yesi yamuwandikaho. Esiha sino yamenya e Budonga Village, Bwaniha Parish, Busime Sub County, Busia District.

Ohutula yindi nende aboluya, husaga lya Lwande Wesonga hwebasa muno handi muno Enosi Ogambo nende omusiani waye Geoffrey Ogambo. Omwoyo mulayi kuhusanga eddaala ne syaalo. Omwoyo mulayi niryo ekumba nomwoyo kwomubiri. Omwoyo mulayi kuleta ehaabi. Mutyosa muno handi muno, olwibulo lwa Lwande Wesonga lwahabeculisenga buli myaka. Mwekesa mbwe OMWOYO MULAFU KUHUSA ESIFO HANDI KULETA EHABI.

V WILSON OKWENJE

Ndaha ohwebasa omusian weffe Wilson Okwenje. Wilson, yafayo muno lukali ohuduhana esiha ohukonya abandu abasoma muno handi muno hubidira ohubiiha epapula bilayi cihaye ohukofula. Yecha yabaduhana batuholera epapula Abner Ekudu ciyatulehera, ecyali cikofule muno handi muno. Abandu bano beca bacihola ebilayi chihaye ohukofula mangu. Handi abandu bano ohuhola omulimu kuno kuyira esende enyingi. Handi omusiani weffe wuno, yeca yafuna esiha ohusomamu mu papula chino nitaciyira mu bandu batekehanga esitabo husyemewo situsibwe. Mani handi ngaluhamo humwebasa lukali muno handi muno. Nasaye atyo ohumuberesa omwoyo mulayi.

VI   WILSON OKWENJE

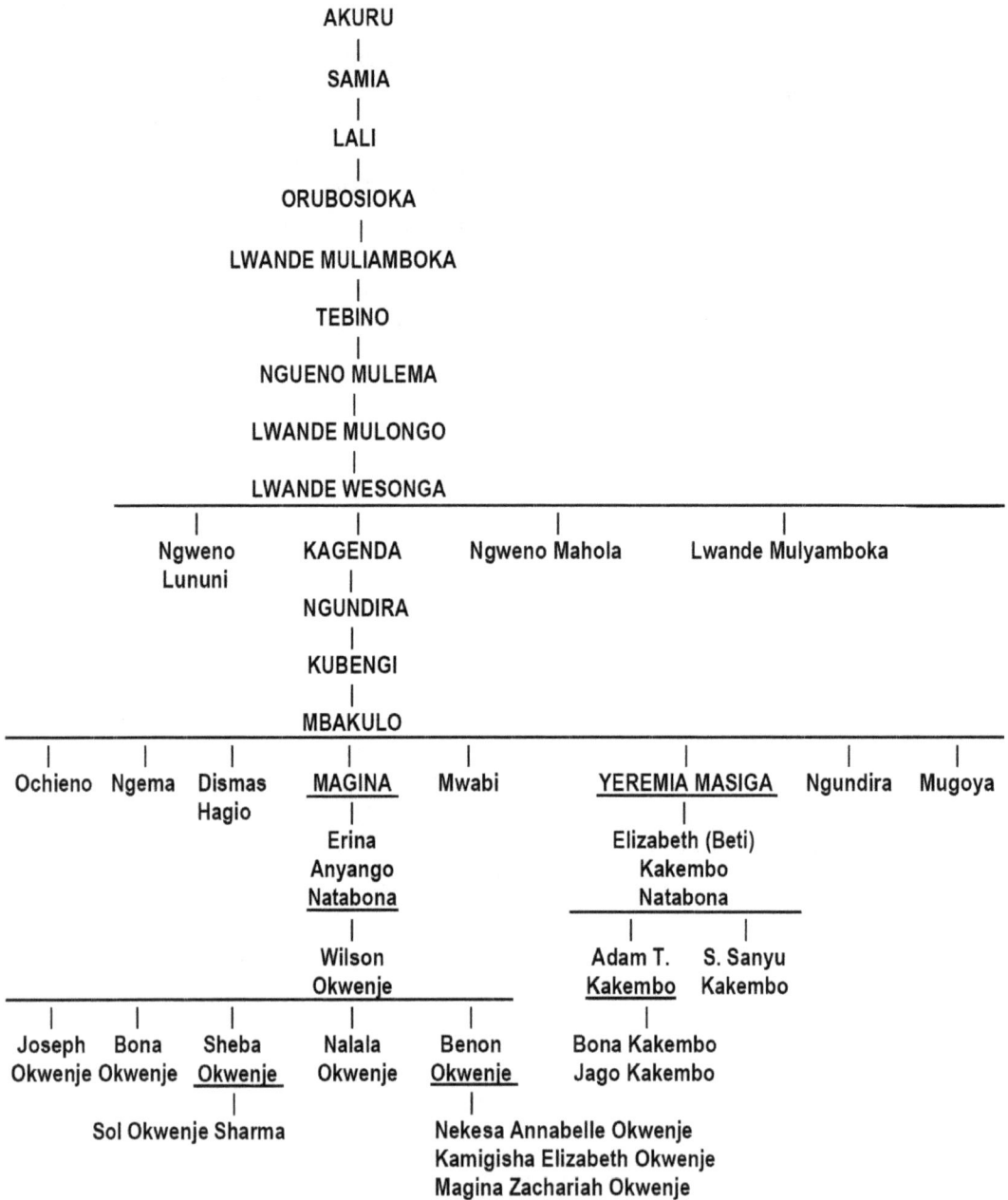

AKURU
|
SAMIA
|
LALI
|
ORUBOSIOKA
|
LWANDE MULIAMBOKA
|
TEBINO
|
NGUENO MULEMA
|
LWANDE MULONGO
|
LWANDE WESONGA

Ngweno Lununi	KAGENDA	Ngweno Mahola	Lwande Mulyamboka

NGUNDIRA
|
KUBENGI
|
MBAKULO

Ochieno	Ngema	Dismas Hagio	MAGINA	Mwabi	YEREMIA MASIGA	Ngundira	Mugoya

MAGINA
|
Erina Anyango Natabona
|
Wilson Okwenje

YEREMIA MASIGA
|
Elizabeth (Beti) Kakembo Natabona

Adam T. Kakembo	S. Sanyu Kakembo

Joseph Okwenje	Bona Okwenje	Sheba Okwenje	Nalala Okwenje	Benon Okwenje	Bona Kakembo Jago Kakembo

Sol Okwenje Sharma

Bona Kakembo

Nekesa Annabelle Okwenje
Kamigisha Elizabeth Okwenje
Magina Zachariah Okwenje

Wilson Okwenje,
Canada, May 2016

VII   DR. PETER W. OBANDA

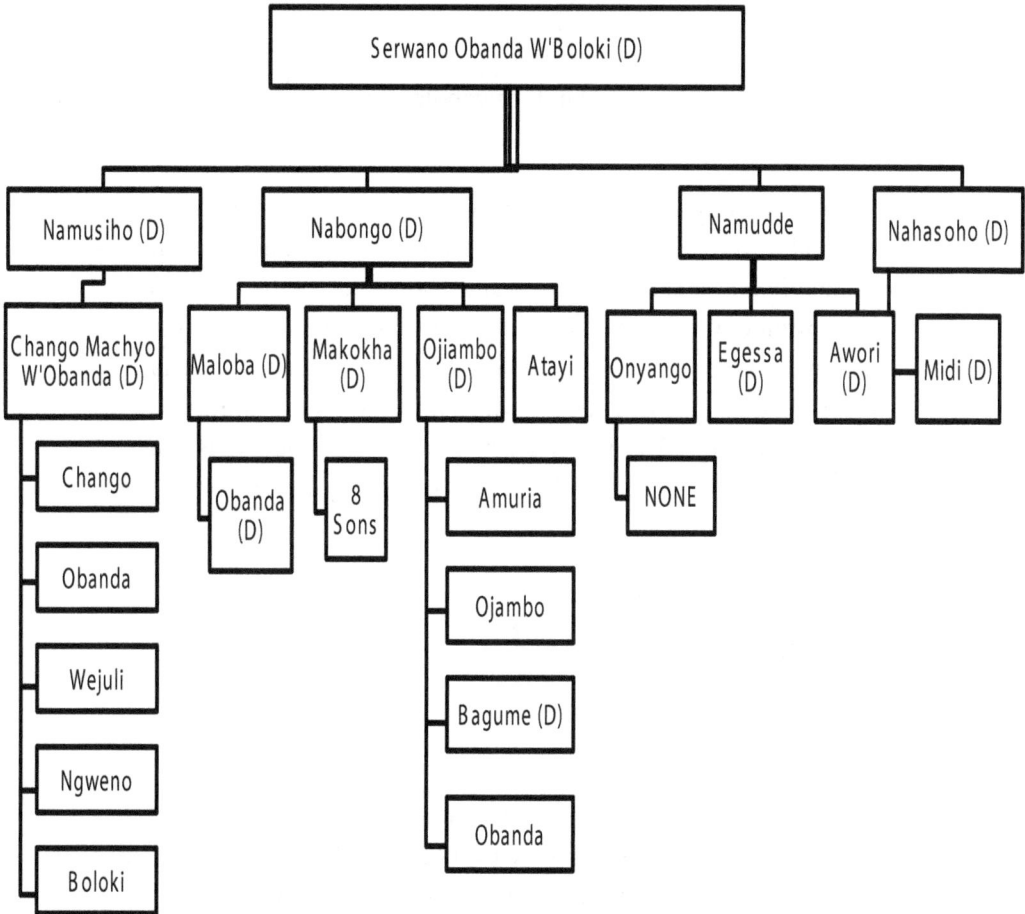

```
                          Serwano Obanda W'Boloki (D)

   Namusiho (D)        Nabongo (D)              Namudde        Nahasoho (D)

Chango Machyo      Maloba (D)  Makokha  Ojiambo  Atayi    Onyango  Egessa   Awori   Midi (D)
W'Obanda (D)                   (D)      (D)                        (D)      (D)

   Chango           Obanda      8        Amuria             NONE
                     (D)       Sons

   Obanda                               Ojambo

   Wejuli                               Bagume (D)

   Ngweno                               Obanda

   Boloki
```

Dr. Peter W. Obanda,
2015

VIII   ABWOKA DAUDI

Bino nibyo Bwire Abwoka Daudi, biyabola ati:

"Ndebasa muno Mzee Ebuneri Ekudu nende eddala lyaye ohumuhonyera niyaali ahola emirimu cino. Yataho esinani esiamani nahoola hu hwibulwana hwa Abatabona be saga lya Lwande Wesonga. Nise mulala hu abo abamuhonyanga nakonyeresa embosi cini mu Sub-County ye Lunyo, Busia District, Uganda. Ese nise Bwire Abwoka Daudi ohutula e Butenge Village, Nalwire Parish, Lunyo Sub-County, Busia District. Ndaduhana Dipuloma mu Secondary Education.

(Signed) Abwoka Daudi

December 2016"

Omusala kulondaho asi anno mu Amasaga kalondaho awo VIII, omu-siani wa Daudi Bwire Abwoka niye owakuhola. Yasoma ebindu bidira hu komputa. Humwebasa muno ohutwekesa esyo huboneraho sino.

(VIII . . .)

LWANDE

TIBINO

ODONGO (TWINS WITH OPIO)

ONYANGO SIKUHU

GINYENDA OMANYI

ABURI

NGWENO MULEMA (OPIO)

LWANDE MULUNGO

LWANDE WESONGA (NABONGO)

NABAHOTO ABALWANDE

NGWENO MAHOOLA NAMUDDU

LWANDE OMULYA MBOKA NAMUDDU NAHALULU

KAGENDA AMALAKULE KANEHAMA

NGWENO LUNUNI NAHOOLI

NGUNDIRA OWA NANJOYA

WANGA OFUMBUHA OWA NANGOMA

OMALA OWA NABAWALA

KUBENGI OWA NAMULUCHA

MBOYO OWA NALUKADA

BUKEKO OWA NASONGA

DIKIDI OWA NASONGA

MUHACHI

MASINDE OWA NALUKADA

KAGENDA OWA NAMULUCHA

ONYANGO HADONDI ABA NASUBO

MAFULU OWA NABEERE

NAMBAKWA OWA NAUMUDDE II

OWORI OWA NAMUDDE II

KAGENDA OWA NAMUDDE

MBAKULO NAHULO

GASUNDI NAHULO

ODUKHO OWA NASIMALWA

MUSA ODUKHO OWA ABWOKAH NAMAKANGALA

HADONDI DANIEL ODUKHO OWA NAMUKUBA

HADONDI BULASIO ODUKHO OWA NANDEECHA

OUMA PAULO ODUKHO OWA NABONGO

DAUDI ODUKHO ABWOKA

MAOBE OWA NASONGA

BWIRI ABWOKAH DAUDI OWA NAMUBACHI

1 2 3 4 5 6 7 8

IX   DR. PETER W. OBANDA

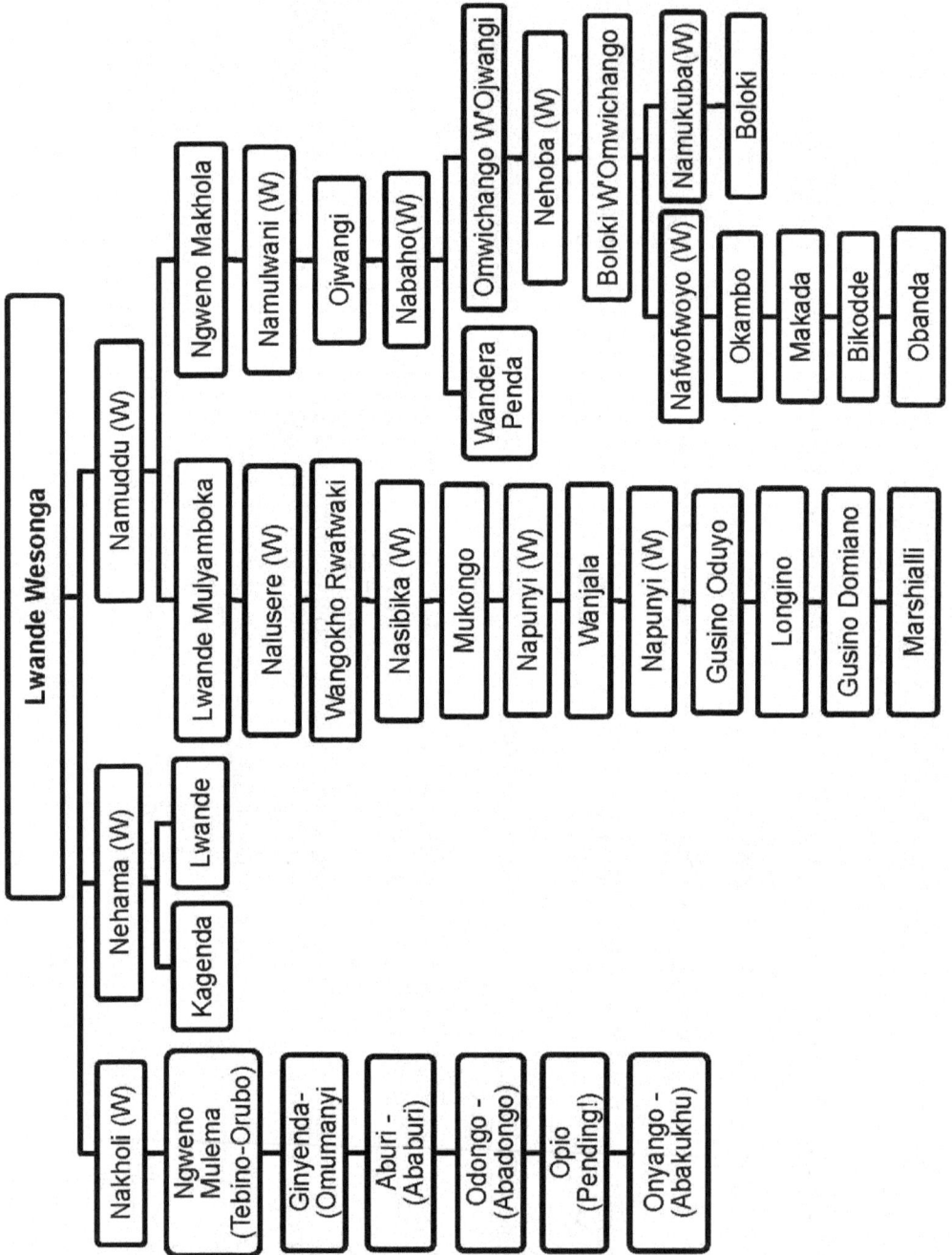

Lwande Wesonga

- Namuddu (W)
  - Ngweno Makhola
  - Namulwani (W)
  - Ojwangi
  - Nabaho(W)
    - Omwichango W'Ojwangi
    - Nehoba (W)
    - Boloki W'Omwichango
      - Namukuba(W)
        - Boloki
      - Nafwofwoyo (W)
        - Okambo
        - Makada
        - Bikodde
        - Obanda
    - Wandera Penda
  - Lwande Mulyamboka
  - Nalusere (W)
  - Wangokho Rwafwaki
  - Nasibika (W)
  - Mukongo
  - Napunyi (W)
  - Wanjala
  - Napunyi (W)
  - Gusino Oduyo
  - Longino
  - Gusino Domiano
  - Marshialli
- Nehama (W)
  - Lwande
  - Kagenda
- Nakholi (W)
- Ngweno Mulema (Tebino-Orubo)
- Ginyenda- (Omumanyi)
- Aburi - (Ababuri)
- Odongo - (Abadongo)
- Opio (Pending!)
- Onyango - (Abakukhu)

X   EMBOSI CINDI ECYOLUYA

Aliwo ebindu bindaha ohubekesa hu bidira huhuwandika esitabo sino. Mani nibyo bino: Enamber cye pegi cindatecanga akati wepapula, cyekesa mbwe onyala watingala hu bindu bya Abner Ekudu, hu pegi ecyo. Esindi siri mbwe Omuyaku Ekudu luyali nabusa embosi cino, yeca yola humbosi yibabola mbwe "Emaddola Ngombe". Beca bamubolere koti abeho beffe abaali e Kenya mubiha ebyo, ebihale badaha ohukaluha ewabwe. Nibabateba ewabwe nena? Bakaluhamo bati "e Maddola Ngombe". Nindaali omuyere, nihwacicanga e Kenya na a be Kenya batuteba bati, e Maddola baaliyo batye? Abahulundu, baliwo esiha esyo, batuboleranga bati e Butenge nisyo esifo sibalanganga bati "e Maddola Ngombe". Hulwohuba Kubengi yaali ne Ngombe enyingi muno. Nabakaali abacyayanga. Hulwohuba cyaali embitirifu, mani abandu bandi nga banyala ohudolamo engombe, abakaali bahaya ohumanya baati, e ngombe cindi siciriwo. Beca bakuliha amakunda oba esifo sya Kubengi bati e Maddola Ngombe. Naye, Kubengi — lala hu kunda lyaaye balilanga baati Butenge. Bino mbiteremo, ohumanyisa abomumoni, esiffo sibalaanga bati e Maddola Ngombe siriena? Abandi bahongereho ebyabwe.

· · · · · · · · ·

AFRICA

EBILONDAHO BIDIRA HUHUKONYERESA
HWA ABNER EKUDU MA

OHUTUMBULA.

Ndi omusangafu muno ohwandiika esitabo sino OLWIBULO LWA NGWENO MULEMA.
Silayi muno ohusisoma nohumanya olwibulo lwa Ngweno Mulema omwana wa TEBINO.
Ngweno mulema niye omwana wohune hu bana Tebino ngina niye Nanyinya; naye
bobbwa amahwana nende ODONGO naye Ngweno niye OPIYO. Ngweno yali yalema,
yatula munda niyalema ngabakingasa.

Bamwanangina: Ginyenda (Omanyi). Aburi (Omuburi), Odongo (Omudongo) nende
Onyango (Omukuhu).

Ngweno yebula omwaana waye Musiani mulala, olangwa LWANDE MULUNGO, Lwande
Mulungo oyo, yakeka abahasi babiri; Nabaholo nende Nabongo, Nabaholo niiwo
omutula abatabona balwande, naye Nabongo niye owebula Lwande Wesonga, ni
mu Lwande Wesonga niye owibula abaana bano: Nahooli; Ngweno Lummni, Namudu;
Ngweno Hadu/Nahola, Kagenda; Nehama, ni bulana humandiika esitabo ndabukulaho
esaga lya Lwande Wesonga lyongene, mamu esitabo sino sihoya siakulihwa
OLWIBULO LWA LWANDE WESONGA, bwene nisitebwaho Ngweno Mulema; siha esia BATABONA
boosi nga aba Lwande baliho nga batula hu Lwande Mulungo.

Bakuka yefwe nende balatayefwe bebusanga hu sioayo nabaana babwe abasimbuha,
bacha ohubakaniayira; ebidira hu luyia, amayee, engano, emibayo, ebyohuluemo-
sesania, ebidira humasika.

Nabona nga bulamu sasisiriwo ebyosio, bulamu esiri nisio amekero Schools
ndahire omwaana eomma esitabo musibongo siohukaniayirwa nabahulundu,
bahulundu boosi mbano sibasiboneha dawe bafwire babwere, bulamu abandu ba
1900 badudu muno sibasiboneha muno haba abahanyalire bakaniayira abaraga
bababonaho.

Mumeta ako akali musitabo esio: sindguhira ameta kabaana ababandi mamu
mbawo sindakandiika dawe nende ameta ka bahasi sakira husaba omulamu olibawo
yahateresa esitabo sino alinyala ohwichusa ameta ako humwene yikediraho.
Manya oti; ochaaka sanyala ohumalayo byoosi ohwola ebindi bimudoondobanaho;
obindi yaba nga sabitekehe bilayi, naye owenyuma niye oteresanga hyahyama/
ebyadoondobaha. Mbasa nimubona ebihyamu mulowe hunjolobya, hunjakire.
Ebikobolwangamo ohuteresa amahabi amangi; sakira kuno nomuka nikwo wesi
chaakiraho nga lwaba obona.

BY. ABNER EKUDU MA
BUTORE V
1995

(Soma obufwimbuli 7.5-8)

Bulanu endaalo chino abaana sibasibucha ali abahulundu, olwohuba saliwo esidiooli, esiosyo siosi sibulawo, manu bulanu abahulundu abahira obungi abemiaka 1800 sibaliwo dawe, bulanu abalwo 1910 noba abahira obungi, naye mwabo simulimo omanyire.

Abaana bulanu engolobe basoma ebitabo, sakira siesi ndahire abaana basomenge ebinhu bino nga esitabo nisyo esibekaniayira nga luhwibulwa nohukabana enyama.

Enyama chiri chiti, Eyoluyimo, Eyomwimo, eyesibiho', eyemisambwa, nende eyomuhana, mbasa echio nichio enyama ehulundu.

Hubbira abami bano abahonyanga ndeberesa (Researches) embosi chino echolwibulo lwa Ngweno Mulema;

01. Eriya Ochieno Ngweno, oyo naye yamanya echiabuli nyumba eyitula mu Ngweno Mulema.

02. Samuel Egondi; Omulo, yambolera ebidira hu Mboyo – Bulondani.

03. Yekoyada Ngundira Ochieno yambolera ebidira hu Mbakulo.

04. Yowasi Nyabola Lwande; Yambolera ebidira khu Lwande II Muliakha.

05. Ekaka Embalwa yambolera ebidira khu Hakwe, Wamira nende Mboko.

06. Morris Ogaani Odooli nende Erisa Odianga Orodi banjekesa ebidira khu Wanga Ofur⸻

07. Patrick Bbala Balongo yanjekesa ebidira khu Namiripo. Paul Ngweno.

08. Zablon Wambete Oguna yanjekesa ebidira khu Olweni Nyambi.

09. George Ouma Sombi yanjekesa ebidira khu Sombi.

10. Yolamu Nasaba yanjekesa ebidira khu Awori.

11. Alfred Omala Olijjo yanjekesa ebidira khu omala.

12. Erasto Obwora Makokha yambolera ebidira khu Ngweno Sisera.

.../3.

OLUKENDO LWA KINTU NENDE MUSAMIA.

Kintu nende Musamia batula mu misiri, Batula boola mu Sudan, North Uganda niboola
hulugulu Masaba (Elgon), babukula ohwo esikoko nibeha a Buganda nga Kintu ali
nomuhasi wa Naambi.

Lubola mu Buganda ali omwalo nibabuluhira aawo, nibataaka esikoko esio. Omwalo okwo
kulangwa MUSAMIA no hwola leero. *Olwanjala Omuhara mawa musamia yakwibula*

Musamia luyatula aawo nadira engira eyomunyanja Sitta Makooli (Lake Victoria)
niyengira obwato, nabodoohana nachia ebuleka Bujaluo nakooba musikobo sia Sakwe, *Esusumu (Kisumu)*
Nakenda nachia namenya musyalo sya Banyore ba nganyi mu Kenya niyohala esiribo
leero balangawo SIRIBA.

MBAKULIKHA (OHUTUBULA) YIBAKULIHA E BUTABONA.

(a) Olunyinyi (Omutuba) niyo engubo yi musamia yofwalanga.

(b) Obwato: nibwo bu musamia yambuhiramo nachia ohukonya yamenya.

(c) Engeso, niyo eyasibanga endiri chio bwato echingisa amachi.

(d) Esyuma.

OHWELAA KWA BATABONA. Orubo Sioka Syalali, Makada momu kafuniranga olukendo.
Orubo nyumba mbi, Efumo lya mahaa.

ABAANA BAMUSAMIA: Lwande, yebula Tebino.

Tebino yebula abaana bano:-

1. JINYENDA (Omanyi), esikera nibamulanga OMANYI, waliwo omwami olangwa Owinyi yali
   Esikoma, yachia yangwesa ongombe amalwa manu niyimera, nalanga enjia chiosi, manu
   onjia chosi nichiebusa ewa OWINYI manu Jinyenda luyali achia nomuhasi mukofu amular
   namuteba ati, Omanyire simwami alangire? Jinyenda yafunyamu ati haba naye omuhasi oyo
   yamuboola ati, syali ahendo oterangaho. Jinyenda yafukirira, namuhasi omuhoolera ati.
   Nabateba olcha abandu bandi bafunyamu naye ewe ofunyamo olunyuma oti "INGWERE AMAIN
   manu Owinyi yatoba enjia nga ateba buli luyia, naye Jinyenda yafunyamo ati "INGWERE
   AMALWA" manu abandu boosi bafunyiramo alala bati niwe Ommanyi omanyire engombe
   niyingwero amalwa nohutula awo, nibulanu yohola enono "BAMANYI" nibali ABABORO.

2. Aburi, niye omwana wa Tebino owohubiri, olwola nisibonoha nga Ngweno Mulema niyo
   owabukula obwami, manu Aburi yaali omunyolefu obwami okhubukulibwa nomwana muyore
   nga niyo omulonda mulwanyi olwo, manu Aburi yakiyanga Ngweno Mulema amwitte abukule
   obwami.

Aburi babechanga mudembi oba Esirimba, manu Aburi luyawulira ati, Ngweno Mulema
mbala bamukingiro Hakati, Aburi yokisa aandu, naye omundu owabona Aburi natokehe
ohwitta Ngweno Mulema, nachia yokosa Ngweno mulema yaboola ati; ese sindi nende
embosi nomwana wefwe Aburi, Aburi natokeha esio Esanga yinamuloba, ese hanjio Ssa.
Ngweno Mulema yabukula obusalo nobuyingo naboola ambamukinga ati, huchie lubali bah
awene Aburi yokisiro, ni Aburi yoyinga ohubbaya Ngweno Mulema nefumo, ati Afumito,

...../4.

nihano ahayingo khayiswo, naye Ngweno Mulema luyalehula esikera namalakho, ni Ngweno Mulema yelaaya ati, "HULIHO Chati AMOLO" ni Aburi luyola mudaala naboolera abana bayo ati, "Simusiriraniranga nende olwibulo lwa Ngweno Mulema obusirandemu do... nise otangire" Nohutula aawo olwibulo lwa Aburi nende Ngweno Mulema sibasirinanga obusirandemu. AMOLO Olwibulo lwa Ngweno Mulema nibaba nibayima manu bafumita esolo nibolayaa bati, hulikho choti AMOLO" nga bechulisa ohwelayaa hwa Ngweno Mulema hwayamitta Aburi.

3. NGWENO MULEMA. Ngina niye Nanyinya, Ngweno Mulema bebulwa amahwana, niye Pio, nende Odongo. Ngweno Mulema nimwo omutula abatabona. Olwola nabawo omwana namira enyuma yasinwana muyere, nayo omwone enyuma nadaha enyuma yaye, naye omwene mwana naboola ati, Leha omwana nachia orwanyi hunayibona hunyaka, nayo omwene nyuma siyafukirisania nende mwanangina dawo yemeda ohusaba enyuma yaye, manu mwanangina oyo muhulundu, yetta omwana oyo yamubaka yatusamo onyuma eyo, Luyatusamo yayiba mwanangina naboola ati, "Otabona enyuma yawo njiyowakera ndanyesa omwene wango : ohutula olwo nibakabuhana, omuyere achia Boro mu Bujaluwo, naye omuhulundu adonga awo. Nihwo ohutula Abatabona olwembosi "OTABONA".

4. ODONGO, nimwo omutula abadongo, ningina niye NANYINYA nibo abebulwa amahwana. Bahindawo muno ohukekana nabatabona, Owachaaka ohukeka Natabona niyo Reuben Onyero Agula, naye ohutula hu basefwe nende bakuka yefwe sisyaliwo dawo. Oluyia nilwingiya lukekananga.

5. ONYANGO (Omukuhu) niye owali claaka wa Tebino, Esiakera yalangibwa Omukuhu, yali nende engombe yaye buli yachia achia nayo naboya (Ohuhungira), yaholanga atio, nibulamu abandu bamulanga bati, "OMUKUHU" okuhula nende engombe, nihwo ohuola balanga enono eyo "ABAKUHU" naye boosi nibali "ABABORO"

NGWENO MULEMA. Ngweno Mulema nomwana wa Tebino, ngina niye Nanyinya. Ngweno Mulema yali nende omwena mulala yengene niye Lwande Mulungo. Lwande Mulungo Yobula Lwande Wesonga, Ngina Lwande wesonga NABONGO.

ABAHASI BA LWANDE WESONGA NIBO BANO:

1. Namudde Hatoke, 2. Nakholi, (3) Namiripo nende Namuddu, Boosi haba sibali nibebula dawo. Lwande atule achie alakule, omulakusi yamuboolera ati, wicha ohwokana omuhasi okenda niyo owahaholore olwanyi olwo. Manu hu Lwande yecha yehale enbaka, nabakaali baye bachia ohwaya hubemewo babukane omuhasi, omuhasi ababoolere ati "Simundoolaho? manu hu bakaali bachie eyiri Lwande Wesonga bamubolere bati "Aliwo omuhasi undi odaha khu mudoole" Lwande yechulisa koti omulakusi yamuboolera, huyomewo atume bayi abo bachie baboolo omuhasi yeche mudaala. Omuhasi oyo luyecha mudaala yeduhira Lwande Wesonga nangwa amalwa, omuhasi oyo yolera husyaki, nibamudayira amalwa mu Sikwada bamuyirira, luyamala ohungwa amalwa ako nibamuba nobusuma yalya, yehala aawo ohwola luwerani Lwande atuma abakaali baye muchie mweyee musidwoli omukeni anakonamo, nibwahya muchuli Lwande Wesonga yalanga abahasi baye, Namudde Ha+ Naholi, Namiripo nende Namuddu omuhasi muyere Lwande yamuboolera ati, ewo chia odehere omukeni oludaabo, hu Namuddu afunyamo at,

... /5.

"Okunyu kululu kundichanga kuno nikwo kundadehere omuhasi womwami. Lwande Wosonga yamufunyamo ati, Analichanga hu mbaki change" okwo nikwo ohwatula olwibulo lwa Namuddu ohulwangwa ABAHWALULU naye nabatabona abolwibulo lwa NAMUDDU naye Lwande Wosonga ohubola ati, Analichanga ombaki, ohwo nihwo ohwatula olwibulo lwa NEHAMA ohulangwa ababakwa.

Omuhasi yibadoola enono yali NEHAMA, yemawo yayera enda, manu abahasi ba Lwande Wesonga, baboolanga bati, siniyo owalukenda manu luyaali niyebula onwana omusiani oyo alangwa KAGENDA.

Abahasi ba Lwande Wesonga boosi abaali bakumba bachaaka ohuyera enda nibamaliro ohwibula Kagonda, Naholi niyebula Ngweno Lumuni, Namuddu niyebula Ngweno Makhola nende Lwande Omuliamboka, Namudde Hatoke haba si siyebula omwana nende Lwande Wesonga dawe.

Lwande Wesonga luyafwa babasa ohubekawo Kagenda mulwanyi olwohuba niye omuhulund owachaaka ohwibulwa munyumba ya Nehama, Namudde Hateke haba siyasima dawo omwana womuhasi wanasikoko ohubekwa oba ohwingira olwanyi, nga ye adaha omwana owamaliriha olangwa Ngweno Lununi Namudde Hateke yemawo yabukula ebindu ebyobwami yakisa. Kagenda luyatcha ati ebindu byobwami biri ena? Namudde Hateke yakania Kagenda ati, amake kabiliya ebindu byosi.

Ngweno Lununi yali obuhochangono Hoanda, Namudde Hateke yamulaka yocha nende bahochangono, oludaalo olulakane lulwola nende esaa Namudde Hateke yabukula esiayi yobwami natta musimwero natula orwanyi wedaala yachia ohulinda ngweno lmuni hungira. Ngweno Lununi luyoola Namudde yabukula esiayi yobyobwami, nasiyaa Ngweno Lununi, Ngweno Lununi yengira mu daala nolukaalakaasa, ohwo nihwo ohwihasa Ngweno Lununi husisala si Kagenda yadaha yehalcho, Kagenda yafwirwas obwami obwo.

Ngweno Lununi niye owakerama Namudde Hateke, yayira olwanyi, manu abandu ba Nemu Hatteke lubecha mudaala nga sibaliho nomwiwa nga sibagyala ohuba nende ekono, bomawo baberesa Ngweno Lumuni omuhana nga nisio esibewo sya Namudde Hateke. Esibewo siya Namudde Hateke siebula abaana babiri abasiani nibo bano Namiripo babiri abasiani nibo Hamiripo, Olweni (Nyambi) nibo abalwangwa abatabona Basembe olwohuba lubatula mu Ruembwa nibamenya e Busembe, naye abaduma nende abadde babalanga bati, Abasembo ba Lununi abasembera hu nyanja, mani nibo abatabona BADDE.

Kagonda siyabona ebilayi dawe ohuta hu mwana muyere obwami naye nga omuhulundu mudaala Kagenda yachaaka ohuyirimbana nende Ngweno Lununi siemawo Kagenda nibakabana engombe chia lata yabwo nibakabuhana. Eickera Kagenda natakeroma edaala lya simwana nohuduhir obwami, ngina yali nasikóko. Handi Lwande yalama Ngweno Lununi. Naye Omwana womuhasi wa nasikoko yakaba yaba okuhulundu mu hwibulwa, sanyala ohuhola emisiro chiedaala eliyo Yakaba omwana muyere ni ngina yocha nolukalakasa oyo niyo ohola emisiro.

...../6.

EYEE LYAKERA IWAKIA EBUNYALA NEBUSONGA.

Amayee akakera nihukwa Bunyala nende Busonga, Amaye kene kali 3.

1. Omuganda nende omusebe nomunia.

OMUGANDA: Mundaalo chie Ekaka abaganda baseta abasamia, manu abandu ba Ekaka
buruha bakwa e Bunyolo ne e Busonga Omwami munyala yali NGIRA nende
simwana OYOLO nende KUNDU.

ODUNGA MUHAYO niye owabona Ekaka nabandu baye, manu Odunga yasaba Ekaka achie
ewaye e Buhayo amenyeyo, hulwo Ojune nga Ojune mululu muno, nga
Odunga abasa ati Ekaka nanocha nende Odunga yecha ohumulasanira. Ekaka nabandu
baye nibatula e Bunyala nende e Busonga, naye abola hanga E'ngombe e Bunyala haba
sibachienda chiosi dawe ohumalaho Busonga nibo abandu be Ekaka badoha, lubola
e Buhayo Odunga yasangalira muno Ekaka, manu abandu b'Odunga bachaka ohubukula
abahasi babandu b'Ekaka abancha bulayi naye nga bola abakuba sibanya ohuba nende
sibabola dawe. Abandu b'Ekaka bahola namaani onwami wabw nga omundu wo Dunga
abulamo. Abasamia bachia eyiri Odunga nibabola bati, esialo siefwe silangwa
MADOOLA NGOMBE manu ewe niwosayo engombe chiawo chino oba onaba ebilayi muno.
Nisio esiakera basikuliha MADOLA NGOMBE niwosayo musialo esio no nibahama eyati
chibiri nga badaha Odunga abakoboso musialo siabwo.

Bulanu Odunga yakobosa abasamia musialo siabwo, Odunga namenya mukina ne Ekaka
amenya ewayo yiyatula nga Odunga yemenya nende Ojune mukina olwohuba Ojune yali
omululu nga amulinda eyiri abasuku baye. Odunga namenyere Mudina nabahayo baye,
nabahasi babahayo babukulengo hubasamia nibabatula nibababola hubamwakwe babatalangaho.
Bulanu abasamia babola bati Bulanu abahasi bengwe bahoya ohutufunyaho nga luhukobela
huba muwabwo abasamia bahola muno amaani. Bulanu abandu abo bachaka ohuba-
nyirisira Odunga nga sibanyireho bati babangula nibali ewabwo; nga bamanyiro bati
Odunga niyo omwene obanyala. Odunga yaboola ati, lubahafunyo hubanagulo.

Odunga yasingira ohulwana nabasamia abahasi bakobole hu bahayo Odunga yaboola
Ojune kenda husete abandu bongirira abandu baye. Ojune yaboola ati eso onwami ndi
omulwaye, chiaho nabandu bandi nga yekadia atio. Odunga yaseta bahuyane nende
basamia. Odunga aseta mahona chungula batabona abahasi, abene bahasi sisinyaliha
ohutusa ano abahasi, olwo eyee nirikwao. Odinga Siawola niyo asseta omundu wo'mundu
Odunga yatula mudaala nadabadaba abolera Ojune nende Ekaka hu Ekaka nabola Odunga
ati basamia mbakamisie bahayiro ewabwe bafunyeyo e Buhayo hu Odunga nafunyayo
e Buhayo hu Odunga nata hu Ojune esulubbi ati sindahaboloro Ojune yakaya ohuyiro
eMakoha yakora Odianga yetta omundu wange. Odunga luyafunyayo e Buhayo yabola ati
Ojune oyo yesi ahaya ohufwa, manu yatuma Odido Omunyanga ati ewe niwo omanyiro
ohukenda esiro, ndaha ochie onjitiro Ojune niwitta Ojune ndahube omuhasi manu
Odido yecha esiro Ojune nakona naye hiboola husiriwa esiolukoba baduhira nabakale
manu batema okusala okulayi boola hulukoba bambuhiraho bengira mukati nabandu

..../2.

b'Odido achire nabo buli mundu yaholanga lulwali lwayamba lwonyumba cha Ojune bamanye bati ali ano, Ojune huyali nga akonere naye omwana yenyala hubuliri bwa Ojune naye Ojune aboola ati, simunyaho omuhasi ono yanyinyaliroho omwaana ni bulamu abasuku bemonya nibalinda, nga bamanyire mwali ni mukota Ojune akoterwe, ni endeolo ohumuyira ni bahwesa olwiki kaala nibasingirira nibafunaka efumu nibamumalaho esoro obabumbula nibakerenia esibachua nibakona nende esikoko manu efumu nisidira obusacha, nibamha batulira homusola kula nibachia ohwekisa musino nibawulira bati, Afwiro nibayira embosi Odunga, lubayira embosi Odunga yasangala muno naberesa Odido Habisinya omuhasi.

BWIRE NANGAGA WAK WANDERA

NAFUNYA: —

SIONGONGO WA EMBAAYA

NAKIROYA: Yebula omukhana:

Nekesa

NAKOOLI Siongongo

SIONGONGO - SIONGONGO

NASICHONGI Yakorama muha Abner Mayende Sombi, niyebulamo omusiani

yafwa! Omuhana niye Oliwo.

NGWENO LUNUNI

'ILAYO Khakwo

Wamira

Mboko

Khakwe wa Ngeno Lununi

Nakwanga Ngweno Odibya.

NASUBO Ouma Fuhi

Ngweno Odibya Khakwe

OUMA FUKHI

NASONGA Ngweno Okiya

NAMUDDE Were Odaari

NGWENO OKIYA WA OUMA FUKHI

WERE ODAARI WA OUMA FUKHI

OMWIKHA WA WERE ODAALI

WAMIRA WA NGWENO LUNUNI

NAMULEMBO Obinda Otambula

OBINDA TAMBULA

Yaboola ati SIMUMBULANGAGA DAWE KWAKHAMULIRE OBWANI

NIBUBINDA. Okhwo nikhwo okhwatula erita erio).

OBINDA OTAMBULA

BWIBO Omanyo Aucha

NAMULUMBA Ekaka

OMANYO AUCHA WA OBINDA OTAMBULA

NALUKADA Ochieno Mugola

Ngweno Rabwori

OCHIENO MUGOOLA WA OMANYO A.

NASUBO Omanyo Mbogo

Ogaando

NAMAKANGALA Ogoola

..../3.

ABAFWSI BA NGWWO LUNUNI.

01. Nanyanga: Yobula Lwando II.

02. Nahono: Yobula Ogoola.

03. Namuddo (esibowa): Yobula Namiripo nonde Olwoni (Nyembi).

04. Nawangale: Yobula Waida, Mudubwa nonde Ngwono Kanga.

05. Namakangala: Yobula Lwando Omolo.

06. Nahore: Yobula Sombi.

07. Nasonga: Yobula Nando, Ngweno Mudamalo.

08. Namiripo: Yobula Awori Nahooli.

09. Noroba: Yobula Lwando Hagongolo.

10. Nahnyo.   Yobula ? - - Hakwe, Wamira nonde Nboko.

11. Nasonga II: Yobula Banga.

—✂—

OMANYO MBOGO WA OCHIENO MUGOOLA

NALILI	Philipo Opio
NAMUYEE	Shem Ouma
NABIRONGA	Richard Ongamo
NAMIRIPO	Musumba
NANYANGA	Musungu
	Sindano

PHILIP OPIO

Omanyo Mbogo

OMANYO OGAANDO WA OCHIENO MUGOOLA

NALALA	Omanyo wa Ochieno.
NAMAINDI	Ochieno wa Ochieno
	Omanyo wa Omanyo Ogaando

NGWENO RADWORI WA OBINDA OTAMBULA

NAMENYA	Otyola Odaaro

OTYOLA ODAARO WA NGWENO RADWORI

NAMAINDI	Lwemba
	Obinda
NAMAINDI II	Yowana Walwala
	Abudasio Hatende
NALALA	Antonio Guloba
NAJABI I	Magero
	Ezekiel Opio
NAJABI II	Gasipabo Walala
	Morris Onganga
	Benard Barasa
NAKUHU	Edward Ekaka
NAWOONGA	Francis Ekaka (Oganga)
	Agnitano Ouma
	Joseph Juma
NADIANGA	Obinda Munyausi
NAMONI	Romano Ouma

LWEMBA WA OTYOLA ODAARO

OBINDA WA OTYOLA ODAARO

NAKUHU	Onyango
	Wanyama
NAMWAGISA:	Okiya

...../4.

	YOWANA WALWALA WA OTYOLA
NABAHOLO	Otyola
	Ngweno
	Namaindi
	Were
	Nalwenge
NAMUKUBA	Wangira
NAMUDDE	Okuku
	Nahwanga

	ABUDASIO KHATENDE WA OTYOLA
NAPOWA	Charles Otyola
	Ben Namaindi
NAKHULO	Wanyama

	CHARLES OTYOLA WA ABUDASIO
NANYILALO	?
NAMUNAPA	-

	ANTONIO GULOBA - OTYOLA
NAMULUNDU	Mangoni
	Oguttu
	John

	NANGENI - ONTONIO GULOBA
NAKHABI	-

	MAGERO OTYOLA
NAKHATIKO	Otyola Makokha
	Okinyo Joseph Wandera

	OTYOLA.MAKOHA - MAGERO
NAMULUMBA	-
NABULINDO	Otyola

	EZEKIEL OPIO - OTYOLA.
NAMAKANGALA	Ochieno

	GASPARO WALALA - OTYOLA
NAHUMIE:	Ouma
	Christopher Otyola
	Taabu
	Were
	Okochi
	Obinda
	Jaja

	MORRIS ONGANGO - OTYOLA
NASUBO	Okochi
NAMWALIRA	Ngeno

..../5.

	LUGUNDA WA MUMBO
NEGEMBE:	Odiombo
	Luseni Juma
Nasubo I	Maloba
NASUBO II	Sigangale
NAMULEMBO:	Wanyama

	ODIOMBO WA LUGUNDA
NAMAGWE:	Samuel Wandera
	Wanyama Muchudde

	LUSENI WA LUGUNDA
NAMWAYA:	Petero Lugunda
	Paul Lugunda
	Muchudde
	Ouma

	SIGANGALE WA LUGUNDA
NEBERE:	Majoni Charles
	Barasa Humpress

	WANYAMA WA LUGUNDA
NAMENYA:	Sunday
	Muchudde

	MALOBA WA LUGUNDA
NAMUNYARA:	Sunday
	Mulima (Yafwa)

	WAMIRA WA NGWENO LUNUNI
Namulundu:	Muhemba

	MUHEMBA WA WAMIRA.
Nakroya;	Ondayo
	Embalwa
NAMANGALE	Omiya
NAMULEMBO	Ochieno

	ONDAYO WA MUHEMBA
N.liali:	Muhemba
	Dakayo
NAMIRIPO:	Okumu
	Bwaku

.../5.

3

MUHEMBA WA MACHIO SIRINGO

NEHOBA:	
NAMUDUMA:	Wanyama
	John Machio
	Odimbe
	Ogoola
NACHAKI:	Tsaka

DAKAYO WA MACHIO SIRINGO

Namahia:	Ondayo

OKUNU WA MACHIO SIRINGO

MABONGO:	

BWAKU WA MACHIO SIRINGO

?

EMBALWA WA MUHEMBA

NAMWINI:	UMA
	Namulundu
NALWENGE:	Adika
NASUBO:	Ogumba
	Ekaka

UMA WA EMBALWA

?

NAMULUNDU WA EMBALWA

NAMWINI:	Muhemba Njoroge

MUHEMBA WA NAMULUNDU

NALWENGE:	
NAMBANJA:	Ouma
	Mbalwa
	Makoha.

ADIKA WA MBALWA

NABONGO:	Matias Nagafwa
NSIWE:	Mbalwa
	Nalwenge
NALIALI	Michael Makoha

MATIAS NAGAFWA WA ADIKA

Nasibwiha:	Oundo
	Adika

MBALWA WA ADIKA

NAHATUBA:	Onyango
NAJABI:	Ojiambo

..../4.

OUMA WA EKAKA

OKUMU WA EKAKA

NAMANGALE: Bwire
NASINYAMA: ??

OMIYA WA MUHEMBA

NANGWANGA: Ojiambo
Kwereho

NANJOSI: Ongari
NABOOLI: Abdulia.
NAMWINI: Olando

KWEREHO WA OMIYA

NAMUHOFWE: Keziron Mugeni
NAHWANGA: Manda

KEZIRON MUGENI WA KWEREHO

NAMUYEE: Odwori
Onyango
Wanyama
Naam

NALIALI: Bwire Wyoliffe
Yosia Ekaka
Moses Onyango
Naande

NAMULUMBA: James Egessa
Muhemba

MANDA WA KWEREHO

NAMINDI: Nasonga
Juma

ONGERI - OMIYA

ABDALLA - OMIYA

NALIALI: Oguttu
NAMUHOFWE: Juma
NALIALI II: Owaka
NAMUBACHI: Barasa.

OGUTU - ABDALLA
JUMA - ABDALLA

NAHONE: Egesa
Kilo
Mbalwa

OLANDO - OMIYA

NAKIROYA: Cornal Onyango
Okochi
Wamira
Egesa
Ouma

CORNEL ONYANGO-OLANDO

NAMULUNDU: —

OKOCHI - OLANDO

NAJABI: Olando
Eli

EGESA - OLANDO

NANYINEKI: —

OUMA - OLANDA

NANYINEKI: —

MANGENI - OLANDO

NAMBANJA: —

✂

	WAMIRA – NGWENO LUNUNI
NAMAKANGALA:	Okino
	OKINO – WAMIRA
NABOHOLO:NAMULAHA	
	NAMULAHA–OKINO
NABULO:	Ngweno Pamp
	Pamba
	NGWENO – NAMULAHA
NAKUHU:	Pamba
	Oundo
	PAMBA – NGWENO
NAMANGALE:	Tambiti
	Oundo – NGWENO

	NGWENO LUNUNI
	MBOKO
NAKIROYA:	Gombe
	Dubasa
	Nasenye
	GOMBE WA MBOKO
NASONGA:	Ojiembo Maramba
NAMUDIBA:	Nababa
NANUMULI:	Ngweno Ngwero
	OJIEMBO MARAMBA WA GOMBE
	?
	NABARA WA GOMBE
NAKUHU:	SANDUKU
	SANDUKU – NABARA
NABURI:	Fwogo
	Wandera Ganja
	Okumu Ngweno
NABURI:	Bwire Obwogo
	FWOGO – SANDUKU
NAHABEKA:	Bwire
	Sunday
	WANDERA – SANDUKU
NASIHUNE:	Ochieno
	Bwire
NALALA	Mangeni
	Wafula
	Wandera Wesonga

	NGWENO LUNUNI
NAMIRIPO:	Awori Nahooli
	AWORI NAHOOLI – NGWENO LUNUNI
NASONGA:	Wamachode
	Wamira
	WAMACHODE – AWORI NAHOOLI
NANGAYO:	Ngweno
NABUYAYI	Balongo
	Okuku
	Muyaanga
	NGWENO WA MACHODE
NAMULEMBO:	Kosima Galande
	KOSIMA GALANDE WA NGWENO
	OGUTU

..../3.

OKUKU - WAMACHODDE

NASONGA	Okochi
NAPUNYI	Wafula Abduheri
NASIBIKA:	Wafwa
	Ogoola
NAPUNYI II	Wanyama
	Ausi Balongo
NAMWANGA	Magero

OKOCHI - OKUKU

NAMUHULA:	John Namayayi
	Ogondo
	Ouma

MUYANGA - WA MACHODDE

Yafwa Nasiri Ohukeka

BALONGO - WA MACHODDE

NABONE:	Yolamu Masaba
	Alex Wanyama

YOLAMU MASABA - BALONGO

NAMAKANGALA:	Difasi Ouma
NASIBIKA:	Egesa Duncan
	Mangoni Humphress
	Wafula Julias
	Geofrey
NAMUTENDE:	Wa Machodde

DIFASI OUMA - YOLAMU MASABA

NASUBO:	Biita
	Sikuku

EGESA - YOLAMU MASABA

NAMULUNDU:	Ewire Bogere
	Bwire Balongo

WAMIRA - AWORI

ODENDE

NGWENO LUNUNI

NEROBA: LWANDE MAGONGOLO- Siboneha enyumba yino yoyambania
hu hamiripo nga yifanana nga aba
namuddu, naye siboneha bosi bali nende nguhwa yabwe, Neroba
muha Ngweno Lununi nibabere balangwa namuddo (Abasembe) niba
Naroba omuhasi yali omumataki

.../8.

	LWANDE MAGONGOLO - NGWENO LUNUNI
WAMULOBAI	Mudenyo
	MUDENYO - LWANDE MAGONGOLO
NABONGO I	Adundo
Nahasoho	Adera
NAMBANJA:	Ofwirho
NABONGO II	Mulindo
	ADUNDO - MUDENYO
NALIALI:	Magongolo II
	Were Ojango
	ADERA MUDENYO
	MAGONGOLO - ADERA
NANJUKU:	Ojiembo
	Muchere
	MUCHERE - MAGONGOLO
NABUKA:	
	OJIAMBO - MAGONGOLO
NAKUUNA:	Ehudu
	OFWIHO - MUDENYO
NALALA:	Osobolo
	Mandu
	OSOBOLO - OFWIHO
NAJABI:	Barasa
	Wandera
Nafwofwoyo:	Odunga
	MANDU - OFWIHO
NASUBO:	Ochieno
	Obuyu
	Sihaha
	MULINDO - OFWIHO
NALALA	Ochieno
	NGWENO LUNUNI - LWANDE WESONGA
NANYANGA	Lwande
	Lwande
	Awori - Lwo
	AWORI - LWANDE
	ODINGA - AWORI
	ODINGA
	Siminyu (Ochooko)

NGWENO LUNUNI
One: Ogoola.

.../9

MUMBO WA WAMIRA

NABIANGU:	Muchudde
	Lugunda
NAMALELE:	Wamira
	Biriko
	Kasaaka

MUCHUDDE WA MUMBO

NABUKAKI I	Mulima
NABAKHO	Grado Ogookha
NAMATOTE:	Nikola Ofwejja
NAKUHU	Oyolo
NAMUDAIRWA:	Wanyama Odongo
NABUKAKI II	Opeke
	Konna
NACHWERE	Baresa
NEBERE	Raphael Musumba

MULIMA MUCHUDDE

NADENGE:	Wanyama Ogooyo
	Joseph Omuya
	Sindano
NANUNYEKERA:	Ganynya
	Ogaara

GRADO OGOHA WA MUCHUDEE.

Nabonwe:	Alexander Luduba
	Simion
	Peter
	Sephiel Lugunda
	Adiriano
	Slivano Apondi
	Paul

NIKOLA OFWEJA WA MUCHUDDE

NAHULO:	Mulima Mumbo
	Stephano Mangeni
NABUKAKI	Peter Muchudde
	Grado Ogoha
	Ojiambo Lugundu
NAMASIKE:	Emmanuel Muchudde
	Grado Ogoha
	Ojiambo Lugunda
NATINGORIAT:	Odongo Gweno Mulema
	Okello Ngeno Lununi

RAPHAEL MUSUMBA WA MUCHUDDE

NANYIFWA:	Peter Ouma
	Charles Mutesa
NALALA:	John Were
ADETI	Moses Ouma, Manuel O
	Manuel Ogutu

...../6.

OUMA WA EMBALWA
?

NAMULUNDU WA EMBALWA.

NAMWINI: Muhemba Njoroge

MUHEMBA WA NAMULUNDU

NALWENGE:

NAMBANJA: Ouma
Mbalwa
Makoha

ADIKA WA MBALWA

NABONGO: Matias Nagafwa
NASIWE: Mbalwa
Nalwenge

NALALA: Michael Makoha

MATIAS NAGAFWA WA ADIKA

NASIBWIHA: Oundo
Adika

MBALWA WA ADIKA

NAHATUBA: Onyango
NAJABI: Ojiambo

NALWENGE WA ADIKA

ADETI: Judge
NASIE: Majimbo
Ojiambo
Ouma

NAKIROYA: Taifa

NEIBIRA(KUMAM) Mbalwa Julias
NASIROL Ojiambo Adika
Wafula siminyu
NANUMA: Ouma Kabwere
Mbakulo Obondo
Odwori
NATIKOKO: Buyoka Hatete
NAKURUKU: Godfrey Nehabi
Barasa Mwengo

MICHAEL MUHEMBA WA ADIKA
NAKIROYA: Macho
Nalwenge
Nahulo

OGUMBA EMBALWA
NAMAINDI: Grado Makoha

GRADO MAKOHA WA OGUMBA
Rojas Wafula
Doinald Lwoma
Fred Ouma
Sailas Namulumba
NAMKIMA: Julias Embalwa
NAMUKUBA: Ben Ogumba

Michael Mayga

EKAKA WA EMBALWA
NALALA: Ouma
Okumu
Taabu
Oundo

..../7.

	OKOCHI — ONGANGO
NAMUDUMBA	—
	BENARD BARASA — OTYOLA
NAMUHULA	Juma Otyola
	Ouli
	EDWARD EKAKA — OTYOLA
NAMUDDE	Peter Otyola
	Ouma
	PETER OTYOLA — EDWARD
NAMUDAIRWA.	—
	FRANCIS EKAKA — OGANGA WA OTYOLA
NAKHULO	—
	AGAITANO OUMA WA OTYOLA
NABONWE	Taabu
	JOSEPH JUMA WA OTYOLA
	OBINDA MUNYAUSI WA OTYOLA
	ROMAN OUMA WA OTYOLA
NAJABI	Odibia Otyola
	Nandunga
	Okello
	EKAKA WA OBINDA OTAMBULA
NASONGA	Ouma Muhaha
NASUBO	Ongango
NAMAKANGALA	Obbondo
NAMULUNDU	Ekaka Masorea.
	OUMA MUHAHA — EKAKA
	ONGANGO — EKAKA
NAHASOHO	Leubon Siriebo
NADONGO	Atanas Ekaka
NAHONE	Charles Obbare
NAMBANJA	Obinda Eriakimu
NAMULUNDU	Ekaka Masorea
NAMAKANGALA	Leston Sikala
	REUBEN SIRIEBO — ONGANGO
NACHAKI	Humpress Wanyama
	ATANAS EKAKA — ONGANGO
BWIDO	David Ongango
	Francis Barasa
	Michael Wangira
	Ekaka Odwori
	DAVID ONGANGO A. EKAKA
NATIKOKO	Biwirin Ekaka
	FRANCIS BARASA — ATANAS EKAKA
NALANGO	Lonald Ekaka
	MICHAEL WANGIRA WA A. EKAKA
NAHUMACHI	James.

.../6.

EKAKA ODWORI WA EKAKA ATANASI

CHARLES OBBARE WA ONGANGO

ADETI	Abahana Bongene
NAFUNYA	Ekaka (Mekanika)
	Nahone
	Odwori
	John

EKAKA MAKANIKA WA CHARLES OBBARE

NAMUKOBE	Obote
	Jogoo
	Kilo
	Siriebo

NAHONE WA CHARLES OBBARE

NAMULUNDU	Mugeni
	Barasa

ODWORI WA OBBARE

NALLALI	Mugeni

JOHN SIRIEBO WA CHARLES OBBARE

NAMULUNDU	Wandera
	Siriebo

OBINDA ERIAKINU WA ONGANGO

NAMUDUMA	Omuhana Yengene

EKAKA MASORE WA ONGANGO

Siyaleha mundu dawe.

LASTON SIKALA WA ONGANGO

OBBONDO WA EKAKA

OCHIENGI NASIKAYE

NANYIWALO	Chore Abwoyo
	Omanyo

CHORE ABWOYO WA OCHIENGI NASIKALA

OMANYO WA OCHIENG NASIKAYE.

OGOOLA WA NGWENO LUNUNI

NALALA:	Mbulu
	Wandefu
	Muniala
	Sibala

MBULU WA OGOOLA

NABONWE:	Ngweno Sigiria
	Siganga
	Ogoola II

NGWENO SIGIRIA WA MBULU

NABUKAKI:	Eria Ochieno
	Ogoola Ongeke

ERIYA OCHIENO WA NGWENO

NAMIRIPO:	Wanyama Zablon
NACHAKI I	Mbulu Yonasani
	Mekhoka Amulamu
	Daudi Odedo
	Ojiambo Gideon Ngweno
	Salomon Okello
NACHAKI II	Mangeni
	Samuel Wanyama
	Wafula Wycliffe
	Wandera
NACHAKI III	Richard Egessa (Ngweno)
	Samuel Nangeni
	Onyango
NAJABI I	Wafula
	Bwire
NAJABI II	Daudi Ngweno (Bwire)
	Fredrick Wandera
	Siminyu
NAJABI III	Aggrey Okuku
	Paul Sitanga

ZABLON WANYAMA - ERIA OCHIENO

NAMUDIBYA:	Onyango
NANUNYORO:	Baguma

BAGUMA WA ZABLON WANYAMA

NANUMAYI:	

YONASANI MBULU WA ERIYA OCHIENO

NANUKOBE:	Peter (Nasiga) Ogoola
	Onyango Geofrey

MAKOHA AMULAMU WA ERIYA OCHIENO

Nafuka:	Wanyama
	Wandera

DAUDI ODEDO WA ERIYA OCHIENO

Ngweno

OJIAMBO GIDION WA ERIYA OCHIENO

NAMUNYAKOLE:	Bwire
	Wandera

Salomon Okello wa Eriyo Ochieno

NAMUSIGE:	Okumu
	Egosa

SAMUEL WANYAMA WA ERIYA OCHIENO

NANYANGA	Ngweno

WAFULA WYCLIFFE WA ERIYA OCHIENO

NAMUNYEKERA: Ogoola

WANDERA WA ERIYA OCHIENO

NADONGO: Ngweno

RICHARD EGESA WA ERIYA OCHIENO
Daudi
Mugeni

SAMUEL MANGENI WA ERIYO OCHIENO

NASIRWA: —

DAUDI NGWENO WA ERIYA OCHIENO

NALIALI: Sitanga
Ngweno
Zekalia

FREDRICK WANDERA WA ERIYA OCHIENO

NADONGO: Ngweno

AGGREY OKUMU WA ERIYA OCHIENO
Ngweno

OGOOLA WA NGWENO

Nabbiangu: —

MBULU WA OGOOLA

NABONWE: Sitanga Obwaso
NABUKAKI: Yosia Wafula
NASIEMA Yosamu Egessa
Okumu Yolam
NACHAKI Wanyama
NAMUPODI: Osinya
NAMUFUTA: Onyango

YOSIYA WAFULA WA SITANGA

NAMALA Charles Mangeni
G. William Ojiambo
NAMBOKO: Peter Juma.
NAMUMAYI: Michael Wandera
Muhongo Stephin
Wilber Bwire
Daudi Ofha
Benard Businge
Simion Sanya
NACHONGA Mugende Sitanga
NAMUSIHO MBULU

MICHAEL WANDERA WA WAFULA

NACHA
NAKUHU Geofrey Sunday

YOSAMU EGESSA - SITANGA

NACHAKI: Samuel Wanyama

Aggrey Ojiambo

James Oundo

George Mangeni

NAMULAKA Opio

NAMUTENDE Odongo

Wandera

NAMUNYEKERA Opio

Mangeni

AGREY OJILMBO – YOSAMU EGESSA
DAUDI NANTONGO
JAMES OUNDO – YOSAMU EGESSA

Namutindie – Rojers yafwa
GEORGE MANGENI – YOSAMU EGESSA.

Nabukaki – Taabu, Richard Wandera.

YOLAMU OKUMU – SITANGA

NAKOOLI
– Bwire
– Mangeni
– Wafula.

BWIRE – YOLAMU OKUMU

MANGENI = YOLAMU OKUMU

WAFULA = YOLAMU OKUMU

OSINYA = SITANGA

NALALA = MUKISA

MBULU HENERY

NGWENO LUNUNI

Namangalo
– Waida.

WAIDA = NGWENO LUNUNI
= Mudubwa
= Ngweno Konga
= Osinya.

MUDUBWA – WAIDA
⊖ Osinya.
= Peter Lwande
= Eriya Achiengi

NGWENO KANGA = WAIDA
= Nasubo = Mbuya
Waida II

MBUYA – NGWENO KANGA
– Waida
– Odimo

WAIDA MBUYA

NAPUNYI:
= Isirael Wafula
= Daniel Achieno
= Peter Mbuya

ISIRAEL WAFULA = WAIDA

NALALA: Julia Nachio
NAMULUNDU: Egessa

NAMUSOGA

JULIAS MACHIO = L. WAFULA.

EGESSA = J. WAFULA.

DANIEL ACHIENO = WAIDA

NANAINDI: Charles Hamala

PETER MBUYA = WAIDA.

JONATHAN OUCHO = MBUYA

NAKUHU: Nasubo.

DAUDI OKUKU = MBUYA

NAMANYI: = Wanyama

= Waida

NALIALI: = ————

ODIMO = MBUYA

= Living Oucho.

LIVINGSTON OUCHO = ODIMO

NAMUTENDE: = (Onyango) Wycliffe Mbuya.

= Ogutu

WYCLIFFE MBUYA

NABONWE: ————

NADIGO: = Moses Odimo

= Waida.

= Daudi Wafula.

NABONGO: ————

OGUTU = OUCHO.

NAMANYI: ————

WAIDA II = NGWENO KANGA

NAHAYO: — Ibulaimu Bwire.

— Erisa Ndiira.

NAMASIRO: — Yowori Wandera.

— Dani Mujugga.

IBULAIMU BWIRE = WAIDA.

NAMULENESI: ——

NAMAINDI: — Magero

NAMUDDE: — Wafula

— Ogutu.

MAGERO = IBULAIMU BWIRE.

NAMULEMESI: — Mangoni.

NAMUKOBE: ——

WAFULA = IBULAIMU BWIRE.

NABOOLI: — Mbuya.

OGUTU = IBULAIMU BWIRE.

NABUKAKI: - Okumu

ERISA NDIIRA = WAIDA

NAMAINDI: - Ali Wandera.
        - Ojiambo Ndiira.
NAJABI: - Wanyama Ndiira.

ALI WANDERA = ERISA NDIIRA.

OJIAMBO = NDIIRA.

WANYAMA = NDIIRA.

YOWERI WANDERA = WAIDA.

NALIALI: ♂ Jackson Ouma.
        - John Ogutu.
NALIALI: - Albert Ojiambo
        - Barasa
NAMANYI: Justin Wafula.

JACKSON OUMA = WANDERA.

ADETI: - Bwire
     - Mareki.
     - Moses.
NAMIHANJA - Ouma.

JOHN OGUTTU = Y. WANDERA.

NAMASESE: - Monday.

ALBERT OJIAMBO = Y. WANDERA

NAHULO: - Wandera.

BARASA = Y. WANDERA.

NAMULUNDU: - Bwiro.

JUSTIN WAFULA = Y. WANDERA.

Namiripo: - Barasa
      - Justo.

OSINYA = MUDUBWA.

NASICHONGI: - Peter Lwande.

        - Eriya Achiengi.

PETER LWANDE = OSINYA

NAHOOLI: - Williamu Ojiambo
      - Wasiko.
      - Wandera
      - Barasa
NAMWANGA: - Ochieno.

WILLIAM OJIAMBO = P. LWANDE.

NAJABI: - Mangoni
      - Bwiro
      - Wafula
      - Okumu

NACHIMO: - Bwire Simion
       - Egessa Amosi
       - Siminyu
       - Mahobbo.

MANGENI – WILLIAM.

NALIALI: Oundo

BWIRE – WILLIAM

NAMAKANGALA: ——

WAFULA – WILLIAM.

NAHANYI: ——

WASIKE – P. LWANDE.

NALIALI: Friday
          Charles.

WANDERA – P. LWANDE

NAMUSOGA: Geofrey Wanyama
          Jimy

OCHIENO – P. LWANDE.

NEKHOBA: ——

ERIYA ACHIENGI

NALIALI: Ofwiri
          Mudubwa.

NAMULUNDU: Prop Opio

OFWIRI – ERIYA ACHIENGI

OPIO – ERIYA ACHIENGI

NASICHONGI:

NUKKA – NGWENO KANGA

WAIDA WA MBUYA

NAMUDUNA: Samuel Musigo

SAMUEL MUSIGO

NASICHONGI: Absolom Ojiambo
          Ekello Firimon.

NAMUDAYI: Waida Tito
          John Wanyama
          Aggrey Oundo.

WAIDA TITO.

ADETI: Nimrod Mbuya.
          Amulam Waida
          Paul Wafula
          Aggrey Oundo.
          Daudi Were

175

	NGWENO LUMUNI
	NABERE
	SOMBI
NAMULEMBO	Obaala
	OBAALA - SOMBI
NALUKADA	Jinga
NASIMALWA	Obwora
	Ngweno
NAHAYO	Lwande
	JINGA - OBAALA
NAKOLI	Ojiambo
NAMANGALE	Kuchihi
	OJIAMBO NINDA
NAMULUNDU	Wanyama Livinstone
	Olwochi
	Ojwangi
	WANYAMA - OJIAMBO
MAHONE	Bwire Livingstone
	Lubega Jinga
	Ouma
	KUCHIHI JINGA
NAKWERI	Onyango Wero
NACHAKI	Wafula Jinga
	OLWOCHI OJIAMBO
NABULINDO	Bwire Godfrey
	Okumu Geofrey
	OJWANGI OJIAMBO
NALALA	
	OBWORA OBAALA
NAJABI	Halogo
	HALOGO OBWORA
NAFWOFWOYO	Firipo Obaala
NAMULEMBO	Musa Hagaga
	Jackson Musumba
Nabonwe	Wero Chabugwe
NAKOOLI	Zablon Himbiri
	Yoward Halogo II
	FIRIPO OBAALA HALOGO
NAHONE	Yosia Ojiambo

176

NAHONE	Nuwa Masurubu
	Daniel Okello
	Bulasio Obaala
NAHONE II	Juma
	Ojiambo
	Wafula
	Barasa
	Ouma
	YOSIA OJIAMBO - OBAALA
NAMUBASIRA	Jimbi
	Lwande
NAHULO	Wafula
	Pemba
	Ouma
	NUWA MASURUBU - OBAALA
NAMUFUTA	wanyama
	Bwire
	Mayende
	DANIEL OKELLO - OBAALA
	Paska
	Ojiambo
	Bogere
	BULASIO OBAALA P - OBAALA
NAKWATI	Wandera
	Amiggo
	Nahone
	MUSA MAGAGA HALOGO
Napunyi	Wanyama
	Ouma
NASERA	Nasimalwa
	Majoni
	WANYAMA MAGAGA
Nandekia	—
	OUMA - MUSA MAGAGA
NABWALA	Musa Magaga
NAMAKANGALA	Musa Magaga
	NASIMALWA - MUSA MAGAGA
NAMAKANGALA	—
	MAJONI - MUSA MAGAGA
NABWIBO	Musa Stephin
	Musa Magaga.

••/3

NADURI	—
	<u>JACKSON MUSUMBA -HALOGO</u>
NEBEERE	Livingstone Halogo
	Obwora
	Mangeni
	Obaala
	Makoha (Sibaki)
NAMBANJA	Egessa
	<u>LIVINSTON HALOGO MUSUMBA</u>
ADETI	—
	<u>OBWORA MUSUMBA</u>
NAMBANJA	Bwire Charles
	Stephin Oundo
	Francis Mangeni
	Sunday Kenneth
	<u>MANGENI MUSUMBA</u>
NAMULUNDU	Musumba Jackson
NAMUTES	Ester Kulaba
NAKOMOLO	Ojiambo
	Ouma
	<u>OBALA MUSUMBA</u>
NANYIBOMI	Ojiambo
	Musa Ojiambo
	Egessa
NABOOLI	Bwire
	<u>MAKOHA MUSUMBA</u>
NANIRIPO	—
	<u>EGESSA MUSUMBA</u>
NABOOLI	Manuel Musumba
	Moses Musa
	<u>WERE CHADUGWE MUSUMBA</u>
NAMUFUTA	Ojiambo
NAMANYAMA	Ojiambo
	Obwora
	Wafula
	<u>ZABULONI HIMBIRI HALOGO</u>
NANYIBOMI	Samuel Juma Halogo
	Najabi
	Wangira
	Barasa
NAHONE	Musa Magaga
	Obaala

178

NAMULUNDU:	Egessa
	Sidialo
	Ojiambo
	Ayonjo

SAMUEL JUMA HIMBIRI

NAMENYA	James Sumba
	Wilson Mangeni
	Humphress Sunday
	Wafula Juma

NAJABI HIMBIRI

NAHONE	Bwire Najabi
	Wanyama
	Charles Najabi

YOWERE HALOGO

NAMWANDIRA	Ogutu
	Wafula
	Sunday Bosi bafwa!
	Nakooli
	Were

OGUTU - YOWERE HALOGO

LWANDE OBALA

NAMAINDI	Samuel Sombi II
NAJABI	Jacob Omondi
Namiripo	Daniel Donga
NACHAAKI	Salimu Wandera

SAMUEL SOMBI II

NABONWE	Abner Mayonde
	George Ouma
NAMUDDE	Zedekia Wandera
	Wilson Mangeni
	Tito Sombi (Onyango)
Nakooli	Anderea Edege
	John Rabongo

ABNER MAYENDE - SOMBI

NASICHONGI	---

GEORGE OUMA SOMBI

NAMULINDA	Bwire (Obaala)
	Onyango (Sombi)
	Ojiambo
	Mangeni
	Wandera
	Okumu

179

NAMULANGIRA	Lwande Wilberforce
	Robert Sombi

ZEDEKIA WANDERA - SOMBI

NAMBANJA	- Obaala (Sombi) Aggrey
NAMULUNDU	Lwande Patrick
	Fred Sombi
	Lwande Jackson
	Obaala Aggrey
NAMUKEMO	Lwande Wilson
NADIDI	Wafula Bernard
NAMURARAKA:	Sombi Samuel
	Ngweno Mulona Wilber
	David Makoha
NAMULUNDU II	Godfrey
	Bon
	Bwire Moses

AGGREY OBAALA - Z. WANDERA

NAMUKEMO	—

RABONGO JAMES BWIRE Z.W.

NAKAROKO	Nambanja Henery
NAMUKOBE	—

LWANDE PATRICK Z. WANDERA

NAMUDAIRWA	Samuel Sombi

WILSON MANGENI WA SOMBI

NAMULUNDU I	Onyango Henrey
	Bwire Geofrey
	Samuel Sombi
NAMULUNDU II	Livingstone Ouma
	Robert Lwande
	Walter Master Bwire
	Benjamin Omenya
NAMUFUTA	Wycliffe Namudde
	Backley Obbala Ojiambo

ONYANGO HENREY WA WILSON MANGENI

NALUBA	Leonard Wafula

BWIRE GEOFREY WA WILSON MANGENI

NANDEKIYA	—

TITO SOMBI (ONYANGO) WA SOMBI.

NAMUSONGE	Samuel Sombi
NALIALI	Kulindi Carmasky
	Hadudu Zadekiea
	Sombi Stanely

Andereya Ndege WA SOMBI

NAKWERI	Obaala Bakari
	Were
	Ojiambo .
NAJABI	Samweri Sombi
	Andere Egessa
	Abneri Stephen

JOHN RABONGO WA SOMBI

JACOB OMONDI WA LWANDE

NAMULEMBO	Yokana Lwande
	Samuel Wandera
	Ngweno Jackson
NABOHOLO	Edward Sombi
NASONGA I	Isaac Oduba
NASONGA II	Joram Musumba

YOKANA LWANDE WA JOCOB OMONDI

NAMENYA	Onyango Alex

ONYANGO ALEK WA YOKANA LWANDE

NAMIRIPO	Omondi

SAMUEL WANDERA WA OMONDI

NABONGO (SINDAMANYA)	Patrick Dwire
NAJABI	Shadrack Barasa
	Omondi Godfrey
	Ouma Bonard

NGWENO JACKSON WA OMONDI

NAMUTORO	Ojiambo
	Bwire
	Fred
	Omondi

EDWARD SOMBI WA OMONDI

NAMWAYA	Tom Okello, Tambiti
NAMULUNDU	Ouma

	TOM OKELLO WA EDWARD SOMBI
ADETI	-
	TAMBITI EDWARD SOMBI
NALALA	-
NAMUGANDA	Maadi
	ISAAC ODUBA WA OMONDI JACOB
NAMUBUPI	Lwande
	Najabi
	Sombi
	LWANDE WA ODUBA ISAAC
NABURI	-
	NAJABI WA ODUBA OMONDI
NASIRISI	Stephin Omondi
	SOMBI WA ODUBA ISAAC.

	NGWENO LUNUNI WA LWANDE WESONGA
NASONGA II	Banga
	BANGA
NAMAINDI	Ombole
	Embaaya
	Ngweno Dambakana
	Odooli
ODWAKO	-
	OMBOLE WA BANGA
	EMBAAYA WA BANGA
NAHWAKU	Mbasiro
	Mulohe
	Siongongo
	MBASIRO WA EMBAAYA
	''
	MULEHE - EMBAAYA
NALIALI	Abahana 4, Akumu, Norima, Guloba ::
	Muohanji Naggaga, Wandora Banana.
	WANDERA BANANA WA MULEHE
NALALA	Stephin Mangoni
	Bwiro Naangaga.
	MANGENI STEPHIN WA WANDA
NAMUTINEIE.	Nangaga
	Bwiro
	Masiga.

	HAMIRIPO WA NGWENO LUNUNI
NAMANGALE	Lwando
	Namudde
	Musebule
	Ngweno Donga
	LWANDE WA HAMIRIPO
	Opio
	Agwanda
	OPIO WA LWANDE
NABONGO	Sembo Madara
	SEMBO MADARA – OPIO
NAMUDUMA	Yowaba Okuku
	Dismas Tanga (Yafwa)
	Baturumayo Nabongo
	YOWANGA OKUKU MADARA
NAMAKANGALA I	Jocob Okumu
NAMAKANGALA II	–
NABUKAKI	Odwori
	JACOB OKUMU – YOWANA OKUKU
NANYIBURA	Masuko – Samu
	Dely Robert
	Lta Tanga
	DISMAS TANGA, SEMEO MADARA, NAMULUMBA
	BATULUMAYO NABONGO – S. MADARA
NACHONGA	OGUTU
	Joseph (Namude)
NALWENGE	Onyango
	Monday

2.	NAMUDDE WA HAMIRIPO
NABONGO	Sikala Agula.
	SIKALA AGULA WA NAMUDDE
NALIALI	Odongo Sihawa
	Were
NAMULUNDU	Sikala Oyoda
	ODONGO SIHAWA – ONGOLI
NANYANGA	Wycliffe Namudde

....../2.

183

| | Opada |
| NAJABI | Ouma David |

INYASI WERE - SIKALA OYODA

| NAMUSIKHO | Atanasi Sikala |

ATANASI SIKALA - INYASI WERE.

NASUBO	Wandera
	Ojiambo
	Makoha Nyasi
	Nyasaga
	Bwire
	Nyasi

WANDERA-ATANASI

NAMWALIRA	Fredrick Wafula
	Ojiambo Atanasi
NASUHUNE	Makoha Tanasi
	NAHULO

WERE WA SIKALA AGULA

| NAMULUNDU | Otengo |

Yakerama Namulundu yali owa simwana khuney-

OTENGO WA WERE

| NANYINEKI | Wilbirond Okumu |

WILBIRONDO OKUMU - OTENGO

NAJABI	Onyango
	Wafula (Yafwa)
	Ojiambo
	Wandera
	Barasa
NAMUTIMBA	Wanyama
	Sanya
	Mugeni
	Barasa

ONYANGO WA W. OKUMU.

| NAMUDDE | Peter Masiga |
| | John Wanyama |

WAFULA - W. OKUMU

| NAMUDEPI | Wandera |

OJIAMBO WA W. OKUMU

NAMUDDE:	Mugeni Barnard
	Denesi Oguttu
	Godfrey Bwire
NAMUMALI	Barasa W. Okumu

..../4.

ONGOLI WA ODONGO SIHAWA

WAIERE	Wanyama
	Odongo
	Odwori
	Okochi

WANYAMA WA ONGOLI

NAHABI	Barasa
	Ouma
	Bwire

ODONGO WA ONGOLI

NAHONE	Okumu
	Ojiambo
	Gusino Mangeni (Yafwa)
WAMAINDI	Egesa
	Orida Bubolu
NEHOBA	Bukalu
	Sibiya
	Lumboti

ODWORI ONGOLI – NANGWANGA.

O	OCHOCHI WA ONGOLI

WERE WA SIKALA A.

SIKALA OYODA

SIKALA A.

NAMUDIBA WA ATIKO SIKALA (ADISI)

ATIKO SIKALA (ADISI)

NACHAKI	Ogutu
	Opio *MANGENI*
	Juma
	Wandera
	~~Ohasa Lazalo~~
WAHONE	Opada (Okumu)
	Ouma David
	Wanyama
	Barasa Oundo
NAHAMENGE	Bwire *OGUTU ATIKO*
	Ouma
	Opio
	Mangeni
WABAHOLO	Richard Ojiambo
	Charles
	Wandera James
NABAHOLO II	Lazalo,
	Okhasa
	Barasa Isaac.

.../3.

WANYAMA WA OKUMU

NAPUNYI   Ochieno Charles

3   MUSEMBULE WA HAMIRIPO

NAMUKOBE   Ngweno Nabulayi

                       NGWENO NABULAYI - HAMIRIPO

NALALA   Walungoli

                       Olunjala

                       Onyuni

                       WALUNGOLI WA NGWENO ARIADA

                       OLUNJALU

NATIKOKO   Eriya Omwene

                       ERIYA OMWENE - OLUNJALU

NAJABI   Stanley Asumanga

                       STANLEY ASUMANGA WA ERIYA OMWENE

NAYIYE   Richard Ojiambo

                       Yovani Mangeni

                       RICHARD OJIAMBO - S. ASUMANGA

                       ONYUNI - NGWENO NABULAYI

NALALA   Paulo Ngweno

                       Seperia Nyegenye (Abbanga)

                       PAUL NGWENO - ONYUNI

NAHONE   Ouma Eriazali

                       Musumba James (Yaffa)

NASIENYA   Mangeni

                       Wafula

                       Wanyama

                       ERIAZALI OUMA PL NGWENO

NAMUDUMA

NAMULANDA

                       JAMES MUSUMBA P. NGWENO

NAMULOB'   Wandera

                       Jason

                       Matinda

NAMULO   Sanya

NASAKAMU   Sanya

                       James Musumba

                       MANGENI PAUL NGWENO

NABONWE   Patrick Egessa

                       BWIRE FREDRICK - PAUL NGWENO

NANYIRUMI   -

NASUBO   Wandera Vincent.

-5-

WAFULA DISHAN WA PAUL NGWENO

NALLA I	-
	WANYAMA DAVID - P. NGWENO
	WANYAMA ERINEYO - P. NGWENO
NAYIYE	Juma
	Wafula
	SEPERIA NYEGENYE ABBANGA
NAMUHOOKOSI	Ochieno Wilfred
NAMANGALE	Onyango Waltet
	OCHIENO WILFRED - NYEGENYE
NASIRWA	Stephin
	OCHIENO WILFRED - NYEGENYE
4	NGWENO DONGA WA HAMIRIPO
	OJWANGI WA NGWENO DONGA
ADETI	- Balongo
NEHOBA	Onyigi
	Ojanji
	Ngweno B.
	BALONGO WA OJWANGI
NACHAKI	Wandera Balongo
	Patrick Bbala (Yafwa)
	Obbamba Balongo
NAHAI I.	Filikis Orembo (Yafwa)
	Asebe Balongo (Yafwa)
	Adeti (Yafwa)
	Ouma Balongo
	WANDERA WA BALONGO
NADONWE	Makoha Lungasa
NAMWINI	John Bwire
	Mangeni Wandera
	MAKOHA WANDERA
NANYANGA	-
NAMUDDE	Bwire Wandera
	Mangeni Wandera
	PATRICK BBALA BALONGO
NAKONWE	John Okonya
NAKIBOYA	Pamba Patrick
NATUKOBE	Ouma
	Godrey
	Ojwangi
	Albert Ojiambo
	Anthony Wandera

✈

	OBETE WA ONYIGI
NAMIRIPO	John Wandera
	Alex Mangeni
	MARIKO MAKANDA WA YOWANA OJWANGI.
NAHAYO	Barasa (ABUHERE)
	BARASA WA MARIKO MAKANDA
NAKUHU	David Juma
NAMULEMBO	Idi Barasa,
	Nyongesa Barasa.
	WANJALA WA ONYIGI
NAMANYI	Bodi
	Abangi (yafwa)
	Maloba (yafwa)
	Onyango
NATIKOKO	Ojiambo
	BODI WA WANJALA
NACHWERE	Wandera Bodi
	Bwire Bodi
	ABANGI WA WANJALA
	ONYANGO WANJALA
NEDERE	Masiga.
	OKAARA WA ONYIGI
NAMUKOBE	Okochi
	Masiga
	OKOCHI WA OKAARA
NAMANGALE	Juma Onyigi
NADEKE.	

end

JOHN OKONYA WA PATRICK BBALA.

NAMUTALA	Barasa (Balongo)
	Okumu Okonya
	Balongo Okonya

OBBAMBA WA BALONGO

NANGAYO	Abahana 3

FILIKISI OREMBO WA BALONGO

NAMUJALA	Wangalwa

WANGALWA WA FILIKISI OREMBO

NASONGA	Okuku
NAKOMOLO	Bubolu
	Fitaleo Osinya

FITALIO OSINYA

Malala	Masinde
	Baati

ASEBE WA BALONGO

NASUBO	Bwire
	Okoowa

OUMA WA BALONGO

NAMUTINDIE	Geofrey Okochi
	Ojiambo
NAHABI	Cornel Bwire
	Mangeni
	Gusino
	Bwire

GEOFREY BWIRE WA OUMA.

NEKEKERE	Vincent Sanya
	Thomas Barasa

OJIAMBO WA OUMA.

NAMUKONO	Ogutu

ONYIGI WA OJWANGI

NAHABI	Yowana Ojwangi
	Obete
NACHIMO I	Wanjala (andeme)
NAMUDAIRWA	Okaara
NACHIMO II	Juma

YOWANA OJWANGI WA ONYIGI

NASUBO	Mariko Makanda
	Francico Obete

..../2.

—※—

MARIKO NAKANDA WA YOHANA OJWANGI

NADAYO   Barasa (Abuhere)

BARASA WA MARIKO NAKANDA

    "

WANJALA WA ONYIGI

NAMANYI   Boodi

    Abangi (yafwa)

    Maloba (yafwa)

    Onyango

NATIKOKO   Ojiambo

BOODI WA WANJALA

NAIWASI   Wandera Boodi

    Bwire Boodi

ABANGI WA WANJALA

    "

OKAARA WA ONYIGI

NAMANGALE   Juma Onyigi

NADEKE   —

OLWENI NYEMBI WA NGWENO LUNUNI

NALYALI	Owori	Habocha
NASONGA I	Siduwa	Owori
NASONGA II		SIDUWA
NALALA		Sidubo

HABOCHA WA OLWENI NYEMBI

Nimurodi Ndongi

OWORI WA OLYENI NYEMBI

Joel Ariada.

SIDUWA WA OLWENI NYEMBI

Ojiambo Agaaya

SIDUBO WA OLWENI NYEMBI

Taimor Hakerwe

Abujar Ekudu

OLWENI NYEMBI WA NGWENO LUNUNI

NACHEKI	Sunu nende Okweyo.
NALYALI	Habocha

SUNU WA OLWENI NYEMBI
Morris Onyango
Manel Wanyama

OKWENYO WA NGWENO LUNUNI
Ogana
Wambete.

HABOCHA WA NGWENO LUNUNI
2

HABOCHA WA OLWENI NYEMBI

NALALA	Ndongi
	Otiende

NDONGI WA HABOCHA

NAJABAI	Obocho

OBOCHO WA NDONGI

NAMANGALE	Nimrod Ndongi

NIMROD NDONGI

NANJOSI	Booker Ndongi
	Apolo Ndongi
	Joshua Sigondi Ndongi
	Jogoo Patrick
	Banda Emmanuel

BOOKER NDONGI WA NIMROD NDONGI
Sigondi
Toti
Ezekiel Odonya

APOLO NDONGI WA NIMROD NDONGI

NAMENYA	Nimrod Ndongi
	Were

OTIENDE WA OLWENYI

NABURI	Bakanya
	Chabbiri (Chabbiri luyafwa babekawo Bakanya)

BAKANYA WA OTIENDE

NAHOONGA	Hadera
	Habuu (Hadera luyafwa babekawo Habuu)

HADERA WA BAKANYA

NANYIBONI	Sigondi (Choroko)

..../4.

NASONGA OWORI WA OLWENI NYEMBI

NAMULUMBA	Opala

OPALA WA OWORI

NAMANGALE	Wamalwa

WAMALWA WA OPALA

NADUKAKI	Musumba George
Nahasoho	Wandera

OWORI II WA OPALA

NADONGO	Sibabalo
NAKOOLI	Joel Ariada Mangoli

SIBABALE WA OWORI II

NAHULO	Odwori

ODWORI WA SIBABALE

NASONGA	"

JOEL ARIADA (MANGOLI) WA OWORI

NALALA	Jackson Ochieno nende Joshua Wandera (Duncan)

JACKSON OCHIENO WA JOEL ARIADA

NAMUDE	"
ADETI	Albert Owori
	David Ojiambo (Kaka)

JOSHUA WANDERA (DUNCAN) WA JOEL ARIADA

NALALA	"
NASONGA II	~~Siduwa~~ Wa Olweni Nyembi.

SIDUWA WA OLWENI NYEMBI

NAMUNAPA	Omuhehe

OMUHEHE WA SIDUWA

NAMAKANGALA	Zefania Agaaya
NAMANGALE	Zadoki Ouma (Ranyosi)

SEFANIYA AGAAYA

NAMUMA	Cornel Malinga
	Ojiambo Patrick

MALINGU CORNEL WA ZEFANIYA AGAAYA

NAMENYA	John Omuhehe
	Egessa Oburra

JOHN OMUHEHE WA CORNEL MALINGU

NAMUKOBE	Malinga (Abbara)
	(Tajiri Mawaya)

OJIAMBO PATRICK WA ZEFANIYA AGAAYA

NAFWOFWOYO	Mafwamba
	Agaaya

MAFWAMBA WA OJIAMBO

NAJABI	"

ZADOKI OUMA WA OMUHEHE

NALALA	Wanyama
	Wandera
	Wafula

..../5

192

	<u>WANYAMA WA OUMA</u>
NALYALI	Ndongi
	<u>WANDERA WA OUMA</u>
NAHONE	Robert
	<u>WAFULA WA OUMA</u>
NAMUSONGE	Ndongi
	<u>OLWENI NYEMBI WA NGWENO LUNUNI</u>
NALALA	Sidubo
	<u>SIDUBO WA LWENI NYEMBI</u>
NABWALA	Ndoro
NACHAKI	"
	<u>NDORO WA SIDUBO</u>
NABAHOLO	Buluma
	<u>BULUMA WA NDORO</u>
NABULE	"
NAHONE	TAIDOR HAKERWE
	Alfunsi Nabwala
	<u>TAIDOR HAKERWE WA BULUMA</u>
NAKOOLI II	Alex Oundo
	Okello Wilson
	Oundo Hakerwe
NAKOOLI I	'
NANJOSI	Nabwala
	Bubolu
	<u>ALEX OUNDO WA TAIDOR HAKERWE</u>
NALYALI	Wafula
	Mangeni
	<u>ALFUNZI NABWLA WA BULUMA</u>
NAMANGALE	Clement Wanyande
	Okumu Nabwala
	Sidubo Nabwala
	<u>NACHAKI WA NYANDE WA SIDUBO</u>
NAMAYAYI	Siyaleha mundu musacha.
	Oundo niye owafweira mu maye e Tanganyika
	nalehawoo Omugyhni - Halengo N'Omuhanax Akumu
	Ng'ina Gideon Wanyama.
	<u>NAHERE MATA DANIEL</u>
NAMUDAIRWA	Siboche
NIHODA	Namukooli
NABULINDO	Okuku (Obaba)

...../6.

193

NABONGO	Buluma
	Dadi nende abahana babiri (2)
NAMAINDI	Abahana 2 Addea, Auma Samia.

OUNDO WA WANYANDE

NAJABI	Yebula Opuli Halango, Manu Oundo yafwira
	mu mayoe ake Tanzania mu 1914.

DANIEL MATA WA WANYANDE

NAMBOKO	Yawawo nachya e Bunyala elya nali nende
	enda ya Mata niyebulayo omwana Achoka,
	Namboko yacha elya olwambalina olwahuba
	Mata yali akerame Leah Ongoola (Odeywa)
	Siboche nafwire.

NAMENYA-LEAH ONGOOLA ODEYWA

Yali mu ha Siboche, Siboche yafwa niyebule
naye abaana babiri omuhana nende omusyani
Omuhana niye Ofwamba — Omusyani niye Muliro
abo nibo abaali abaana ba Siboche. Mata
niyakeram yebulamo abaana 8 abo boosi bali
abahana berere, olunyuma niyebula abasyani
2 ABUNERI EKUDU nende YEKOYADA MBUNDA nibo
abekala enda.

ABUNERI EKUDU WA DANIEL KATA

NAHABUKA I	Reubeni Namenya
NAHABUKA II	Jophiter Okumu, Julius Onyango,
	Samuel Beker Dwire.
NAGENI	Eridadi Ongoola, Wilberforce Edudu Dwire,
	David Nafula, Benard Handra.
NALYALI	Ouma Yefusa (Jophiter)

REUBENI NAMENYA WA ABNER EKUDU

NADONGO	Wilber Dwire.

ERIDAD ONGOOLA WA ABNER EKUDU

NACHAKI	Moses Namenya

JUSIAL ONYANGO WA ABNERI EKUDU

NAMUKULWA (NEREKE)	"

WILBERFORCE EKUDU WA A. EKUDU

NABOHOLO	"

DAVID WAFULA WA ABNERI EKUDU

NACHIKI	2

BERNAD WANDERA WA ABNERI EKUDU

NALYALI	Wilber Dwire.

YEKOYADA MBUNDA WA MATA

NACHONGA	Bonya Dwire, Michael Wanyande, Okello & Oji
NASIYEE	Charles Mata Wandera, Leuben Leah Ojiambo,
	Godfrey Ouma (Singuba)
NAHIBE	Ngweno Dickson (Mugaluka)
	Samuel Sidubo, Benard (Acid) Manyande,
	Joseph Ndyaba, Nuwa Mamenya.

BENYA BWIRE WA YEKOYADA MBUNDA

NACHAAKI   Ronald Ojiambo
Yona Mbunda.

MICHAEL WANYANDE WA YEKOYADA MBUNDA

NANKIMA   Fred Wanyande.

CHARLES MATA (WANDERA) WA Y. MBUNDA.

NABUWI   Buleyan Masiga, Timoth Mukisa, Andrew.

LABANI LEAH OJIAMBO WA Y. MBUNDA

NABBYANGU   "

OUMA GODFREY WA YEKOYADA MBUNDA

NAGEMI   Mbunda Levi

JORAM WAFULA WA DANIEL MATA

NASIYEE   Stephen Mulehe, Namukooli, George Ojiambo
Were Godfrey Ojiambo, Joseph Ogutu,
Julius Wanyana (Nalyali).

NAMUSOGA   William Egessa, David Oundo.

STEPHEN MULEHE WA JORAM WAFULA

NAMUDIRA   Eli Mata (Chubbani), Emmanuel Oguttu,
James Ojiambo.

JOSEPH OGUTO WA JORAM WAFULA

OWEFUMBE
NAMAGANDA   "

   Mata Daniel Raymond.

GODFREY OJIAMBO WA JORAM WAFULA

NAMAGANDA   Livingstone Were

SIBOCHE WA WANYANDE

NAPUNYI   Sitefano Okiya.

SITEFANO OKIYA WA SIBOCHE

NAMANGALE   David Odunga, Clement Ojiambo (Obbimbo)

CLEMENT OJIAMBO (OBBIMBO) WA OKIYA

NADONGO   "

NAMUKOOLI WA WANYANDE

NAHERE   Burocho, Burocho Yatula ano hale mu 1918
nachira mu Syalo sya Tanzania nohwola J
sihumanyire ngalwali.

OKIKU (OHABA) WA WANYANDE

NAMUDDE   Egessa Peter, Anderea Sidubo

EGESSA PETER WA OKUKU (OHABA)

NEBERE   Yobula abahana bahaya.

ANDEREA SIDUBO WA OKUKU (OHABA)

NAMANGALE   Akello Wanyande, Moyi.

SIPEMI WA SIDUBO

NALYALI   Oduba

ODUBA WA SIPEMI

NASITWOKI   Wasiguli

WASIGULI WA ODUBA

NAMAKANGALA   Wamalwa.

	WAMALWA WA WASIGULI
NAMUTENDE	Pantaleo Wanyama
	PANTALEO WA WAMALWA.
NAIDI	Luka Egessa
NAMAKANJA	Mangeni, Wafula, Ngolobe.
	OLWENI NYEMBI
NACHAAKI	Sunu, Okwonyo, Ondero.
	SUNU WA OLWENI NYEMBI
NANYANGA	Nangenge, Onyango Sigoma, Obongooya.
	NANGENGE WA SUNU

	OLWENI NYEMBI
NACHAAKI:	Sunu
	Okwenyo
	Ondero

	SUNU WA LWENI NYEMBI
NANYANGA:	Nangenge
	Onyango Sigona
	Obongooya

	NANGENGE WA SUNU
NASUBO:	Hadooke
	Ngweno Dwaara
	Odwooli.

	HADOKE WA NANGENGE
NANYANGA:	Nabbaya
	Obwaso Potero
	Enosi Onyango

	OBWASO WA HADOKE
NAMUHOOKOSI:	Abahana 3 Bongonge.

	ENOSI ONYANGO WA HADOKE.
NASIBUNG:	Samuel Wanyama
	David Mangeni

	AMUEL WANYAMA WA ENOSI ONYANGO
NAMUCHERE	Allan Wanyama
	Enosi Wanyama
NAMUGANDA	Waiswa Wanyama
	Kato, Nabangi, Hadoke.

	DAVID MANGENI WA ___ ONYANGO
NASICHONGI	Enosi Onyango
NASONGA	George Wangira

	NGWENO DWAARA WA NANGENGE
NAKUROYA:	Olowo Obbando
	Morris Onyango
	Francis Adenya

	OLOWO OBBANDA WA NGWENO DWAARA
NAJABI	Ngweno J.
NABUKA	Wanyama

	NGWENO II W'OLOWO OBBANDO
NABUKA	Wanyama

	MORRIS ONYANGO WA N'GWENO
NAKUHU I	Hillary Boniface Ngweno
	Anthony Onyango
	Archilens Oundo

	HILARY BONIFACE NGWENO
NAMUSUNGU	Abaana Bahana (2)
	ANTHONY ONYANGO WA MORRIS ONYANGO
NAMUDDE	Patrick Ngweno
	Henrey Muluka
	Namwanga Justin
	Archileus Sidda
	Regina Adikinyi
	ARCHILEUS OUNDO WA MORRIS ONYANGO
NAMUGABO:	Stephin Oundo
	Charles Oundo
	Joseph
NAMUGANDA	Morris Oundo
	Junior Oundo
	FRANCIS ADENYA WA N'GWENO DWAARA
NAMULUMBA	Wandera Black
	Syaalo
	WANDERA BLACK
NABULAGAYE:	
	ODWOOLI WA NANGENGE
NAMANGALE	Ogono Stephin
	Were Odwooli
NAKOOLO	Mikairi Ngweno
	Namuel Wanyama
NASONGA	Sotoka
	OGONO STEPHIN WA ODWOOLI
ADETI:	Okumu Wilfred
	Mudina
	Ouma Jackson
	Wanyama David
	Clement Kilo
	OKUMU WILFRED WA OGONO
NAHONE	Wanyama, Ngweno, Barasa Richard Buluma
NASUBO	Wandera Bamson, Sanya Fred, Moses Okumu
	MUDINA WA OGONO
NABOTWE	Sam Wandera
	Eriya Bwire
	OSINYA WA OGONO
?	David Ogono
	Silas Onyango
	WERE ODWOOLI WA ODOOLI
NAMUSIHO	Wandera
NASYENYA	Muzee
	WANDERA WA WERE
NGEMI	.....

../3.

196

NALYERO	Naloba Odwooli
	Bwire Fred
	MANUEL WANYAMA WA ODWOOLI
NASIHUNE	Enosi Onyango Luyafwa, Manuel Wanyama nakerama NASIHUNE niyobula,
	Oguttu Wilson
	Stephin Wafula
	Kwoba
	Oundo
	OGUTU WILSON WA MANUEL
NAMUTESO	
	STEPHIN WAFULA WA MANUEL
NALALA	Oliver
	WILLIAM KWOBA WA MANUEL
NAMUSOGA	....
	OUNDO WA MANUEL
NALALA:	....
	OKWENYO WA LWENI NYEMBI
NABONGO	Oguna
	Olowo
	OGUNA W'OKWENYO
NALYALI	Zablon Wambeto
	Asumanga George
	ZABLON WAMBETE W'OGUNA
NANYILALO	Wilson Oguna (Okumu)
	Yokana Egessa
NAMENYA	Abahana (4)
	WILSON OGUNA (OKUMU) WA ZABLON WAMBETE
NABURI	Ongudi, Wandera, Maliro
NAMUHOOKOSI	Omuhana mulala Yongene.
	YOKANA EGESSA WA ZABLON WAMBETE
NANYANGA	Ojiambo Egessa
	Wandera Egessa
NAMUKOBE	....
	ASUMANGA W'OGUNA
NAJABI	Onyango
	ONYANGO WA ASUMANGA
NAMUTESO	Wandera Moses
———	———
NACHAAKI II	**NACHINI WA OLWENI NYEMBI**
NANYANGA	Ouma Olyeddo
	Nachini Luyafwa Omijjo nakerama Nanyanga niyebulamo Matayo Matalo:
	OUMA ORYEDDO WA NACHINI
NAJABI	Bubolu

..../4.

BUBOLU WA OUMA ONYEDDO

NANYANGA   Nachiri II

Nadoke II

NACHINI WA BUBOLU

NAHUMACHI   Kenneth Bwire, Dev Wafula, Milton Barasa,
Vincent Tibiita, Makilin Wandera.

ONUJJO WA NACHINI

NANYANGA   Matayo Natalo

MATAYO NATALO WA OMUJJO

NAJABI: Owori John

Zablon Kitari

Jackson Onyango

OWORI WA MATAYO MATALO

NANULEMBO   Ouma Patrick

Walter Magambo

Bwire Nelson

NAMANGALE   Bwire

JACKSON ONYANGO WA MATAYO NATALO

NASIMALWA   Goofrey Onyango

Peter Onyango

Frod Onyango

Wandera

end.

53

NGWENO HADU MAHOLA

NAMUTAMBA, Namutamba yaali ohasi ya Awori Nahooli.

Abe BANDA badaha Lwande ababe abandu bachye babahonye eyeo, nga ABASIBIKA baali
badaha ohuseta enono ya BAHOOLI balasene habo, bu BAHOOLI nibecha eyiri Lwande
Wesonga nibamusaba ababe abandu bechye babahonye. Naye abandu ba Lwande nibaboola
bati liwenya omuhana wundi, olwohuba omuhana mulala sanyala ohwidisa amabanga
Kabandu, hu bulamu ABAHOOLI nibameda omuhana oyo NAMUTAMBA.

LWANDE WESONGA WA LWANDE BIRUNGO NAMUDU
(NAMUTAMBA): NGWENO MAHOLA.

NGWENO MAHOLA WA LWANDE WESONGA.

NADONWE	Dwobo nende Mulyaha
NALALA	Lwande II
NAMULWANI	Ojwangi Obinda
NADONWE II	Masaba Ngundira (Osinjo)
NASIBWOCHI	Mutika, Ngweno Sibera.

DWOBO WA NGWENO MAHOLA.

HAMAKANGALA	Ochwinga

OCHWINGA WA DWOBO

NEHOBA I	Oyula Wandera
NEHOBA II	Nambudye, Mangoni Henry, Okwomi, Mukaga.

OYULA WA OCHWINGA.

NALALA	Olowo, Thomas Ouma
NANYANGA	Ojiambo, Odundo
NASERA	Orabi

NAMBUDYE WA OCHWINGA.

NABONGO	Ochwinga
NALALA	Nyabbola, Siganda.

OKWOMI WA OCHWINGA

NALALA	Oyula yamukerema hu niyebulamo Ojiambo.

SIGANDA WA NAMBUDYE.

NANYANGA:	Amosi Egondi
	Yolamu Hasibante.

YOLAMU HASIBANTE WA SIGANDA.

NABULO	Charles Onyango

PASCAL ONYANGO

NABUKAKI	Mukaga
	Owori
	Siganda

MULYAHA WA NGWENO MAHOLA.

NABONGO	Andrew Nyanja
	Omolo
	Ianduha

ANDREW NYANJA WA MULYAHA.

NAMULUMBA	Okuku
NASUBO	James Ogoola
NALWENGE	William Odera
	Barnabba Masinde
	Yovani Wafula
	Nathanael Ouma
NAMIKANGALA:	Ochilo, Wanyama.
	Wangalwa Nende Omala
NASUBO	Mulyaha
	Lwande

OKUKU WA NADREW NYANJA.

NAMENYA:	Dwire

JAMES OGOOLA WA ANDREW NYANJA.

NAMULUNDU:	Vincent Lugendo
	Wilberbad Sifuna
	Sylvester Dwire
	Patrick Gozza
	Okumu
NASIBAYI	Wandera

WILLIAM ODERA WA ANDREW NYANJA.

NAMULOBA	Moses Ouma
	Daudi Wanyama
	Salomon Mangeni

BARNABBA MASINDE WA ANDREW NYANJA.

NAHABI	Wandera

YOVANI WAFULA WA ANDREW NYANJA

NANGOHO	Dwire Joseph
NASINYAMA	Henery Ojiambo

NATHANAEL OUMA WA ANDREW NYANJA.

NATANZANIA	George Opiyo
	Charles Odongo
	James Okello
	Stephin Hamala.

OMOLLO WA MULYAHA

ERIEZA LWANDE

ERIEZA LWANDE WA OMOLLO

NAMUTALA	Edward Wasike
	Albert Siminyu
	Paul Nyegenye.

OSODO WA.........

NANYIBBONI	Dwire

....../3.

—✂

CHILLO WA ANDREW NYANJA.

Wanyama

Wangalwa

WANGALWA WA ANDREW NYANJA

NADONGO	Nyanja

ONLLA WA ANDREW NYANJA

NANOOHO	Ogutu

Namulu

Masiga

VINCENT LWANDE WA: ....

NAMUGANDA:	"
NALALA	"

LWANDE II WA NGWENO MAHOLA

LWANDE MULYAHA WA LWANDE II

Dangi

DANGI WA LWANDE MULYAHA.

NASUBO	Lwande

LWANDE WA DANGI

NAKOOLI	Yowasi Buluma

Erukana Wandera

Yolamu Mabbachi

Dani Were

YOWASI BULUMA WA LWANDE

NALIALI	Living Wanyama

Gidioni Dwire

Dickson Magero

ERUKANA WANDERA WA LWANDE

NAMULUNDU	Oundo

YOLAMU NABBACHI WA LWANDE

NANYANGA	Richard Egessa

Aggrey Lwande

William Wandera

Honery Namalwa

MULYAHA WA LWANDE

NALYALI	Francisco Ojiambo

Rowrence Wanyama

AGGREY LWANDE WA YOLAM MABBACHI

NABAHO.	Nafwa

Egossa

Nabuyiya

Maritino Otyola

Elezali Guloba

...../4.

202

	EGESSA WA............
NAMUKOBE	"
	DANGI WA LWANDE
NAMAKANGALA	"
	JEREMIAH NGWENO WA......
NAMAINDI	Absolom Masinde
	Peter Egessa.
	ALONI ADIKA WA...
NAMUKUBA	Dwire
	NGWENO MAHOLA WA LWANDE WESONGA
NAMULWANI:	Ojwangi
	OJWANGI WA NGWENO MAHOLA
NABAHO	Wandera
	Omwichango
	WANDERA WA OJWANGI
NAMANGALE	Achoode
	Ognando
	Penda
	Ongango
	WANDERA WA PENDA
	ONGANGO WA WANDERA
	Dangali
	OMWICHANGO WA OJWANGI
NEHOBA:	Boloki
	BOLOKI WA OMWICHANGO
NABWOFWOYO	Okombo
	Makaada
	Obbanda Sirwano
NAMUKUBA	Boloki Pantaleo
	MAKAADA WA BOLOKI
NAPUNYI	Manuel Ojwangi
	MANUEL OJWANGI WA MAKAADA
Nakuhu	Muluka
NAMAKANGALA I	Ojwangi Boloki, Obbanda.
NAMAKANGALA II	Makaada,
NAMADI	Gablier ONYANGO
	SIRWANO OBBANDA WA BOLOKI
NAMUSIHO	Benjamin Machyo
Nabongo	Maloba Akisoferi
	Ojiambo
	Makoha

.../5.

NAMUDDE: Onyango
            Egossa

                        BENJAMIN MACHYO WA OBBANDA
NANGANDA: Obanda
            Wejuli,
            Boloki
            Omwichango
            Ngweno.
                        MALOBA AKISOFERI WA OBBANDA
NANJOSI   "
NADECHO   Obbanda

                        OJIAMBO WA SIRWANO OBBANDA.
NAMANGALE   Amuria
            Willy Ojiambo
            Magume
            Obbanda

                        MAKOHA WA SIRWANO OBBANDA.
   ?   Mwichango
            Obbanda

8

BATALEO BOLOKI WA BOLOKI

NASUBO I	Malingu,
	Dwire
NAPUNYI	Opondo
	Mugeni
NASUBO II	Mangeni
	Obanda

MALINGU WA PANTALEO BOLOKI

NAKURUKU	Boloki

OPONDO WA PANTALEO BOLOKI

NAMULUNDU	"

MANGENI WA PANTALEO BOLOKI

NGWENO MAHOLIA WA LWANDE WESONGA

NABONWE II   Masaba

MASABA WA NGWENO MAHOLA

Ngundira (Osinjo)

NGUNDIRA WA MASABA

NAMAINDI   Dujubo

Mwanga

Indoro

NADWANGI   Zefania Okumu

Eward Owori

Ongomo

ZEFANIYA OKUMU WA NGUNDIRA OSIJJO.

NASUBO I   Wandera

Mika Dwiro

Okollo

NAKULO   Ojwangi

NASUBO II   Ouma

EDWARD OWORI WA NGUNDIRA OSIJJO

NANYANGA   Wycliffe Oundo

WERE WA......

Asango

Onyango

Odungo

NGUNDIRA:

Bati yaali nende ebyayo ebingi, naye bamuletera ok
bindi bati yayenge, naye yaboola ati, ese omwono nd.
nga hu Ngundira chyango echi mbula onanjayire, nih
ohwatula erita NGUNDIRA, erita niye OSINJO.

NGWENO MAHOLA WA LWANDE WESONGA.

NABONWE   Masaba

MASABA WA NGWENO MAHOLA.

Awori

Ogaanga

Onyango Hatera

Onyango Odyonga

AWORI WA MASABA

NADONGO   Lwande

HOBA   Gwato

Mugenya

EYAILA   Odunga

	DANIEL WANJALA
NAMUKUBA	Nekasio Egessa

	ODUNGA WA MUGENYA
NANDAKO II	Lwande
	Awori
NACIWERE	Lwande
NANDAKO II	Mugenya
NACHAAKI I	Ouma
NACHAAKI II	Lwande (Monday)
	Mayende

	AWORI II WA ODUNGA
NANKIMA	Nanyanga

	LWANDE WA ODUNGA
NACHAAKI	Mugenya

	MUGENYA WA ODUNGA
NADAARE	Ojiambo
	Bisse
	Samba
	Daniel ~~Wanyama~~ WANJALA
	Ojuku

	DANIEL WANJALA WA MUGENYA
NAMUKOBE I	Mukaga,
	Were
	Okello
NANYANGA	Wilson Nayaala
	Dwire
	Barasa
	Ojiambo
NAMULUNDU	Onyango
NATIKOKO	Egessa
NAMUTKOBE II	Okumu
	Wafula
	Wandera

	MUKAGA WA DANIEL WANJALA
NAMAINDI	Wanyama (Were)

	WILSON NEYAALA WA DANIEL WANJALA
NAJABI	Toyota
	Wabwire
	Daniel Wanjala
	Mangoni

	AWORI WA MASABA
NAMANGALE	Slvanus Wangalwa
	Cosma Gwato
	William Sikaala
NAMUDDE	Ogooya Anderea
	Slyvanus Wangalwa Wa Awori
NAMULUCHA	John Wafula
	Fredrick Bwiro
	Vincent Opio
	NELSON ODONGO
NANYANGA	Andrew Bwiro
	Gedi Sangalo
	John Wanyoma
	CORNEL OKELLO
NASINYAMA	
NAILABI	Wanyoma
	JOHN WAFULA WA SILYVANUS WANGALWA.
KABALEGA	Wanyama
	Onyango
	Oune
	Wandera
	FREDRICK BWIRE WA SLYVANUS WANGALWA
ADETI	Saiya W
	Wandera
	Barasa
NAYINGANI	Opio
	Okello
NAMUTINDYE	Joseph
	Ogutu
	VINCENT OPIYO WA SILYVANUS WANGALWA
	Awori, Osbon
	OKELO CORNEL
NASUDO	Sunday Denes
	Sam Barasa
	WILLAM SIKALA WA AWORI
NAMANGALE	Ogooya Anderea
	Jared Wandera
Nalala:	George Bubolu
	Joshua Ogutu
	NGWENO MAHOLA WA LWANDE WESONGA
NASIBWOCHI	Mutika
	MUTIKA WA NGWENO MAHOLA
?	MUTIKA WA NGWENO MAHOLA
	Wanga
	Bhaali
	Kodeka

208

ENNALI WA MUTIKA

FUDIEMBE

FUDIEMBE WA ENNALI

NALIALI — Musa Fidiembe

MUSA FUDIEMBE WA FUDIEMBE

WANYANGA — Yosia Gusinja

James Okinda

NAMULUNDU — Enosi Otika

Jonathan Ouma

Mangeni

Buchunju

NAMUKOMBE — Erieza Mugenda

Grisom Wandera

NAMULUNDU — Abisayi Wanyama

NAMUYEE — Ouma Daudi

YOSIA GUSINJA WA MUSA FUDIEMBE

NASIBIKA — Wafula

Wanyama

NASIMALWA — Wandera

Ouma Patrick

NAMURWA I — Ojiambo

Bwiro

NAMURWA II — Mugeni

Bwiro

Mangeni

JAMES OKINDA WA MUSA FUDIEMBE

NAHABI I — Machyo Alupakusadi

Wanyama

NAHABI II — Darasa

Martin Musa Fudiembe

ENOSI OTIKA WA MUSA FUDIEMBE

NANGAYO — Egessa

YANASANI OUMA WA MUSA FUDIEMBE

Musisi

Mutika

.../

	WANYAMA WA DANIEL BULUMA
NACHAKI	Muganda
	WAFULA WA DANIEL BULUMA
NABAHOLO	Muganda
	Dwiro
NACHAAKI	Daniel Buluma
	OKOMBA WA MUGANDA
NAMULWAANI	Eridadi Ouma
	Okumu
NAKIROYA	Wangira
NAMAKANGALA	Osinya wa Eridadi
	Odwori
	DANI NALEBE WA MUGANDA
NYARUWA	Kadeka
	Muganda
	Judh Wanga
	Ochoola
	DAUDI OUMA WA MUGANDA
NAYIGAGE	Wafula
	Muganda
	Wandera Musa
	NGWENO MAHOLA WA LWANDE WESONGA
NAMULWANI	Ngweno Sisera
	NGWENO SISERA WA NGWENO MAHOLA
NAHUMACHI	Hamala Halanga
	Makuda
	HAMALA WA NGWENO SISERA
NAMANGALE	Obwora
	OBWORA WA HAMALA
NAMAINDI	Agoola
	Odieso
NACHONGA	Zekalia Osolo
	ODIESO WA OBWORA
NABONGO	Wasike
	WASIKE WA ODIESO
NAHOSOHO I	Juma
NAHOSOHO II	Okochi
	Obwora
	Okoohi
	Ogutu
	Odwori

.../13.

NASUBO I	George Hamala
	Richard Ngweno
	Wilson Ogana
	Agoola Edward Namangale
	Samuel Makuda
	Christopher Nachonga
	Friudi Odwori

NASUBO II	Wycliffe Ouma
	Fred Osolo

NAMULEMBO	Obwora Isaac
	Nachonga Opyo
	Okello
	Namwonja

OGUTU WA ZAKALIA OSOLO

?	
"	Odioso
	Geofrey Ogutu
	Hamala

GEORGE HAMALA WA ZAKALIA OSOLO

NAMACHOLE	Situma
	Charles Dwana
	Tom Mulongo

NENOBA	Nathan Hamala
	Aludda
	Peter Henry Hamala

RICHARD NGWENO WA ZAKALIA OSOLO

?	
"	JOShua Osolo

WILSON OGANA WA ZAKALIA OSOLO

?	
"	Daniel Auma
	James Ognana
	Peter Ogfana
	Tom Osola
	Fred Ognana

ERASTO OBWORA WA MAKOHA LUNGASA

NASINYAMA	John Makoha

JOHN MAKOHA WA ERASTO OBWORA

NAMBIRI	Jackson Osolo
	Francis Makoha
	Benlicto Obwora
	Ochiongi Mayu
	Budoro
	Idamba

WALTER MAKUDA WA ZAKALIA OSOLO

?	Dvani Wandora
	Dolifis Wandora

FRED NGWENO WA.........

?	
	Kenneth Ngweno
	Anthony Ngweno

MAKUDA WA NGWENO SISARA

NAMANGALE	

MBALWA WA......

NAMANGALE   Paulino Omedda
Ognale
Okuku

PAULINO OMEDDA WA MBALWA

NASINYAMA   Alfred Sisera

OUMA WA MAKUDA

NABONGO   Esekiel Makuda
Onyango
Ochiengi
Wandera

NANYIFWA   Zablon Wanyama
Ahenda Benjamin

EZEKIEL MAKUDA WA OUMA

NAMUDDE   Samuel Makuda

NAMUHOMA   Ouma

NASONGA   Ochieno

NAMAKANGALA   Ouma

OCHIENGI WA OUMA

NAMULUMBA   Ouma

ZABLON WANYAMA WA OUMA

NAMAINDI I   ..

NAMAINDI II   ...

NACHAAKI   Ngweno

Makuda

BENJAMIN AHENDA WA OUMA

NABURI   Ouma

NAMAKWE   Ouma

NGWENO SISERA WA NGWENO MAHOLA

NAMULEMBO   Halanga.

HALANGA WA NGWENO SISERE

.:....   Olunjalu

OLUNJALU WA HALANGA

NAMAYERO   Nicodemu Ngweno

NICODEMUS NGWENO WA OLUNJALU

NAHOOLI   Ngweno

APIYO WA HALANGA

NALALA   Nangweri

Ngweno (Alego)

ERASTO OBWORA WA MAKOHA

NASINYAMA   John Makoha
Walter Makuda
Fred Ngweno Lununi

NABORO   Patrick Ojiambo
Vilian Edbang Makoha

....../15.

212

6₇

NAMUNULI	Enosi Ochiengi
NACHAAKI	Godfrey Osodo
	Luka Stephin Opyo

MAKUNDA WA NGWENO SISERA

NAMBANJA	Munyuwalo
	Makoha
NASONGA	Mbalwa
NAMANGALE	Ouma

MAKOHA WA MAKUDA

Ouma luyafwa, Makoha yakerema muha simwana, na Makuda Obbara.

NADIBBONYO	Buluma
	Ohaba
NAMAINDI I	Jacob Bwire
NAMAINDI	Jeremiah Wandera
	Ombunga

Obwora niyafwa Makoha Lugasa yekerama Nachong Erasto Obwora niyebulamo Erasto Obwora.

BULUMA WA MAKOHA

NALALA	Jastas Namanyi
	Wawuya

JASTAS NAMANYI WA BULUMA

NAHULO	Ojiambo

OHABA WA MAKOHA LUNGASA

NACHONGA	Solomon Makoha

SOLOMON WA OHABA

?	BARASA
	Ochiengi
	Makuda
	Makuda
	Nafwa
	Sihaba

JACOB BWIRE WA MAKOHA

NABURI	Julias Obwora
	Israel Onyango

OGESSA WA JULIAS ODWORA

NABBYANGU	?

JEREMIAH WANDERA WA MAKOHA

ADETI	Augustino Omondi
	Wycliffe Makoha
	Slyvaster Ochiengi

AUGUSTINO OMONDI WA JEREMIAH WANDERA

NASUBO	William Omondi

WYCLIFFE MAKOHA WA J. WANDERA

?	Juma

OMBUNGA WA MAKOHA LUNGASA

?	Washingston Juma
	Albert Okumu

Agamay Taabu
Ojwangi

WASHINGTON JUMA WA OMBUNGA

Ogola
Odwori

LWANDE BIRUNGO WA NGWENO

NABONGO   Lwande Wesonga

LWANDE WESONGA WA LWANDE BIRUNGO

NAMUDU   Lwande Mulyamboka

LWANDE MULYAMBOKA WA LWANDE W.

?   Wangoho Rafwaki I

WANGOHO RAFWAKI WA LWANDE MBOKA

NASIBIKA   Mukongo

MUKONGO WA WANGOHO RAFWAKI I

NAMANGANDA   Wanjala
NACHWERE   Wangoho Pendo II

WANJALA WA MUKONGO

NAPUNYI   Oduyo
Mayingu
Wangoho III

ODUYO WA WANJALA

NAMAINDI   Roman Cusino & Macial Doloko
NALWENGE   Longino, Ouma, John Ogema & Macial Doloko

ROMANO CUSINO WA ODUYO

NAMUSIHO   Domiano Ouma

LONGINUS OGOHA WA ODUYO

NASUBO   Ogola, John Ogema,
Mbok Clement and Patrick Okumu.

JOHN OGEMA

NABULINDO   Charles Wanjala
NANGWE   Joseph Oduyo
NABULINDO   Luberuto Malingu
Patrick Mugeni
Morris Cusino
Fred Makoha
NENAME   Taabu Robert

CUSINO ROMANO

ADETI   Patrick Ouma
Ogola
Oduyo
Tambiti
Mbolu

NAMUBACHI   Bubolu

NABURI   John Wandera

NAMUTALA   Fred Ochiengi
Godfrey Obbanda.

DOMIANO CUMA WA ROMANO CUSINO

NABULO   Oduyo
Kabuli

.../17.

69

LWANDE WESONGA WA LWANDE BINUNGO

NAMUBU	Lwande Mulyamboka
NABILYACHO	Odemi

ODEMI WA LWANDE MBOKA

	Muhula
	Odemi

MUHULA WA ODEMI

NASUBO I	Wanyande
NASUBO II	Ngweno (Osiyo)
NABBONYO	Ongenge

WANYANDE WA MUHULA

NACHONGA I	Haluba
NACHONGA II	Petero Nabahunya

PETERO NABAHUNYA WA WANYANDE

NAKUHU	Joseph Wandera
NAKIROYA	Nabbangi
	Ouma

NGENO (OSIYO) WA MUHULA

NASABI	Asumanga
	Wilson Wangalwa
	Sengeri

WILSON WANGALWA WA NGWENO OSIYO

NACHWELE	Wandera
	Mangeni
	Ouma
	Onyango

ONGENGE WA MUHULA

NACHIMO	Yeremia Ochimi
	Okello
	Ajongo

YEREMIA OCHIMI WA ONGENGE

NAJAAYA	Mikaya Namangale
	Mesusera Muhula

OKELLO WA ONGENGE

	Mayo, Muhula

MIKAYA NAMANGALE WA YEREMIA OCHIMI

NAWONGA	Ongenge James
NAMUDEMO	Ochimi
	Muhula Daglas N

MESUSERA MUHULA WA YEREMIAH OCHIMI

NAMUDAIRWA	Wandera
	Muhula
NAKOYI	Ongenge
	Ochimi
	Okumu
NAMANYI	Barasa

OJONGO WA ONGENGE

NAKEWA	Odemi
	Nasanael Ouma

...../17.

215

-18-

<u>NASANAEL OUMA WA OJONGO</u>

Abangi

Okollo

<u>ODEMI WA ODEMI</u>

Mayondo

Ogulo

<u>OKUMU WA ODEMI</u>

NALUKADA	Ajongo yakerema muha simwana
NAKIROYA	Matayo Odemi

<u>MATAYO ODEMI WA ODEMI</u>

NACHWERE	Onyango
	Ngweno Osiyo
NAHABI	Obbakiro

_____ONGA WA LWANDE MULUNGO.

"KAGENDA AMALAKULE KA NEILMA"

OMALA WA KAGENDA

ABAHASI BA KAGENDA

NABWALA	Omala,
	Sichimi
NANGOMA	Waecha Ofumbuha
NANJOWA	Muhachi
	Ngundira

OMALA WA KAGENDA

NAKUHU	Lwande.

LWANDE WA OMALA.

NABONGO	Ndumwa
NASINYAMA	Achiengi
NAMANGALE 1.	Okuku
NAMANGALE II	Malibo

NDUMWA WA LWANDE

NAMENYA	Ochaso
NALALA	Clijjo
NAMENYA	Ohuya

OCHASO WA NDUMWA

NAHABI	Owayya
NAHABI	Yafesi Namenya
NAHABI	Kosea Junge
NAMBURBI	Charles Oundo
NAHABI	Iginatiyo Mudambo

OLIJJO WA NDUMWA

NAHABI	Stephine Ndumwa
NAMUKUDA	Mutanda
	Nonga
NACHAAKI I	Wafula
NACHAKI 11	OMALA
	WILSON OPIYO
NACHAKI IV	Yovan Makoha
NACHAKI V	Yanasani Godan

STEPHIN NDUMWA WO CLIJJAO

NABYANGU	Mangoli
Nachaki I	Dudaha
NACHAKI II	Ndumwa

BUDAHA WA STEPHIIN NDUMWA

NASUBO	

(1)

OMAALA

MAKOHA OSOGGO

NASIBIINGA	Ayimbi
	Omaala
NAMUHUMWA	Oguba
TEREZA OKOOLA	Alfred Bwire
	Pascal Ouma
	John Ogutu
	Manuel Mangeni

ALFRED BWIRE WA MAKOHA SOGGO

NABURI	Okochi Bwire
	Julias Juma
	Majoni
	Peter Mayende
NASERA	Jophiter Barasa
	Moses Onyango

PASCAL OUMA WA MAKOHA SOGGO

NALALA	Musumba Ouma
	Patrick Lumumba

JOHN OGUTU WA MAKOHA SOGGO

NASIKAANI	Ouma
	Ogemba
	Teresa
	Sitabi

MANUEL MANGENI WA MAKOHA SOGGO

NAHULO	Ogemba Francico

OGEMBA WA KUBADI

NAMANGALE	Mangeni Ogemba

MANGENI WA OGEMBA

NANYIREMI	Stanley Wanyama
	Bwire Wilber

STANELY WANYAMA WA MANGENI

NASITWOKI	Mukaga Wanyama
	Friday Wanyama
	Odembo Wanyama

BWIRE WILBER WA MANGENI

NAMULUNDU	Wangira Robert

end

	TEFIRO WAFULA WOLIJJO
NAMAINDI	Erisa Mangoni
NAMINDI	Ochaso
	ERISA MANGENI WA TEFIRO WAFULA
Nahasoho	Wafula Juma
	OPIO WILSON
NAMAKANGALA	Olijo,
	Omala
	Wafula
	Nahulo
	Okumu
	JUMA WA ERISA NANGENI
NAMUTENDE	"
NAMAKANGALA	"
	ALFRED OMALA WA OLIJJO
NAMUFUTA	"
NAKALYOKO	Dwire
NAKALYOKO	Ochieno
NAKALYOKO	Kagenda
Nakalyoko	Okumu
	OCHIENO WA ALFRED OMALA
NAPUNYI	"
	NONGA WA CLIJJO
NEHODA	Achwada
	WILSON OPIYO WA CLIJJO
NAMAKANGALA I	Okijjo
NAMAKANGALA II	Wafula
NAMAKANGALA III	Okuku
NAMAKANGALA IV	Nahulo
Nalwnge I	Ouma
Nalwenge II	Wandera
NAMAKANGALA V	Majoni
NAMAKANGALA VI	Osaamo
NAMAKANGALA VII	Musumba (Yafwa)
Namulundu	Bitijei
	Junior
	Birungi
	CLIJJO WA OPIYO WILSON
NAMULUNDU	Simon
	Birungi
	Junior
NAMUGANDA	"
NAMUNYANKOLE	"

...../3.

220

	WAFULA WA OPIYO WILSON
NAFWOFWOYO	"
	MAKOHA YOVAN WA OLIJJO
NAPUNYI	Mayindi
NAPUNYI	Ouma
NAPUNYI	Wandora
Nakooli	Majoni
NAKOOLI	Oboto
NAKOOLI	Sajja
NAKOOLI	Opondo
NAKOOLI	Nabuhya
NAKOOLI	"
NAMAYOGA	Okello
	Makaanda Ojiambo
	OUMA WA YOVANI MAKOHA
NAHULO	Amosi
	Jamy
	Mukisa
	YONASANI GADAN WA OLIJJO
NAMAKANGALA	
NAMUFUTA	Samuel Oundo
NASONGA	Omala
NAMAKANGALA	Aringo
	YAFESI NAMENYA WA OCHASO
NAMAINDI	Wandera
	CHARLES OUNDO WA OCHASO
NAJABI	Wanyama
NAJABI	Ochaso
NAMAKANGALA	Mugeni
NAMAKANGALA	Ochaso
	KOSEA JUNGE WA OCHASO
?	BBITA
	IGINATIYO MUDAMBO WA OCHASO
NAMAINDI	Tanga
	WANYAMA WA CHARLES OUNDO
NANYIHODO	"

.../4.

	ACHIENGI WA LWANDE
NAMULEMBO	Gaunya Oguro
NAMULEMBO	Chwango
NAMULEMBO	Okuku Nalibbo
NAMULEMBO	Okuku Ngendo
	GAUNYA OGURO WA ACHIENGI
NABUNJE	Ombale
NABUNJE	Ochiengi Okaalo
NBUNJE	Darasa Oguru
NABUNJE	Peter Kadimba
NALWENGE	Pantaleo Wandera
NALWENGE	Juma Lucas
NAJABI	C. Kwahde Agunga Kongo.
	CHWANGO WA ACHIENGI
NAMUSIHO	Mugenda
NAMUSIHO	Omala
NAMUSIHO	Wandexa
	OKUKU MALIBBO WACHENGI
NAJABI	Oundo
NAJABI	Abbele Yosamu Wanyama
NAJABI	Aimbi
NAJABI	Clement Lwande Oguro
NAJABI	Ochiengi Semeyo
NAJABI	Pantaleo Oguro
NAJABI	John Omala
	OHUYAA OHONJO WA NDUMWA
NALUBANGA	Cheto
NALUBANGA	Okumu Nakubo
	OHETO WA OHUTAX
?	Omala Lwande
	OKUMU NAKURO WA OHUYAA
NABULINDO	?
	ERINEYO KATA WA OGENDA
Nahasoho	Wandera
NAHASOHO	Ouma
NAHASOHO	Bwire
NAHASOHO	Mangoni

..../5.

WANDERA WA KATA

NAMULUNDU	GUMA wa Kata ℝ\ℙ.
MAGO,ARE	Abahana 3

OGEMBA WA ACHIENGI

NACHONGA	Kubadi
NACHONGA	Nduku

KUBADI WA OGEMBA

NANYIFWA	Okello Mayunga
NAMUDDE	Ogemba II
"	Oundo
"	Wafwa

OGEMBA II WA KUBADI

NAMANGALE	Kata
"	John Osaalo
"	OKELLO AUGUSTINO

OSAALO JOHN WA OGEMBA II

NAMANYI	Obukya MAKOHR.

OKELLO AUGUSTINO WA OGEMBA II

NANUFUTA	Ouma
	Opiyo

OUNDO WA KUBADI

NACHAAKI	Omala
NAMIRIPO	Okello
NAJABI	Wandera

OMALA WA OUNDO

NAHABI I	Bendicto Wangalwa
NAHABI II	Anyango (Wanyama)
	Wandera Stephen
	Albert Okumu
	Barasa Stephin
	Ojiambo Milton
NAHASOHO	Alex Juma
	Wilson Mangeni
NAKOOLO	Oundo
	Bendicto
NEWUNJE	Egessa Wilber
	Ouma Stephine
NAMAKWA	Wafula
	Sanya

ANYANGO (WANYAMA) WA OMALA

NAMUKUBA	Robert

WANDERA STEPHIN WA OMALA

NAMUMALI	Leonald Wandera
	Moses

ALEX JUMA WA OMALA

NEBERE: Dwire Patrick

Ouma

Oundo

WILSON MANGENI WA OMALA

NAMALELE   Wandera (Solo)
Godfrey Dwire

WANDERA WA OUNDO

NAMWAYA   Kubadi
Oundo
Wafula
Peter Ouma
Hagai
Godfrey

OSAALO WA MAYUNGA WA KUBADI

NANYIFWA   Okuku Rabwogi
Makoha Sogo

OKUKU RABWOGI WA OSAALO

OHETO WA OHUTAA

?   Ouma Edward
Wasike

MAKOHA WA OSAALO MAYUNGA

NAMULU   Ayimbi
Omala

AYIMBI WA MAKOHA

NAMBASI   Aggrey Musungu
Peter Ouma
Joseph Majimbo
Clement Lwande

AGGREY MUSUNGU WA AYIMBI

NAKOMOLO   Fred Wanyma
Simon Dwire

PETER OUMA WA AYIMBI
NAMUKEMO   Elijah Peter

OMALA WA MAKOHA

NAJABI   Milton Taabu Omala
Wilson Mangeni

MILTON TAABU OMALA WA OMALA

NAHASOHO   Benard Sanya
Wilber Ojiambo
Onyango Geofrey

OMALA WA KAGENDA

?   Onyoobo
Ogemba

ONYOBO WA OMALA

NAHALANDA WA ONYOBO

NAPUNYI   Julias Wangalwa
Ouma (Pusi)

..../7.

JULIUS WANGALWA WA NAMALANDA
NASIYEE	Ogutu
NAJABI	Wandera

OUMO PUSI WA NAMALANA

NABBYANGU	Mangeni Jackson
NAMENYA	Wandera
	Wanyama
	Juma

WANDERA WA OUMA (PUSI)

NEKUNYE	Wafula
	David

WANYAMA WA OUMA (PUSI)

NATONGI	Mugeni
	Loenald Ouma
	George Wanyama

JUMA WA OUMA (PUSI)

?	Onyango
	Dani Ouma
	James

SICHIMI WA KAGENDA

2

LWANDE WESONGA

NEAHAMA	Kagenda

KAGENDA WA LWANDE WESONGA

NABWALA	Omala Nende Sichimi
NANGOMA	Wanga Ofumbuha
Nanjowa	Muhachi Nende Ngundira

WANGA OFUMBUHA WA KAGENDA

NACHAKI	Ogaara
	Obbiero
	Sichimi

NAHONE	Syawola
NAMULEMBO	Ogaara
	Sichimi
	Omuli
NANJOWA	Muhachi

OGAARA WA WANGA OFUMBUHA

NAHASOHO	Michael Okuruma
	Edward Mugeni
	Dishan Okello
	James Mukaga

OBIERO WA WANGA OFUMBUHA

NABWALA	Hamonye
	Ouma Osodyo

HAMONYE WA OBIERO

?	Muhenyo
	Nasibu Obero

OMULI WA WANGA OFUMBUHA

NAMUDDE	Hamonye
NAMIRIPO	Muhadda

NASIBO OBBIERO WA HAMONYE

NANGANDA	William Nachoye

.../8.

WILLIAM NACHOYEE WA NASIDU OBERO

NAMWALIRA   Okuku
    Ouma
    Wafula
NALWENGE   Ouma

SYAWOLA WA WNAGA OFUMBUHA

NAHULO   Odyanga
    Mukuhu
NADEKE   Ongwe

ODYANGA WA WANGA OFUMBUHA

NAJUNHA   Orodi
NAMULUNDU   Dwonya
NAMAINDI   Ongodde

ORODI WA ODYANGA

NASIBAYI   John Ngwabe
    Onyanga II Erisa
NAMUKUBA   Mageni
NAMULUNDU   Okuku

JOHN NGWABE WA ORODI (MAWAA)

NADEKE   Orodi II

ONYANGA II WA ORIDI (MAWAA)

NALALA   GMP (William Ouma)
    Orodi Wycliffe
    Samusoni Kwoba
    Osinya

MANGENI WA ORODI (MAWAA)

NAMUDDE   ?
NAMUHOMA   Sunday

SUNDAY WA MANGENI

?   Wankya

ONGWE WA SYAWOLA

NABAHOLO   Oherero
    Wanga

OHEBERO WA ONGWE

NAMULUNDU   Bwonya
    Daudi Magunda

DAUDI MAGUNDA

NAMUDDE I   Dwonya luyafwa Daudi Magunda nakerema NAMUDDE I
    niyebulamo Wilson Mahulo nende Living Chobero

NAHULO WILSON WA DAUDI MAGUNDA

NALALA   Wandera Simon
    Patrick Odwori

LIVINSTON OHEBERO WA DI MAGUNDA

NANGENYA   Living Chebero
NAMURWA   Odianga
    Onyango Stephin
    Owori Moses

....../9.

226

NAMULEMBO	Juma Ohebero
	Mugeni Ohebero
NAJABI	Okochi Ohebero

WANGA WA ONGWE

NAMWENGE	Barasa
	Mulyedi Agaitano

BARABARA WANANGA

NANYANGA	Ouma (Humber) Julias
	Andrew (Magero) Wanga

OUMA (HUMBER) JULIAS

NANGWE	?
NAKIROYA	Bwire
	Mugeni
	Egessa
	Wandera Benard

AGAITANO MULYEDI WA WANGA

NAHABI	Yamukerama niyebulamu Wanjala
NANYANGA	Barabara yamukerama muha Barabara mwanangina, Huniyebula Barabara nende Wanjala.

SICHIMI WA WANGA OFUMBUHA

?	Dibondo
	Ognara II
	Mungweno
	Paul Musungu
	Zakalia Sibero
	Daali

DIBONDO WA SICHIMI

NASIHUNE	Batolomayo Bwire
	Samuel Wandera
NAHASOHO	Mahondo Eriakimu

BATOLOMAYO BWIRE WA DIBONDO

NAHONE	George Mulucha
	Gilbert Bwire

GEORGE MULUCHA WA BATOLOMAYO BWIRE

NAMUHOKOSI	Majaliwa
	Batolomayo Bwire

GILBERT BWIRE WA BATOLOMAYO BWIRE

NAMIRIPO	Batolomay Bwire

OGAARA II WA SICHIMI

NAHASOHO	Edward Mugeni
	James Bwire
	Dishani Okello

ANDREW (MAGERO) WANGA WA BARABARA

NAMUDDE	Bosco
	Wanyama
NABAKOOLWE·	John Mangeni
	Bwire David
	Egessa

....10.

TAIDOR NGUNDIRA WA OMOLO

NALWENGE	Yowana Mujabi
NALUKAADA	Alexander Wanga
NAMULEMBO	Slivester Ochieno
	Christin.

YOWANA MUJABI WA TAIDOR NGUNDIRA

?	Benard Mujabi
	Boniface Owino Mujabi
	Peter Mujabi
	Michael Mujabi
	Okello Mujabi

ALEXANDER WANGA WA TAIDOR NGUNDIRA

| NAMULEMBO | Michael Omondi |
| | Walter Ojwangi |

MORRIS OGANI ODOOL

ADETI	Fedrick Barasa
	Paul Ogani
ADETI II	Odwori Ogaani
	Vicent Owino

Wanga OFUMBUHA

| NANJOWA | Muhachi |

MUHACHI WA WANGA OFUMBUHA

| NAHULO | Oheto |
| ADETI | Mulayaa |

NAKOOLI HAUNWA

OHETO WA MUHACHI

| NABONGO | Obbiero |

OBBIERO WOHETO

| NAMULEMBO | Oheto II |
| | Ouma |

HAUNWA WA MUHACHI

| NABONGO | Obbiero |
| | Kagenda |

OBBIERO WA HAUNWA

NAMAINDI	Gawunya
BADUNI	Ngabi
NABUKAKI	Magero

GAWUNYA WOBBIERO

NASIWE	Okochi
NAMBENGERE	Kanoti
	Oligo

MULAYAA MUHACHI

| ADETI | Oligo |
| | Ongala |

OLIGO WA MULAYAA

| NABONWE | Oduki |
| | Ombogo |

MUGENI WA OLIGO
ONGALA WA MULAYA

NAKUHU	Ojwangi
	Osinya
NAMUNYEKERA	Ouma.

.../12.

BOSCO WA ANDREW (MAGERO) WANEA

NAMUSOGA	Eric Ivan
NAKIROYA	Deness

ORODI WYCLIFFE WA ERISA ODYANGA

NAMULUNDU	Jack Laban
NACHAAKI	Dauso Bwire (ongodde)
	Fred Orodi

SAMUEL WANDERA WA DIBONDO

NANYANGA	Stephin Dwire
NAMAKANGALA	DIBONDO
NAHONE	Geofrey Oundo, George Mulucha
	Aggrey Bwire.

ERIAKIMU NAHONDO WA DIBONDO

NAHWAYA	Wycliffe Mulucha, Bwire Henry, Sanya Mangweno.
NAMULEZI	
NAHONE	Ojiambo, Omaajjo.

MUGWENO WA DIBONDO

NASIYE	Zakaliya Sibeero
	Paul Musungu

ZAKALYA SIBEERO WA MUNGWENO

NAMULUNDU	Wilson Ouma

PAUL MUSUNGU WA ZAKALYA SIBEERO

NAMULUNDU	Absolom Magaga
	Iginatyo Wafula

DALI WA SICHIMI

NAFWOFWOYO	Masinde
	Yekosafati Musumba
	Gidion Wandera

ANDEREA DALLI III

NAKIROYA	Jackson Ojiambo
	Charles Ouma
	Humproyss Onyango
	George Wafula
NABUKAKI	Living Mugeni, Richard Mukaga, Stephin Wandera
	Nende Robert Mangeni

OMOLO WA WANGA OFUMBUHA

NANYANGA	Omolo
	Siduhu
	Odooli

OMOLO WA OMOLO

NAMENYA	Domas Were
	Taidor Ngundira
	Augustino Were

AUGUSTINO WERE WA DOMAS WERE

NAMAYERO	Clement Odooli
	Cornel Odipo
	Boniface Nachona
	Paul Were
	Alfred Were
NAMULEMBO	Henry Were

/11.

	BUKEKO WA NGUNDIRA
NACHONGA	Omijja
	OMIJJA WA BUKEKO
NEHOBA	Ngweno
	Bukeko II
	Muniala
	NGWENO WOMIJJA
NAMULEMBO	Gaunya
	Joshua Musungu
	GAWUNYA WA NGWENO
NAMULEMBO	Omijja Kedereyo
	Bubolu
	Odwori Tinga
	ODWORI TINGA WA GAUNYA
NAMUDDE	Taabu
	BUKEKO II WA OKIJJA
NASUBO	Osinya Pamba
	OSINYA PAMBA WA BUKEKO II
?	Nanyibbomi
	Nambisa Bulasio Ouma
	MUNIALA WA BUKEKO II
?	LWANDE
	LWANDE WA MUNIALA KAGENDA II
	KAGENDA II WA LWANDE
	Nadobu Bwonya
	Buluma (Musamia)
	BULUMA WA KAGENDA II
NADEBU	Yowana Hafulu
	YOWANA HAFULU WA BULUMA
NADEBU	Mujuofa Elias
	BUKEKO II WA OKIJJA
NALALA	Wanjala
	Ololo
	OLOLO WA BUKEKO II
NAJABI	Mesusera Olowo
NAMATE	Nikola Ogessa, Benya Odwori
NAMWENGE	Anthony Ngonga
	Bendicto Ngweno
	MUNIALA WA OKIJJA
NAMULEMBO	Obwege
	Hagondi
NAMAINDI	?
NAMULEMBO	Hagondi
	Pedda
	OBWEGE WA MUNIALA
	ZABLON OBWOLO
NAMULEMBO	Hagondi
	Pedda
	ODONGO
NAHAYO	Zablon Obwolo
	ZABLON OBWOLO WA OBWEGE
NALYALI	Okochi
	Wilson Wandera
	James Mumal
	Fredrick Wandera
	Naming Kaisofasi
	HAGONDI WA OBWEGE
NAHABI	Patrick Ominjja
	Okombo
	OPENDA WA MUNIALA
NAKWEDDE	Firimoni Bubolu
NALWENGE	Muniala
	Odongo
NACHIKI	Nyegenye Charles
NAHABOCHA	Nyangweso
	James Barasa.

	ODUKI WA OLIGO
NADEKE	Mengo Okigo
	Ogoola Oduki
	Wandera Oduki
	Juma Oduki
NAMAINDI	Onyango Oduki
	Juma Okudi II
	Ogutu Oduki
	Oundo Oduki
NAMAINDI	Okello Oduki
	Oundo Oduki
	Gaunya Oduki
	Ojiambo Oduki
	MBOGO WA OLIGO
NABONGO	Ochiengi
	Sikuku
	Akumu
	Nekesa
NADEKE	Nabboro
	Muhachi
NAMUNYEKERA	Oriero Gawunya
	MUGENI WA OLIGO
	LWANDE WESONGA
NEHAMA	Kagenda
NANJOWA	Ngudira wa Kagenda
NASONGA I	Bukeko
NASONGA II	Dikidi
NAMULUCHA	Kubengi
NALUKADA	Mboyo
	NGUNDIRA WA KAGENDA
NAMULUCHA	Kubengi
	KUBENGI WA NGUNDIRA
NAHULO	Gasundi
	Mbakulo
NAMUDDE I	Owori
NAMUDDE II	Nambakwa
	NGUNDIRA WA KAGENDA
NASONGA I	Bukeko

YONASANI NGWABE WA BUKELLO III

NAKOLI	Hitler	
	Onyango	

OMIJJA ABBALA WA NGWENO

NAHASOHO	Omuhana

NGUNDIRA WA KAGENDA

NASONGA II	Dikidi

DIKIDI WA NGUNDIRA

NALYALI	Namwiwa
	Agaaro
NANYIBBOMI	Lusimbo

NAMWIWA WA DIKIDI

NABONGO	Ouma Nyaroya

OUMA NYAROYA WA NAMWIWA

NAKAALA	Aloni Omondi	
NAMANGASA	Oulo	Stephin Omochi
	Dikidi	Petero Wandera
NAPUNYI	Toas Mabbachi	Juma
	Simoni Nasude.	

ALONI OMONDI WA OUMA NYAROYA.

NAMIRIPO	Ngundira

PETERO NAMWIWA WA ALONI OMONDI

NAMUNYEKERA	

CALASTO SUMBA WA WAMBUDO

NANGAYO	"
NAKOOLI	Ojiambo

STEPHIN OMOCHI WA OUMA
COMULUS (NGUNDIRA) WANDERA

NEHOBA	
NAKOOLI	Were
	Charles Omondi
	Opio
	Odongo
	Mukaga

PETERO WANDERA WA OUMA.
CAMLUS (NGUNDIRA) WANDERA

NASUBO	Ouma, Egessa, Stephin Omochi.

OCAARO WA NAMWIWA

LUSIMBO WA DIKIDI

NAHULO	Ogengo
NAMWALIRA	Oduyu

OGENGO WA LUSIMBO

NASIWE	Kuucha
NABOOLI	Juma
NASUBO	Ignatio Ogutu
	John Wandera

KUUCHA WA OGENGO

NABONGO	Wanyama Francis

WANYAMA FRANCIS WA KUUCHA

IGINATIO OGUTU WA OGENGO

NAMENYA	Maloba George
NALIALI	Okumu Jackson
	Odwori Richard
	Ogengo Milton
	Oduyu Patrick
	Kuucha stephin (Fredrick)

...../15.

	MALOBA GEORGE WA IGINATIO OGUTU
	OKUMU JACKSON WA IGINATIO OGUTU
	MUTULA WA DIKIDI
NAHASOHO.	Wambudo
	Ngundira Ondyedye
	WAMBUDO WA MUTULA
	NGUNDIRA ONDYEDYE WA MUTULA
NEYINDA	Abuner Omunya
	ABUNERI OMUNYA WA ONDYEDYE
NALALA	Jolamu Egondi
	NGUNDIRA WA KAGENDA
NAMULUCHA	Kubengi
	KUBENGI WA NGUNDIRA
NAHULO	Gasundi
	Mbakulo
NAMUDDE I	Owori
NAMUDDE II	Nambakwa
	GASUNDI WA KUBENGI
NAMANGALE	Orubo
	ORUBO WA GASUNDI
NASIMALWA	Buya
	BUYA WORUBO
NABONGO	Gidion Odiedo
NAMBANJA	Wandera
NALWENGE	Ojiambo
NALWENGE	Mabbachi
	Juma
	Onyango
NAHEMBA	Lucas Onjaalo
	GIDEON ODIEBO WA BUYA
NASONGA	Josophat Odwori
	Charles Ochieno
	Edward Ogoola
NABUKAKI I	NABUKAKI I Joseph Nyongesa
	Joseph Nyongesa
	Joseph Ohito
NABUKAKI II	George Wandera
NASONGA II	Apola Obbala
	Andrew Obbala
	Charles Juma
	Fredrick Omondi
NAPUNYI	William Ogrino
KASONGA III	Ojiambo

-16-

	OJIAMBO WA BUUYA
NAPUNYI	Oohiengi
	Okochi
	NABACHI WA BUYA
NASONGA	Buuya
	Odwori
	JUMA WA BUUYA
NANYINEKI	Orubo
	Nadede
	Okite
	ONYANGO WA BUUYA
NAPUNYI	Buuya
	Otika
	Obbala I
	Obbala II
	LUCAS ONJAALO WA BUUYA
"	Odenga
	Okumu
	Buuya
	Cotton
?	ODENGA WA LUCAS OJAALO NGUNDIRA BUUYA
	LWANDE OMUNYISA WA...........
NASONGA	Oyanga
	Ottiro
NAMAINDI	Kwereho
NABONGO	Wanjala
?	OYAAGO WA LWANDE
	Opondo
	Ogutu
	OTTIRO WA LWANDE
NATMUDDE	Yokana Kadima
	YOKANA KADIMA WA OTTIRO
	MESO WA OWORI
NAJABI	Comulus Wandera
	COMULUS WANDERA WA MEESO
NADEKE	Cornel Ojiambo
NEHOBA	Onyango
	Keya Ochiengi
NADEKE II	Osuwo
	Odwori
	CORNEL OJIAMBO WA COMULUS WANDERA
NABUKAKI	Omondi
	Ochieno
	Meja
	Ojwangi
	ONYANGO WA CAMULUS WANDERA
NAMAINDI	Furango
	James
	Omooro
	Peter Ochiengi

..../17.

	KEYA WA COMULUS WANDERA
NAPUNYI	Ombere
	Mejja

	OCHEINGI WA COMULUS WANDERA
NAPUNYI	Ochieno
	Odwori Fredrick
	Wandera

	OSUWO WA COMULUS WANDERA
NAMAINDI	Ouma

	CHWALA WA OWORI
NABOOLI	Clement Were
NAJABI	Oundo

	CLEMENT WERE WA CHWALA
NASIREKU	Ocheingi

	OUNDO WA CHWALA
NAMUNAPA	Kubengi
	Inginia

	ABWOKA WA OWORI
NABONGO	James Odwori
	Ouma
	Kubengi

NADEKE	Joseph
	Nikola

NABONGO II	Daudi Buluma
NAMUDEUMA	Owori

	JAMES ODWORI WA ABWOKA
Naburi	Ochiengi
	Pius

	KUBENGI WA ABWOKA
NASONGA	Barasa
	Ojiambo
	Pius Okongo

	JOSEPH OWORI WA ABWOKA
MERELE	Abwoka
	Wandera

	DAUDI BULUMA WA OWORI
NABURI	Anyesi
	Wandera
	Mugubi
	Jengo

NAFUNYU	Tinga
	Namwenge
	Idi

	ANYESI WA DAUDI BULUMA
?	DAUDI ROMY

	WANDERA WA DAUDI BULUMA
NABURI	Nikola
	Daudi

-18-

BULUMA WA OWORI

NAJABI	Kanoti Odwori
	Owori Ramunya
NAGWANGA	Pius Onyango
	Mahulo
NAJABI II	Okechi

KANOTI ODWORI WA BULUMA

NASIMALWA	Oyaanga
	Makanga
	Ramisi

OWORI RAMINYA WA BULUMA

NAHULO	Okumu
	Oundo
	Onyango
	Charles Odwori

PIUS ONYANGO WA BULUMA

| NALUKADA | Grado Odoowo |
| | Ndenga |

NDENGA WA PIUS ONYANGO

NALALA	Ochieno
	Bukeko L. Masonga
	Muniala
	Naminjoo Ngundira

NGUNDIRA WA ALONI

| NAMAKWE | Ouma |
| | George |

end.

OKECHI WA PIUS ONYANGO

NANYANGA	Onyango
	Egessa
	Ochiengi

Onyango Wa Okechi

NAMAKANGALA	Buluma

LWANDE WESONGA WA LWANDE MULUNGO

NAHAMA	Kagenda

KAGENDA WA LWANDE WESONGA

NANJOWA	Ngundira

NGUNDIRA WA KAFENDA

NAMULUCHA	Kubengi

KUBENGI WA NGUNDIRA

NAHULO	Mbakulo

MBAKULO WA KUBENGI

NAHAALA	Ngundira II
	Ochieno
NAMAINDI	Ngema
	Dismas Hagyo
NAMUDDE	Magina
	Mwabi
	Mugoya
NACHAAKI	Heremia Masiga
	Echibbi

NGUNDIRA II WA MBAKULO

1. NASIMALWA	Yusufu Nakuhu
NAHEMBA I	Yosia Were (Butonya)
	Grisom Ohonga
NAHEMBA II	Obbonyo

YUSUFU NAKUHU WA (NGUNDIRA II)

NAMULEMBO	Jonathan Mbakulo
NAHONE	Yse Mugeni
	Emmanuel Wanyama
	Saul Ouma

JONATHAN MBAKULO WA YUSUFU NAKUHU

NAMUDDE I	Kubengi Exekiel
	Jacob Ochieno
	Saul Ngundira III
NAMUDDE II	Robert Oyaaka
	Akisoferi Oundo
	Yekonia Rojas Masiga
NANGABI	Damulira
NAKAHYA	Geofrey Ohonga (Bwire)

KUBENGI EXEKYERI WA JONATHAN MBAKULO

NAKOOLI	Wandera John
NAKOOLI	Joseph Ojiambo
	Bwire John
	Kazi Kenneth

..../2.

JACOB OCHIENO WA JONATHAN MBAKULO

NACHAKI	Godfrey Ouma (Yafwa)
	Kazi Mbakulo
NAMAINDI	Robert Ochieno

SAUL NGUNDIRA WA JONATHAN MBAKULO
NYALUWO	Martin Ngundira

DAMULIRA WA JONATHAN MBAKULO
NACHAAKI	Joseph Wanyama G. W.

EMMANUEL WANYAMA WA YUSUFU NAKUHU
NACHAAKI	Ojiambo

OCHIENO WA MBAKULO
NAMUNYALA	Yosia Obbienyo
	Yekoyada Ngundira

ISAAC FAHIRI
NAMANGALE	
NAMUKUBA	Jackson Ochieno
NASONGA	Stanley Mbakulo
	Dishan Mbakulo Bwire
	Bhilimon Wanyama

NEKEDERA	Gideon Oundo (Gasundi)

YOSIA OBBIENYO WA OCHIENO
NAMWINI	

GEDION OUNDO (GASUNDI)
NALWENGE	Bwire
	Okumu
	Kubengi, Ojiambo

YEKOYADA NGUNDIRA WA OCHIENO
NAMULEMBO	James Mbakulo
	Edward Oguti

JAMES MBAKULO WA YEKOYAADA NGUNDIRA
NADONGO	Richard Kubengi
	Wilber Ouma

EDWARD OGUTI WA YEKOYAADA NGUNDIRA
NAMAKANGALA	Charles Kubengi

NGEMA WA MBAKULO
NAMUDDE	Wanjala
NASONGA	Ojiambo (Budaha)

OJIAMBO (BUDAHA) WA NGEMA
NAMAKANGALA	Kubengi Aggrey
	Ramadhan
	Bwire

DISMAS HAGIO WA MBAKULO
NAKKOOLI	Gabriel Ochieno
	Buluma

MAGINA WA MBAKULO
NALALA	Colonio Luduba

	MWABI WA MBAKULO
NAMUKOBE	Stephin Wandera
	Muchere
ADETI	Ouma
	Ngundira III
NASUBO	Wanyama

	YEREMIA MASIGA WA MBAKULO
NALALA	Daudi Mbakulo
NAKOOLI	Abahana Bahaya

	DAUDI MBAKULO WA YEREMIA MASIGA
NAMUTENDE	Martin Luther Mbakulo
	James Kubengi

	OWORI WA KUBENGI
NANYINYA	Abwoka
	Buluma
NAJABI	Omingo
	Okelo
NABONGO	Sicha
	Messo
	Achwala

	OMINGO WA OWORI.
NASIYE	Raphael Owori
NAKOOLI	Oroma.

	RAPHAEL OWORI WA OMINGO
NABURI	Barasa
	Odongo

	ODONGO WA RAPHAEL OWORI.
NAMUDE	Ojiambo Gilbert

	ROMA WA OMINGO
NAMULEMBO	Ogoola
	OKELLO WA OMINGO
NEBERE	Masudi
	Ouma
NAMENYA	Majanga
NEBERE II	Manuel Ojiambo
	MASUDI WA OKELLO
NAJABI	Okello
	MAJANGA WA OKELLO
NAHULO	Sunday
	Wandera

../4.

MANUEL OJIAMBO WA OKELLO

NADONGO   Hilary Bwire
                     Peter Wafula
                     Barasa
                     Aginga
                     Ogutu
                     Ongunyi

SICHA WA OWORI

NAMULEMBO	Oseno
	Opiyo
NASUMBA	Juma
NAMULEMBO II	Abenda
NAMUDEMBO III	Omondi
NASUMBA II	Wanyama
NAMUNAPA	OWORI

OSENO WA ASICHA

NAMULUMBA	Omondi
NAMUNAPA	Owori

OPIYO WA SICHA

NANYANGA	Obwora
	Kubengi
	Ochiengo

JUMA WA SICHA

ADETI	Ogoola

NGUNDIRA WA KAGENDA

NAMULUCHA	KUBENGI

KUBENGI WA NGUNDIRA

NAMUDE I	Nambakwa

NAMBAKWA WA KUBENGI

NAHULO	Ngundira
	Nambasi
	Ogessa

NGUNDIRA III WA NAMBAKWA

NAMBYANGU	Ngwabe
NACHAKI	Odongo Osewa
NAMAKANGALA	Kadima

NGWABE WA NGUNDIRA III

NASINYAMA	Kubengi III

ODONGO WA NGUNDIRA III

NALYALI	Were Sande Osena

PETERO OKUMU WA NAMBASI

NAEOFOYO	Guloba Egombe and Bwire

NAMBASI WA NAMBAKWA

NAMBOOLI	Ayunga and Okumu.

..../5.

	AYUNGA WA NAMBASI
NALALA	Okochi, Oguttu, Mangeni, Ochieng
NEHOBA	Okaro, Omujo, Ouma, Midi and Wafula
	OGESSA WA NAMBAKWA
NAMULUNDU	Basirio Masiga
NABYANGU II	Magunia, Wanyama, Okumu
NAHASOHO	Osyeko
NABYANGU I	Pataleo Ngundira III
	BABIRIO MASIGA WA OGESSA
NAMUKOBE	Barasa, Okochi
NAMULUMBA	Oguttu and Were
	WANYAMA WA OGESSA
NAHULO	Ogesea II
Nabulindo	Mangeni
NAMUKEMO	Ogessa II
	MAGUNIA WA OGESSA
NAMUGANDA	Odongo and Opio
	OKUMU WA OGESSA
NAMANGALE	Bebi, Wafula
Nereke	Bogare
	KUBENGI WA NGUNDIRA
NAMUDDE II	Kagenda
	KAGENDA II WA KUBENGI
NAMIRIPO	Ogaale
	Bendicto Ochimi
NAHASOHO	Albert Malejja
NASUSUNGWA	.....
NAMULUNDU	....
	OGAALE WA KAGENDA II
NASONGA	Masusera Muchanji
NAHABEKA	Gabriel Konna, Pataleo Ogutu
NAHASOHO	E. Okuku
NAHONE	Juma.
	MESUSERA MUCHANJA WA OGALE
NAHASOHO	......
NEHAMA	Kagenda III
	GABRIEL KONNA
NAHASOHO	Matias Wanyama, G. Sande, John Ojiambo
NAHONE	Bwire, Byasi and M. Oundo
NAMUGISU	Kagenda III and Ochimi
NEINDA	Kagenda III
NACHAKI	Ogale II

..../6.

	E. OKUKU ERINEO II
NASINYAMA	F. Wanyama, Changa, Kubengi II, Siminyu and Odeng
NEHAMA	Kage II
	OGUTU P. MALEO
NAMUKUBA	Wandera, Mugeni, Egessa, Ouma.
NAHASOHO	Barasa, Bwire, Tabu and Ouma.
	JUMA
NAGEMI	Tito Ogale II
	ALBERT KAGENDA III
NAMUKUBA	Ojiambo and Okumu
	BENEDICTOR OCHIMI
NAMAMBA	Joseph Onyango
	KUBENGI WA NGUNDIRA I
NEBERE	Mafulu
	MAFULU WA KUBENGI
NACHAKI	Ohoddo
	Semeo Wandera
NAMAINDI	Ondato
NASOHO	......
	OHODDO WA MAFULU
NAMUFUTA	Oundo Manuel
	Ouma Peter
	MANUEL OUNDO WA OHODDO
NAMIRIPO	Ojiambo John (Yafwa)
	Charles Kubengi
	Bwire Ejore
	Ogutu Oundo
	Bwire
	OJIAMBO JOHN WA MANUEL OUNDO
NALYALI	Charles Kubengi
	BWIRE EJORE WA MANUEL OUNDO
	OGUTTU WA MANUEL OUNDO
	BWIRE WA MANUEL OUNDO
	OUMA PETER WA OHODDO
NAPUNYI	....
	SEMEO WANDERA WA MAFULU
NAMWINI	Barnaba Abwoka
	Manase Wanyama
	Owori Joel

..../7.

BARNARBBA ABWOKA WA SEMEO WANDERA

NAKUHU	Kubengi
NASUBO	Fred, William Odira Abwoka.
	Wilberforce Wafula, George Robert Bwire
	John Stephin Ogaali
	Moses Geofrey Ondato

FRED WILLIAM ODIRA WA BARNARBA A.

ADETI	....

WILBERFORCE WAFULA WA BARNABBA A.

NANJALA	Humphres Ivani Wafula

GEORGE ROBERT BWIRE WA BARNABBA A.

STEPHIN ABWOGA

NABUKAKI	Fred Mafulu
	Vincent Semeo

MOSES ONDATO.

MANASE WANYAMA WA SEMEO WANDERA

NAMIRIPO	Richard Wafula
	Dickson Sanya
	Wilfred Sunday
	Godfrey Bwire

RICHARD WAFULA WA MANASE WANYAMA

NALYALI	Martin

DICKSON SANYA WA MANASE WANYAMA.

NAMUHOKOSI	....

JOEL OWORI WA SEMEO WANDERA

NAMUDANDU	James Bwire
	Sam Semeo Wandera

JAMES BWIRE WA JOEL OWORI

NAMWANDIRA	Harbert Kubengi
	George

STEPHIN

NAMUDANDU	....

SAM SEMEO WANDERA WA JOEL

ANDAATO WA MAFULU

NAMUFUTA	Barasa (yafwa)
	Vincent Siminyu

BARASA WA ANDAATO

NAMUSOGA   Chyambi

VINCENT SIMINYU WA ONDAATO

NEGOMA   Ojiambo

KUBENGI WA NGUNDIRA

NaSIMALWA   Oduho, Nabongo, Guyoni

KUBENGI WA NGUNDIRA

NASUBO   Hadondi, Onyango and Okwomi

HADONDI WA KUBENGI

NASIMALWA   Oduho, Nabongo, Guyoni.

ODUHO WA HADONDI

NAMAKANGALA   Daudi Abwoka, Musa Abwoka.
NAMUKUBA   Daniel Hadondi
NANDEKYA   BULASIO Hadondi
NABONGO   Paul William Ouma.

DAUDI ABWOKA WA ODUHO

NAMUBACHI   Salomon Hadondi
NAMULUNDU   Charles Olumbe
NAMULEMBO   Jackson Wanyama.

SALOMON HADONDI WA DAUDI ABWOKA

ADETI   Sunday Robert Abwoka
NABULINDO   Monday Abwoka Julius, Masiga Evan Ngundira.
NABULINDO   Nimrod Saando Bwire
NASIGABA I   (Kiiga) Onyango Samuel
NASIGABA II   Ojiambo Godfrey, Sanya.

CHARLES OLUMBE WA DAUDI ABWOKA.

NABWOLA (MUGISHU)   ....

JACKSON WANYAMA WA DAUDI ABWOKA

NABBYANGU   Bwire Frank,

Wafula Fred

Wandera Desmond

Jimmy Wanyama

MUSA ABWOKA WA ODUHO

Yakorama muha Daudi Abwoka niyobulamu
Daudi Bwire Abwoka.

NAMUBACHI.

Daudi Bwire Abwoka.

<u>DAUDI BWIRE ABWOKA. MUSA ABWOKA.</u>

NAMUDDE
 Tito Wafula Abwoka
 Victor Okumu
 Timothy Bwire
 Moses Eli Okido
 Thomas Were

<u>DANIEL HADONDI WA ODUHO</u>

NAMULIRO
 James Masiga Namukuba
 Willy Were
 Daudi Wiling,Ojiambo Henry

NEREKE
 Samuel Nasubo Hadondi
 Namukuba Godfrey
 Abwoka Bwire

NAHULO
 Wandera Ronald, Manyama Robert, Samuel Were.
 John Hadondi, Saanda.

NAMACHEKE
 Samuel Were
 Kubengi

<u>JAMES MASIGA NAMUKUBA WA D. HADONDI.</u>

NAMULUNDU

<u>WILLY WERE WA DANIEL HADONDI</u>

<u>SAMUEL NASUBO WA DANIEL HADONDI</u>

NAMUDDE
 Tobby Abwoka,

<u>LESTER JUMA GUYONI.</u>

NAKUHU
 Collins Bwire Hadondi

<u>WILLINGSTONE BWIRE WA DANIEL HADONDI</u>

NADONGO
 Bwire George Mark N.

<u>BULASIO HADONDI WA ODUHO</u>

NAMWINI
 Stephin Bubolu
 Were
 Ojiambo
 Ouma
 Malingu

NAMUBACHI
 Milton Egessa
 David Bwire
 Denes Odong.

<u>STEPHEN BUBOLU WA BULASIO HADONDI</u>

NAMAINDI
 Bwire Odu

NAMUGANDA
 Godfrey......

<u>WERE WA BULASIO HADONDI</u>

<u>OJIAMBO WA BULASIO HADONDI</u>

<u>PAUL WILLIAM OUMA WA ODUHO</u>

NAMULISA
 Naphtal Mugeni Ouma
 Wycliffe Wandera Ouma
 Rachffe Onyango
 Harrison Wafula
 Kalori Okumu

NASALWA
 David Okello
 Godfrey Wanya.a

NAPHTAL MUGENI WA PAUL WILLIAM OUMA.

NAHASOHO	Moses Opio
NAMAKANGALA	Kubengi

WYCLIFFE WANDERA WA PAULE WILLIAM OUMA.

NAMUKIGA	Junior Ngundira Nelson Sanya,
NAMUGANDA	Richard Hadondi.

NANYIHODO
Isaac Wandera

FRANCES

RACHFFE ONYANGO WA PAUL WILLIAM.

M	Musa Abwoka

WAFULA WA PAUL WILLIAM OUMA

David Okello
Keniddy.........

MBOYO WA NGUNDIRA

NANYIBBOMI	Nambedu —
NASUBO 1	Obbino
NASUBO II	Onyango
NAMULUMBA	Sikwekwe
NAMAINDI	Obbande
	Nafwa
NALIALI	Omulo
	Odooli
	Ngundira
NASONGA	Masinde Akadda

NAMBEDU WA MBOYO

NAHONE	Daudi Ngundira
NAMUDDE	Okuku, Yakeram Huniyebula SAALA, Nambedu n' Owakerama Namudde Muhokuku, niyebula SAALA HALOBE

DAUDI NGUNDIRA WA NAMBEDU

NAMUYEMBA	Michael Bubolu
NAMAKANGALA	Enosi Ogaambo

MICHAEL BUBOLU WA DAUDI NGUNDIRA.

NAHASOHO	Ngundira James Wanyama
	Ojiambo Patrick DAVID BWIRE OGAMBO
	Were Moses.

.../11.

ENOSI OGAMBO WA DAUDI NGUNDIRA.

NAMUPODI   Taabu — MANGENI JOHN
  Bwire.
  Joseph
  DAVID NGUNDIRA MAKOHA

NAKAMONDO   Masiga
NAKAMONDO   Jared
  Oundo   ABOKI MAKOHA
NAWRUNDU   BENYA MASAHALYA
  OMUNYORO —

OBBINO WA MBOYO

NAMAKANGALA   Okoko
  Sigube
  Nonga

NASONGA 1   Onyango Yakerama muha Basulira
NASONGA II   Yebula abahana bahaya.

OKOKO WA OBBINO

Yakerama omuhasi wa NONGA NAMAINDI niyebula
ODONGO WA OKOKO.

ONYANGO WA MBOYO

NASONGA   Magina, Basulira

MAGINA WA ONYANGO

NADIDI   Okello
  Asiro

BUSULIRA WA ONYANGO.

NASIMALWA   Barasa Charles
  Surusa Festo

SIKWEKWE WA MBOYA.

NAMAKANGALA   Daudi Mudonga
NAHULO   Jones Were (Kenya)
  Kagenda
  Ngundira

DAUDI MUDONGA WA SIKWEKWE.

NAMAYERO   Haba siyaleha musyani.

JOANES WERE WA SIKWEKWE

NANGAYO   Ywana Sikwekwe
  Joseph Onyango
  Domiano Obwaro
  Nahulo
  Omondi

OBBANDE WA MBOYO

NABONYE   Ngundira Ogwayo
NAOLEKONGE   Mboyo
  Sauli

NGUNDIRA OGWEYO WA OBBANDE.

NAMUKUBA   Nabasebe
  Dani Okuku
  Seuli
  Otoyo, Egessa
  Lukiri Ngundira.

-12-

MOTOKA BULLE WA NGUNDIRA OGWEYO

NAMULUCHA	Ogutu
	Olaago
	Wanyama
	Wandera

MBOYO WA OBBANDE

NAPUNYI	Wandera Anderea
NADIDI	Abahana.
NASIBWAHI	Jackson Onyango
NANYIMARO	Guy Mboyo

NAFWA WA MBOYO

NAMULOBA	Haba siyaaleha Musyani dawe.

OMULLO WA MBOYO

NAMANGALE	Yafwa wangu natebula

AKADAM WA MBOYO NASOAGA

NANIMWOTI. 1	Okochi (Yafwa)
NANYIMWOTI II	Yona Buluma Ngundira
NAHONE	Yawawo anwe nafwire.

OMULOO WA MBOYO (HANDI)

NAMULUMDU	Mboyo Yafwa ssa
NASIMALWA	Ouma
NAMAKANGALA	Ngundira, yakerama NAMAKANGALA huniyebulamo SAMUEL EGONDI.

SAMULE EGONDI WA OMULLO (NGUNDIRA)

NANYIBBOMI	Peter Makoha
	Semu Omullo
NALIALI	Siyaleha musyani.

SEMU OMULLO WA SAMUEL EGONDI

NAHASOHO	Bahana (4).

NAMBWEDU

NAHABI	Yobu Namudde
	Erisa Ogombo
	Absolom Wandera

YOBU NAMUDDE WA SALA

NASIMALWA	Adonia Onyango
	Henry Wandera
	Adisoferi Namunapa
NANJAYA	Anania Bwire.

....../13.

ADONIYA ONYANGO WA YOBU NAMUDDE.

NAMAKANGALA	Ouma, Nahabi
	Masahalya (Ngundira).
NAMANGALE	Yobu
	Ojiambo, Ngundira, Paul, Senya.

ERISA OGAMBO WA SAALA

NANYIBWOTI **3**	Ouma

BUSULIRA WA MBOYO

NASIMALWA	Onyango
	Barasa Charles (Bobbo)
	Festo Sumba.

MASINDE WA KAGENDA 1.

NASONGA	Okuku

OKUKU WA MASINDE

NAMUDDE	Ouma

OUMA WA OKUKU

NAMULEMBO	Erieza Lwande

ERIEZA LWANDE WA OUMA.

NAMUSIHO	Paruti Wandera
NAMACHEKE	. . . .
NABONWE	Charles Onyango
	Ouma.
NAMUFUTA	Wanyama Lwande
	Kagenda III
	Odongo

PARUT WANDERA WA ERIEZA LWANDE.

NACHONGA	Lazaro Mugeni
	Johnson Odwori
NABAHONO	Obbanda Honard
	Namiripo: Henrey

NAMACHEKE	. . . .
NASUSUNGWA	. . . .

CHARLES ONYANGO WA PARUT WANDERA

NALWETA	Ouma
	Erieza Lwande II
NABWALASI	Wanyama

NANYAMA WA ERIZA LWANDE.

NEREKE	Moses Oguttu
	Jonathan Mbakulo

NAMUNAPA	Kagenad III wa Erieza Lwande
NABONWE	Lwande.